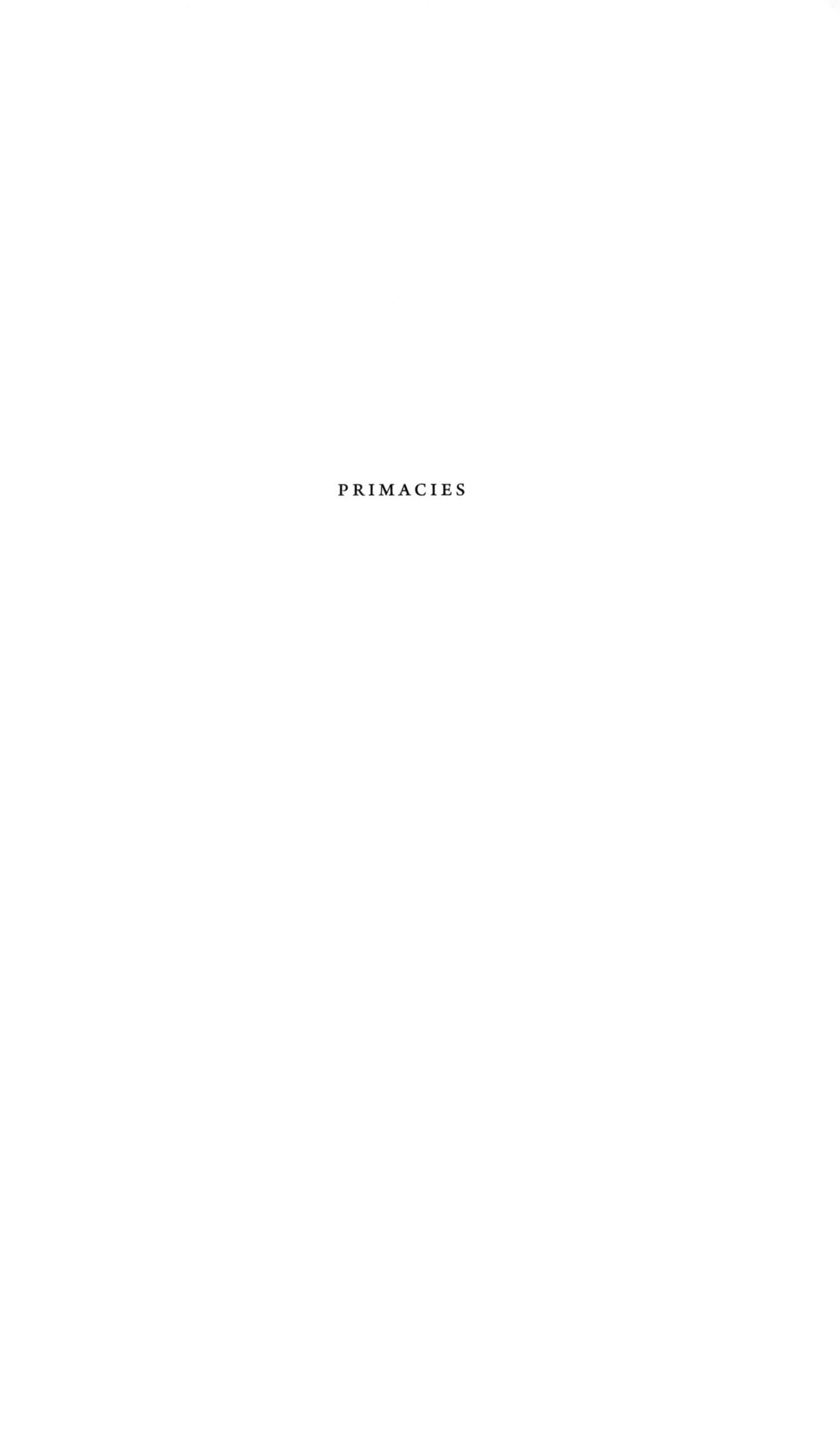

PRIMACIES

PRIMACIES

EXPERIENCE, EXPRESSION, AND THE JEWISH IMAGINATION

Michael Fishbane

The University of Chicago Press Chicago and London

The University of Chicago Press, Chicago 60637
The University of Chicago Press, Ltd., London

Published 2025
Printed in the United States of America

34 33 32 31 30 29 28 27 26 25 1 2 3 4 5

ISBN-13: 978-0-226-84211-0 (cloth)
ISBN-13: 978-0-226-84212-7 (ebook)
DOI: https://doi.org/10.7208/chicago/9780226842127.001.0001

Library of Congress Cataloging-in-Publication Data

Names: Fishbane, Michael, 1943–, author.
Title: Primacies : experience, expression, and the Jewish imagination / Michael Fishbane.
Description: Chicago : The University of Chicago Press, 2025. | Includes bibliographical references and index.
Identifiers: LCCN 2024061768 | ISBN 9780226842110 (cloth) | ISBN 9780226842127 (ebook)
Subjects: LCSH: Emotions in literature. | Psychology and literature. | Jews—Psychology.
Classification: LCC PN56.E6 F57 2025 | DDC 809/.9353—dc23/eng/20250131
LC record available at https://lccn.loc.gov/2024061768

♾ This paper meets the requirements of ANSI/NISO Z39.48-1992 (Permanence of Paper).

for

MONA

Contents

Introduction 1

PART I

1 · Lamentation and Loss: The Poetics of Anguish 11

2 · Making "Sense" of Things: Searching High and Low 34

3 · Correlations and the Imaginal Between 58

4 · The World, Numina, and the Challenge of Theology 82

5 · The Inner Point: Spiritual Consciousness and Attentive Regard 109

PART II

6 · Tears and Testimony: A Literary Meditation 135

7 · Poetic Longing, Mysticism, and the Ontology of Language 156

8 · "The Between": Spaces of Meeting, Language, and the Abyss 178

9 · Alone-Together: Contemplation and Community as Intersecting Values 194

10 · Spiritual Hermeneutics and Appropriation: The Ḥasidic Sermon 218

Conclusion: Forms of Presence 244

ACKNOWLEDGMENTS 249

INDEX *251*

Introduction

What are "primacies," and how do they express themselves? What, in fact, is something primary, and how might we track its tradition? These are questions that interested me long before I could find language to give them verbal or intellectual expression. At some point in my formation, I encountered a transformative essay by the immortal (and very historical) Hebrew poet Chaim Nachman Bialik, whose views of language and creativity have been of primary significance in my thinking. Like a magnet, his words drew many fragments into alignment. In later chapters I shall return to his work more fully, but here it may suffice to summarize his central proclamation. There are several primary languages, he avers, before ordinary and social language, and these are preverbal enunciations that give voice to the depths of the human condition. Principal among these expressions are tears, the cry, and laughter. In his poignant crescendo, Bialik goes so far as to assert that any literary formulation that does not derive from such core experiences betrays language and is inauthentic to the core.[1]

So here, if you will, is a first statement about primacies: they give voice to the most instinctive and raw emotions of our existential condition, and they are at the root of all authentic literary expressions—of sorrow, loss, joy, and fulfillment. In addition, other sentiments or emotions must be included, such as our sensations of voluminous

1. See Haim Nahman Bialik, *Revealment and Concealment: Five Essays* (Jerusalem: Ibis Editions, 2000), 11–26.

space, or the experience of awesome magnitudes and visual spectacles. Each begins with an event that overwhelms consciousness—be it a personal or historical happening or a natural event. The sounds emitted in response are instinctual (such as a wail or shriek of woe), as are their physical manifestations (expressed by tears or bodily tremors). Their impact suffuses our natural being and reorients us in crucial ways. Words come later.

❋

Primacies are felt and enunciated by individuals even when their modes of expression are shaped by traditional literary forms or cultural archetypes. Latter-day readers must therefore strive to attune themselves to the generative factors that elicited these stylistic expressions and sense their ongoing resonance. As the bulk of the ensuing pages will focus on such literary formulations, I wish to specify, at the outset, some of the primary experiences to be explored.

I begin with the voice-opening sounds of the individual as they meet or long for people who constitute their primary reality. This is a cry of personal presence, born of hope or loss, and beseeching immediate care and sustenance. Only later (but never exclusively) are these evocations transformed into a verbal communication. In addition to such voiced occasions of human sound, there are all the eye-opening manifestations of the world that appear unbidden or unexpected. Suddenly, one receives the world in its varieties—both natural and social—and with it all the conditions one must account for or respond to. Repeatedly, we become aware of our interconnections with things: we are not isolated monads but selves-in-relation who are influenced by multiple connections with worldly realities. The lived space between us and others is also filled with shared experiences and memories. These, too, are primary in their valence and validity. It is therefore necessary to attend to the primacy of the "between," with its varieties of mental intention and interactive deeds. This dimension can be a moral zone, where the connections may be reciprocal; or it can be a negative space, where ethical values may be ruptured or undermined.

In the mute world of nature, primary experiences can also stimulate real or imagined connections "between things," and we may express these links through similes that expand our experience of the lived world. And beyond these affects, sensations of radical height or depth may leave us dumbstruck by their primal or brute quality, evoking transcendent wonder or the abyss of terror. Ineffable at the outset, such moments elicit the bedrock of one's personal (experiential) truth. How might we align ourselves to such realities within and without; or to boundaries both perceived and inchoate? What is the interface between feelings and their formulation, or the shifting fault lines experienced on different occasions?

The chapters of this book shall explore such primary experiences through a variety of literary expressions. Two components lie at the base of each study: one is catalytic, the other analytic. The catalytic component is the generative condition or stimulus that evokes the subsequent articulations. Accordingly, at the outset of each chapter, I present a concise phenomenological description of the experiential issues involved. These are followed by the analytic component, which focuses on the literary forms themselves. To be sure, this bifurcation and sequence requires qualification in many cases, since it is often the literary compositions that provide the (phenomenological) evidence for the primary emotions being studied. Hence there is inevitably an active interplay between these two components. Withal, the formal sequence just noted may be justified by the fact that one first lives the reality that is subsequently articulated (and this holds for the literary formulations as well).[2]

Despite a broad overlap, the topics are divided into two thematic parts. Part 1 is particularly unified by issues that mark our concrete human existence: the origin and limitations of speech; the sense of depth and height; the impact of awe-inducing powers manifest in the cosmos; and the search, from within existence, to locate a speculative or contemplative center point. Part 2 also considers themes of primary experience but focuses on how they relate to issues of personal identity—be it the individual quest for poetic authenticity, dimensions

2. See the trenchant remarks of F. Kaufmann, "On Imagination," in *Philosophy and Phenomenological Research* 7 (1947): 369–75.

of interiority and integrity, or interrelationships between one person and another. In both parts, the examples are explored through a broad range of literary types and sensibilities; and in both sections the topics and texts selected reflect a lifetime of personal interests. Others could fill the same slots. To give the preceding remarks specificity, I offer here a succinct précis of the chapters involved.

Chapter 1 opens with an essay titled "Lamentation and Loss: The Poetics of Anguish." It deals with the primal evocation of a cry—charged with the pathos of loss, need, and the yearning for life. The initial cry is fundamentally a scream, and even when it evolves into explanatory words, it retains the primary anguish at its core. The cry has assorted literary expressions, including the personal lyric and the communal threnody. The examples chosen reflect cases of individual loss and national tragedy. The implosion of meaning evident here connects this chapter to its sequel. Chapter 2 focuses on attempts to construe the sense of existence based on several primary orientations. It is titled "Making "Sense" of Things: Searching High and Low," and examines some ways that our standing or positionality in the world affects our attempts to construe meaning and transcend its distressful and deleterious effects. Various authors from antiquity to the present (beginning with *Ecclesiastes* and Marcus Aurelius) give expression to these issues and offer prisms for the self-conscious evaluation of our lived experience. I take special note of the studies of "depth" by philosophers of perception (like Merleau-Ponty) and consider how this spatial sense affects meaning and one's experience of the world.

In addition to the existential modalities of height and depth, our "sense of the world" includes horizontal perspectives whereby we compare diverse experiences to one another. Chapter 3 is titled "Correlations and the Imaginal Between," and it considers varieties of perception (emotional and natural) and their interrelationship through similes. These constructions join experiential realities to the imagination, and thereby expand our sense of context and consciousness of its significance. The genre of similes is further extended by means of parables, which correlate a verbal text and a narrative figure. The cultural use of parables to teach the Song of Songs (or the *Iliad*, for that matter) provides exemplary cases in point.

If similes propose types of likeness between perceptions in heaven and earth, mythic consciousness evidences the elemental primacy of numinous realities on human sensibility—resulting in their attribution as divinities with all-powerful names and a vital will. Chapter 4, titled "The World, Numina, and the Challenge of Theology," explores this phenomenon and focuses on the epistemic dangers when some "likeness" (an anthropomorphic configuration or name) is presumed to be the "thing itself." Such attitudes pose a challenge to monotheistic theology and evoke the polemics against idolatry. This notwithstanding, humans have variously sought the significance of the external phenomena and their inner, animating core. Aspects of this matter are considered in the final chapter of part 1 in chapter 5, which is titled "The Inner Point: Spiritual Consciousness and Attentive Regard." The focus here is on the intellectual and spiritual quest to perceive the inner center of worldly matters (be it as an ultimate truth or the center point of perception and action). The opening section is based on an analysis of a collection of traditional Ḥasidic homilies, focused on spiritual guidance in cultivating attentiveness to religious and existential realities. The concluding part presents a meditation on the theme of having (or attaining) "attentive regard" in one's daily life. It builds on various features treated in earlier chapters.

Part 2 gives particular emphasis to the entwined issues of language and personal identity. Their interrelationship is first considered in chapter 6, titled "Tears and Testimony: A Literary Meditation." Focusing on the phenomenon of weeping as an expression of suppressed emotions and their dramatic release, the essay explores texts ranging from the *Odyssey* and Hebrew Scripture to medieval and modern poetry. It highlights the role of weeping in the struggle for personal poetic expression. In these cases, the concern is with individual identity and self-testimony. The second half of this chapter explores the relationship between tears and the experience of tragedy and suffering and literary exemplars consciously formulated to provide testimonies of certain cataclysmic events. In contrast to the way tears are either initially suppressed or mark the sentiment of the private self, in the latter cases the texts exemplify the incapacity of individuals to restrain their feelings and the imperative to give them public expression—so that others might witness the horrific events (albeit at secondhand) and attest to them for future generations.

Along a different spectrum of language and personal testimony, chapter 7, titled "Poetic Longing, Mysticism, and the Ontology of

Language," explores the attempt by the poet Bialik to mourn his own loss of inspired speech and then speak of the recovery of authentic words as the culmination of periods of inner strife and sorrow. At the emotive core is the sustained hope for renewed creativity and inspiration—whose realization only the seeker can validate. The potential breakdown or the crisis of language explored here takes an interpersonal turn in chapter 8, which is titled "'The Between': Spaces of Meeting, Meaning, and the Abyss." Hereby, I evaluate Martin Buber's notion of "the between," this being an ontological dimension achieved via interpersonal dialogue. To the degree that an individual is focused on self-centered issues, whether these are subjective moods or proclivities, authentic language and authentic meeting are often aborted. By contrast, dialogue is a testament (through the mutuality of lived personal interconnections) that engages the primacy of their singular relationship at a given moment. To a certain degree, both human presence and the "word that is given" (Buber's parlance) are as existentially fundamental as the cry or the scream. How the "abyss" of meaning or significance can be crossed is a recurrent question. Silence, speech, or patience are interrelated issues to be considered and cultivated.

The complex relations between individual and community are considered in the next discussion, chapter 9, which is titled "Alone-Together: Contemplation and Community as Intersecting Values." The central topic considered here is how an individual maintains their authentic self (or desire to remain true to themselves) in the context of transcending (or even transcendent) social or religious obligations. This tension is exemplified through the study of a homiletic discourse by a spiritual teacher in early nineteenth-century Ḥasidism. The contrasting positions and their resolutions are culturally marked and provide an instructive lens as to how authentic religious language (and its reinterpretation) can mediate the tension for the parties involved. The type of hermeneutical creativity that is exemplified in this case provides a connection to the final essay, in chapter 10, which is titled "Spiritual Hermeneutics and Appropriation: The Ḥasidic Sermon." In this context I attempt to integrate assorted themes related to language and hermeneutics treated in earlier chapters. Among the themes taken up is a phenomenology of speech and hearing, both of which are of primary significance in this culture. The first feature, speech, highlights the modalities of a preacher's inspired delivery to their audience; the second notes the auditory situation of the receivers of the message. These two primary realities are supplemented by the shift to text and reading as the original situations of instruction are fixed and formalized through the medium of printed texts. Sacred books now become a new and significant primacy for exposing inductees or students to the given teachings, and this process requires different modes of thematic receptivity and appropriation. For a religious culture, such literary evidence has its own impelling primacy and elicits new linguistic experiences and formulations—including forms of life and behavior thereby stimulated or evoked.

Taken altogether, the chapters of this book reflect a multifaceted attempt to consider the intersections of life experiences and their literary expressions via two interrelated types of phenomenology: a phenomenology of primary emotions and a phenomenology of the literary formulations that give shape and significance to the former. If I would highlight any overriding influences, Gaston Bachelard's phenomenology of experience and poetics of its expression comes immediately to mind.[3] It is from his work that I first sensed how "the mere physical world" might be transformed through poetic language and help us to experience it anew via such resonant formulations. The ramified creativity of Bialik, for all the reasons stated earlier, is another dominant influence. Both have helped shape my sense of a lived hermeneutics, personal and cultural.

This latter point deserves separate emphasis, since the diverse forms of literary expression cultivate (or sponsor) correlative forms of life and their lived embodiment. These may be limited offshoots of behavior or ritualized practices. Each has its own dynamic, as we shall explore, insofar as the action is limited to a specific stimulus or a pattern of gestures that directs consciousness and guides a person to a coherent (and reflective) life of value. How the conjunctive modalities

3. See *The Poetics of Space*, translated by M. Jolas (New York: Orien Press, 1964). Other work will be cited in due course.

may bear on each other is one of the recurrent aspects of the ensuing explorations. The emergence of life events (experienced in primary moments) that may give shape to an informed life is fundamental. It is at the center of this book.

PART I

1

Lamentation and Loss

THE POETICS OF ANGUISH

First Feelings

The cry of life is primordial and recurrent from birth to death: from the first intake of air to the last; from the first gasp of expressive being to one's final breath. Nothing suppresses this cry: it bursts through pain and torment, from the innermost core of our nature. The cry of life is a primal life force that evokes our very being and longing. It precedes language: all the vocal shapes of breath that become the sounds and markers of our yearning for connection and communication. But our breath is evanescent and inevitably subsides into silence and solitude. The cry for care and presence—born of a visceral sense of insufficiency or need—suffuses the cry of life with inchoate lament. Life is bound up with loss and longing from the beginning. Our cry of life is a primal howl with infinite reverberations: lament is at its core.[1]

Life begins with the hitch of breath, a sudden intake of air and its ensuing release. That is the rhythmic ritual of our mortality.

1. Ever since I read Gershom Scholem's youthful meditations on lamentation and language, originally published in *Tagebücher nebst Aufsätzen und Entwürfen bis 1923*, ed. K. Gründer, 2 vols. (Frankfurt: Jüdischer Verlag, 1995–200), 2:128–23 (English translation by A. Skinner, in *Lamentation of Youth: The Diaries of Gershom Scholem 1913–1919* [Cambridge, MA: Harvard University Press, 2007]), I was inspired to return to my own recognition that lament is a genre at the heart of Jewish civilization *and* it reflects a primary truth of human existence (at the core of language). While Scholem's essay was a stimulus, the present discussion is more personal and reflects my sense of the various intersections of language and lamentation. Other chapters below supplement this discussion.

Expression and hope are reborn with each breath, and with the sounds through which we formulate intent and purpose. With each burst of voice we sense the limits of expression and the elision of hope. Possibilities must be resuscitated with every verbal exchange. Words carry our hopes and intentions into the world, seeking to bridge the silence between one speaker and another. Attention to breath is attention to the rhythms of life and loss. Since we cry before we think, our cries of longing give voice to each hesitant hope; but simultaneously they intone despair for all that may falter and die. Lamentation mourns all the longings and loss that expire in anguish during the course of life.

The inaugural and concluding hitch of sound may be a consonant or a vowel depending on its place in the word and the rhythms of breath; whereas the medial flow of tone carries sound across all these vocalic articulations, gathering diverse sounds and an accumulated sense. Each enunciation bears its own rhythmic key; for each enunciation is a life-form that breaks the rifts and hollows of silence with the modulations of existence. Every expression is a new rupture of the absolute realm in which we exist, cleaving the inexpressible Logos of creation into human acoustical shapes—creating meanings and significations large and small. Every vocal burst says "here"—"here I am," a living being in this place; and from this place the individuals reorient to relations in the world (and to those who would, correspondingly relate back, in return). Yearning for connection or social bonding, words may succeed or fail, overburdened by natural desires or fear. The verbal cry of life (of presence and possibility) thus contains lamentation at its source: a sense of lack and longing is entwined from the outset. This is a primal condition of our mortal lives. Drawing breath from the infinite resources of being, we vocalize the world with human sounds that only approximate its sense and reality. Naming is an assertive intonation, denotations anchored in individual insight and tradition, both, each and all, trying to give vocalic cognition to existence. These are often bolstered imitations of worldly sounds and idiosyncratic expression, but mostly by shared conventions and innate structures of syntactic order. This notwithstanding, without reflective thoughtfulness, such successes merely mask the tragic sorrow that every nomination is wrought from a merely seeing "as"—and is not the thing as such.[2] For the world we verbally call into being is more than all our linguistic expressions, and we only, at best, redeem parts of sound and meaning *for us*. We hardly ever approximate the infinite Logos of Divinity that encodes the totality of existence. This is the tragic nature of language, whose end is its origin: longing and limit. The task is to embody and resonate with the mute reality of being, to respond as faithfully as possible to the primordial truths of life.

Consolation comes one word at a time through the audacious concatenation of syllables and silence and the social success they may achieve. But this remains a tragic consolation: the resonance of lamentation inheres in all our speech acts, it being the limited possibilities of its hope for effective meaning. According to an old rabbinic legend, King David tried to jam the upsurge of the primordial abyss with a potsherd on which was inscribed the Divine name.[3] We are far less fortunate, having only allophones of this omnipotent Word—mere fragments of human names or terms whereby we try to contain and filter the inchoate upsurge of existence. It is a fundamental challenge to counter the presumption that our words can truly quell the mysteries of existence.

The innate fear of failure at the source of language—and especially the daily experience of its limits—is one recurrent reason that speakers resort to magical thinking. This latter is induced by the longing for assured communication and by the primary perception (born of our own experience as native speakers and learners of new languages) that our words are not (and palpably different from) the things to which they refer. But the resort to magical notions is enforced by the fact that we "do" things with words, that they have manifest power and effectivity—whether that be due to social success in influencing others or by dint of authoritative edicts and law. Certain ways of saying something, or designating objects, clearly give words their veritable power and agency—for weal or woe. The palpable effectiveness of words gives them the appearance (and practical import) of being inherent parts of the "real"—of qualities truly embedded in existence,

2. See G. N. A. Vesey, "Seeing and Seeing As," *Proceedings of the Aristotelian Society* 56 (1955–56): 121–23.

3. See the text in *Babylonian Talmud, Sukkah* 53a–b; translated and discussed in my *Biblical Myth and Rabbinic Mythmaking* (Oxford: Oxford University Press, 2003), 126–29.

merely needing their proper vocalization to become effective. Such a presumptive positivity contributes to the sense that language has an innate, incantational character. Unfortunately, this is reinforced in any number of ways; but fortunately, as well, the ambiguity of words or our inability to construe a conversation or a text teach us otherwise. Precisely the disorders of language, or a radical change of consciousness, may save words for the truth of poetry.

How is poetry an antidote to magic? Precisely through the realization that every word is humanly purposed; that it is not the actualization of a primal code in the depth of existence, but an act of intention; and that its terms are only "like" their worldly depictions—not the thing made verbally manifest. From this perspective, language is a series of linguistic resemblances that intend to correlate one thing to another, and its approximations of sense are the truth and force of all similes and metaphors. Thus, if magical thinking falters through the presumption that verbal meaning is somehow latent within being, waiting to be activated, poetry is both more humble and exceedingly far reaching. For at its core is consciousness of the verbal construction of meaning, one association at a time. It is the triumph of the instability of language, at every turn. Similes both evoke the gap between things, and simultaneously provide the suture that binds them together. Similes are thus an antidote to verbal illusions. Experiencing the abrupt conjunction between two seemingly unrelated aspects of reality is catalytic for the poet and also allows us, if only momentarily, to overcome our normally focalized orientation through new linguistic correlations. We now do more than see just this, from this perspective—bound as we may be to a mental or physical locale. Somehow, truly wondrously, a simultaneous pair of distinct realities is perceived, and we become aware that we are somehow "between" two types of cognition: the one as physically seen (though not by necessarily being aware that "sight" is itself a construct of sense); the other as spiritually intuited (a likeness that somehow comes to mind). Between the two is a "seeing as": a bifocal perception, with oneself in the middle. In the process, a new order of the "real" becomes manifest.[4]

4. Cf. the comment in W. Stevens, *The Necessary Angel: Essays on Reality and the Imagination* (New York: Vintage Books, 1951), 63: "*I am myself a part of what is real and it is my own speech and the strength of it, this only, that I hear or ever shall*" (italics in the original).

Arising from the depths of a speaker's isolation, words may burst across the rupture that separates personal intention from public formulation. The "I" says to a "you" that what I mean is that this word or reality should be understood "like" this—and then I ask you to hold this likeness in mind so that we might communicate and you can know my intentions. When we articulate this simile structure of language, the magic spell of words is broken. Even if one feels that the terms utilized make good sense, one may still try to make use of some added analogical rhetoric to enforce a point (in some comparative manner) by linking it to other elements in the world—and then one is speaking in similes and animates the world with a new resonance. This can take diverse expressions, depending on context or purpose. Think of the desire of the male beloved in the Song of Songs, who tells his beloved that "your hair" is "like goats that ramble down the hillside" (4:1); whereupon she, in turn, responds with images drawn from her own desire. In the process, through charged dialogue and similes both speakers expand their love—overcoming, temporarily, the separation and longing that drove them to accentuate their love in verbal song. The precise proportion between a topic and its likeness is ever a matter of intuitive genius, which reorganizes the world for the soul—amending the inadequacies of language in creative ways. Similes evince new testimonies of the world and the latent powers of language to evoke them. Indeed, by means of similes, the sensed difference between things is overcome from within language itself, and the feared inadequacy of expression is countered by creative acts of correlation.

The Homeric simile elicits a related dimension when the brutalities of war and corresponding acts of the gods are compared to some more irenic dimension of hearth and home—thus evoking a counterpoint to death and the longing for family life that stirs the souls of the warriors. In a certain sense, these similes close the wound of war by summoning, even supplicating, the return of peace and the *nostos* or "return" to one's homeland. These psychic expressions of supplication encode the lines of the *Iliad* with the tears of longing and lamentation, and dramatize the numerous acts of *hiketeia*, or "supplication," that emblemize this poem.[5] Moreover, these expressions of appeal between

5. See the classic study of J. Gould, "*Hiketeia*," *Journal of Hellenic Studies* 93 (1973): 74–103.

one hero and another, or a specific human and their god, demonstrate the great yearning for life so evident in the epic and evoke the shared world of feelings (love and death) that bind these persons to the earth. Verbal connections to remembered experiences are never far from the mind of each individual, and the similes and evocations sear the heart of every reader. Our inner world is thereby elicited, evoking our own similar sense of anguish and despair.[6]

The felt and expressed "correspondences" between ourselves and the world invest lived experience with deep interconnections (a "forest of images," to invoke Baudelaire's famous figure) between the gods and human life. Such creative acts are more (or so it seems to me) than some primary urge to discover a metaphysical alignment in the depth of things. It is our unyielding desire to bind ourselves to the full panoply of life, to be correlated with its rhythms and forms, and to be resonant with their seeming likenesses, as they are brought to mind by a simile. In so doing, ancient divinatory tables that mark physical and natural correlations are discovered in one's heart; and the hesitant cry (the intake of breath) turns this relationship into a poetic saying: an enunciation of both distance and connection, a voluble, death-defying lamentation—evocative of our primordial grasping for life.[7] It is perhaps for this reason, that Gaston Bachelard, in his many meditations on poetic speech, said that "the poetic image places us at the origin of the speaking being,"[8] or that the poetic image not only "becomes a new being in our language" but "at once a becoming of expression, and a becoming of our being."[9] In a related observation, stated in reflections on the poetics of reverie, he added that becoming a new being in language is an "increment to consciousness"—"a growth of being."[10] Hereby the lament of language is overcome through itself, and poetic

6. That grief and anguish are a primary theme in the *Iliad* has been given admirable analysis by E. Austin, *Grief and the Hero: The Futility of Longing in the Iliad* (Ann Arbor: University of Michigan Press, 2021).

7. And not "mere life," but the rich "fullness of existence"—hence this is something like a primal quest for a lost plenitude. See E. Minkowski, "*La plenitude de la vie—image premiere: Nostalgie du bien recherché*," in *Tijdschrift voor Filosofie* 24 (1962): 507–23.

8. See *The Poetics of Space*, translated by M. Jolas (New York: Orion Press, 1964), xix.

9. Ibid.; see also xx.

10. See G. Bachelard, *The Poetics of Reverie*, trans. D. Russell (Boston: Beacon Press, 1971), 3–6.

creation is a means of self-transformation. It takes the cry for life and meaning into its very being.

It is therefore worth asserting directly: beyond the primary sense of limit and longing that catalyzes the drive for significance, the interpretative act is an equally fundamental element of our human condition. It arises from a deep desire to cross the gap of difference and otherness that confronts one's viewpoint and everything else. The sounds that emit vocalic connections are primordial acts of naming and self-expression, combining to form instances of a habitable social sphere. These patterns are interpretative exchanges of sound and sense that go to the core of human life, and through ongoing acts of clarification and explanation they help form the canon of a community. And what pertains to shared speech pertains to the central expressions that enter canonical texts for recitation across the generations. Here, too, the gaps of difference and otherness emerge (for historical or epistemological reasons), and these, too, must be overcome by one hermeneutical process or another: whether horizontally, as when we attempt to explain the meaning of some term or sentence through another on a similar plane of discourse, or vertically, when we want to reveal some other level of meaning purportedly embedded in the first, so that the external vocabulary is deemed an allegorical expression of a concealed register of thought or discourse. Such correlations or resignifications are therefore, au fond, culture-generating (and fundamentally) hermeneutical similes. Seeing or saying one thing in relation to another continues the primary longing for meaning and significance. Whether these relations emerge from intuitions of apparently similar features of the world, as in poetry, or from studied exegetical acts that elicit textual or other meaning by some art of correlation, such acts are at the heart of the human enterprise.[11] Devoid of the analogical imagination, we'd be ever stuck in the closed circuitry of the "same."

11. Note the remark by O. Barfield in *Poetic Diction: A Study in Meaning* (Hanover, NH: Wesleyan University Press, 1973), 55: "The ability to recognize significant resemblances and analogies, considered as an action, I shall call *knowledge*."

What happens when events destroy every sense of a meaningful existence and the longing to reach beyond oneself is stifled by pain? What happens when tragedy bores into the heart, and a life-shattering cry is all that remains? Lament is then all anguish: an evocation of emptiness. In such cases the breath of life chocks in one's mouth, and the only longing is the desire for death and silence. The catch of breath enunciates the wish never to have been born, and the speaker breathes out the nihility of despair. The voice of lament bursts from a dark nowhere, crying I am "here—just here" with a bottomless anguish. In such laments, every limit has been breached—except for the final one: the need to testify and produce a verbal memorial to pain.

Personal Expressions

The play of light and dark recurs in rhythmic cycles: in one we see the world of things; in the other "all cats are gray," and nothing has color or local distinction. Night has the pallor of gloom for the brokenhearted: the dimensions that light offer fade, and there remains only a flat monochrome of utter despair. Initially, the voice also fails: heaving in sobs, depriving the breath of life the extended rhythms of air within which words might be formed. This chocked breath is like death itself and gives it expression—the raw sounds of lament before language. The mind, too, is listless and dull, and everything seems dead and without vitality. Hardened groans alternatively throb with an abyssal loneliness. When suddenly there erupts the raw certainty of a ruined life. From the depths, more elongated breaths shriek a voluble death wish. Just here is a primal expression of lamentation.

Job understood this situation all too well and strived to stave off its acknowledgment. He stood at the abyss of being, filled alternatively with silence and platitudes—resisting the aching hole in his heart, until it burst out on its own.

A life of tradition and ritual grounded Job's habitual universe; they were the primary basis for his motivations and action. As we learn from the prologue to the Book of Job, which recounts the background and onset of his travail, Job led a life of exceeding piety and performance.[12] So much so that God readily succumbed to the satanic Inciter's proposal to test Job's inmost resolve—whether he could truly serve God with integrity, for its own sake; or whether, to the contrary, he was bent on receiving Divine beneficence, as a positive recompense for his obedient behavior. It was therefore decided that Job be put to the test, though not to the ultimate brink of his life but to a sufficient extreme to see whether he would curse his fate and God to boot and thereby reveal the self-serving underbelly of his piety. Circling the earth, the Satan certainly knew that Job performed his rites conscientiously and that he even repeated the sacrifices of his family in case that they had sinned inadvertently or were not wholeheartedly devoted to God and erred through rote actions or ill intent. This small detail is the psychological crack and suggests that there is something deeper motivating Job, his surface piety notwithstanding. This inner split is his tragic flaw—even though he remonstrated with his wife that one must accept the evils of existence along with the good, since they all ultimately come from God. Physical and spiritual nakedness, he protested, is our condition from birth to death. Job proclaims these assertions a bit too much; so his pleading has an ironic bite and induces us, even before Job himself, to perceive a rupture in the monotheistic order he has vocally defended. But the test itself is unnerving in this religious universe. Do we not perceive in this drama something bordering on a tragic universe, where more than one power exists in heaven? The Book of Job comes as close as seems possible in the Hebrew Bible to presenting multiple Divine-like counterforces.[13] Perhaps something of the spirit of the Greek age has infiltrated the author's mind, for there is good reason to suppose that the age of Job is the "time" of Aeschylus, and leaves a bone to chew as the drama of woe unfolds.

12. I have presented a full presentation and interpretation of the Book of Job and place it in the context of a renewal of Jewish theology in *Fragile Finitude. A Jewish Hermeneutical Theology* (Chicago: University of Chicago Press, 2021), see the introduction. The treatment of Job 3 revises various lectures to health professionals dealing with trauma in the United States and Israel.

13. See the stimulating remarks of B. Kurzweil, "Job and the Possibility of Biblical Tragedy," in *Arguments and Doctrines*, ed. A. Cohen (New York: Harper & Row, 1970), 325–44.

This noted, the tragic reality of Job's situation goes well beyond his specific theological universe, or the rupture of a particular system of explanation. It goes to our fragile core as creatures of sorrow and suffering, when psychic pain sucks the sense out of life, leaving a gasp of woe and silence. In his case the remonstrations of piety (directed to Job's wife but, in truth, a desperate personal theodicy) needed the rupture of pious silence offered by the friends who came to console him. Upon seeing Job's external woes, they were struck dumb. And their gaze of silent horror became, as it were, the inner visage of Job's mind as he faced his life and prior experiences. This social expression of limit became the mirror of emptiness into which Job's benumbed soul gazed—and he sank into a dark despair. The narrator seizes this moment and provides a vocal transition to language so that we might hear the sound of his stricken being. Suddenly, "Job opened his mouth and cursed his day" (3:1)—meaning that he assailed his existence, symbolized by the day of his birth. With tremulous pathos, Job enunciates a raw lament of human limit, and his language reveals what he had stifled all along.

Perish the day I was born, and the night it was announced:
"A son has been conceived!"
May that day be darkness, may God above not seek it out—
and not shine light upon it!
May darkness and thick gloom reclaim it, beclouded in pall—
stricken by the bitter bile of day!
May that night be seized by obscurity—and be not joined to the
days of the year, or numbered among its months!
Let that night be desolate, without joyful sound:
May those who curse the times damn it, those able to arouse
Leviathan!
May its twilight stars remain dark; its hopes for light foiled,
and never see the glimmer of dawn—
Because it did not close my mother's womb,
and hide trouble from my eyes!

Why did I not die at birth, stillborn from the womb?
Why were there knees to precede me, and breasts to give me suck?
For now I would lie in silence, be asleep and have peace! (3:3–13)

More follows, along with a poignant climax; but we must pause to assess this sudden shriek of despair. It arises from the silence of sorrow, deep within his personal pain, and it seeks to blot out the universe as if it were a womb of his own birth. Silenced by the desire of its eradication, it hovers over the lament as a dark density of inconsolable "nothing"—somehow, for the sorrowing Job, this terrifying lament is the objective correlative of his wound and echoes the gasp of an infant, stillborn. This is the language of limit: a breath cry cursing one's origins, trying to reverse by verbal sorcery the external world in which he wallows. It screams his deep subjunctive wish as incantatory invectives, saying "May" but always intoning "Would that!" the light of life were swallowed by the primal monsters of chaos; by Leviathan and the broods of darkest gloom. Repeatedly, the speaker shouts these impossible wishes, for his wound is evidence of his birth into the consciousness of sorrow. The lament is thus like a chant that tries to undo the created order and fill it with the rubble of loss. It is a supplication cast to the winds, floating like verbal vapor into the abyss. There is no longing for life that stifles the shriek. He intones death itself.

Job's lament arises from the total nothingness he feels, the inconsolable loneliness of this crisis of despair. It is filled with the emptiness of its origin, and the vacuum that is one's living void. Thus his repeated wish to stifle speech at its core; indeed, in his wail Job repeats the gasping breath of the newborn child he so personally condemns. If his words emerge in patterns of redundant sense, it is because the cry of Job can only repeat its choked pain; and if his words have some social verity, it is because the speaker is still alive, and his lament is the whip lash of protest snapped toward the friends who represent the world he is condemned to endure. One should therefore not substitute the lament for the silence at its core. The hollow of lament meets the hollow of the universe: for the speaker, they are one and the same, and the saying of it reaffirms this sensation. To hear a personal lament is to perceive its vacuous tremor, to feel the sob of sorrow stifled within the spaces of the consonants. It speaks from the tragic depth of supplication: Would that this pain were stifled and eradicated in death. "For now I would lie in silence" he moans, numb to life and its pain.[14]

14. One must recall here, of course, the cultural precedent of Job's anguish found in Jeremiah's own death wish in Jer. 20:13–17. With related pathos he "curses" the day

Every time Job enunciates the negative particle *al* ("may . . . not") or its rhetorical variants, he is filled with remorse over the failure of meaning—and we suddenly sense, as he comes to his conclusion, what lay behind the ritual piety, so assiduously rendered, to make sure that outer deeds were matched by inner intent. Surely he was a person known for being *yarei' Elohim* (a "God-fearer," reverent and dutiful); but we must also take Job at his word when he says, at the end of his lament, that one's "groan" of daily despair expresses the cruelty that "surrounds" human life at all times (vv. 23–24). Then finally, in the starkest terms, his hidden truth comes out (vv. 25–26):

> What I feared most has befallen me; what I dreaded has come:
> I have no quiet: I am without rest and halt, and torment recurs!

Here it is: the inner pulse of anxiety, sensing the silent void that underlies the rites of order that suppressed his fears, inducing countermeasures of piety to allay the gnawing terror. The pain of life, as a torrent of sorrows, is poured into the soil as an evaporating travail: the fearsome uncertainty of existence was never quite out of his mind, and never fully eliminated by the compulsive cycle of rites embossed by tradition. One day, this time, the fears came crashing in—as the messengers, one by one, announced the truths of misfortunes that severed his heart and overturned his universe. Job's lamentation is, therefore, an expression of his deepest anxieties—resisted and repressed for so long. Lament bespeaks the cry of pain through the terms of tradition; its words are the broken rage of heartbreak.

The lament in Job 3 shrieks to high heaven. It is dense with the tears that every honest heart knows, even when covered by social forms. To whom can one turn in such dire circumstances? Job's lament has

---

of his birth and the announcement of its occurrence—for his words bring sorrow and suffering, remain unheeded by his peers, and are without Divine consolation, despite earlier promises of protection and aid from the womb (1:5–8). The traditional format of the lament allows each speaker to find expression for what chokes their heart. But at bottom both enunciations are gasps of woe. A contemporary of Jeremiah, the prophet Ezekiel, emblemized the cry of lament as "a keening, a vocal gasp, and a shriek" (*qinim va-hegeh va-hi*; Ezek. 2:10). The Septuagint preserves the more probable reading of *qinah*, rendering here *threnos*).

no addressee. It is a death wish turned on itself—silence made voluble. Language merely articulates the despair of ineradicable pain. Its scream is its inner truth; it testifies to the certainties of a ruined self. Only those who hear it can truly sit with Job. The friends came too soon.

Communal Grief

The most inconsolable terror is the cold feel of silence sensed as a hollow reality that absorbs all words and cries without consolation. It is a silence without resonance, carrying off the sorrowing spirit without remainder. The heartache that is enunciated congeals like ice in the cosmic crevices, expanding these fissures into gaping holes of unhallowed space. Lamentation enunciates the ruptures of human life, for the fissures of time and people lost—and the horror of remaining a witness to death. Temporality trickles into the cosmic waste. Only the lament remains to tell the tale.

This is a horror nearly unendurable, and some cultural lamentations can only repeat the gasp of "why?" and "how?" in endless variations—as the chords of an incantation. The gasps of despair express the vocal void swelling each enunciation—both part and whole. This is also a reason that these laments repeat stock phrases from old words of sorrow—projecting situations of loss through ancient paradigms that recount old events of Divine care and long for their recurrence. But for all that, the elegiac syntax is only the metric measure for a disconsolate wail—the rhythmic substitute for disheveled loss. Other cultures modulate these ritual forms with the ululation of screeching sorrow or try to join the chorus of lamentations with human and animal gasps—emitted like the caw of carrion birds dismembering memory.[15] All these are the languages of silence in ritual expression. For nearly a millennium the Jews of Worms and their heirs have recited

15. For a study of linguistic dimensions in the ancient Greek tradition, see M. Alexiou, *The Ritual Lament in Greek Tradition*, 2nd ed., rev. D. Yatromandolakis and P. Roilos (1974; Lanham, MD: Rowman & Littlefield, 2002). In addition to the ethological material cited in the bibliography, see also P. Leino, "The Language of Laments: The Role of Phonological and Semantic Features in Word Choice," *Studia Fennica* 17 (1974): 92–131.

Psalm 83 after their prayers[16]—a poignant lament that cries out "Elohim (God) do not be silent (*al domi lakh*); / O God (El), be not deaf (*taḥarosh*) and dumb (*tishqoṭ*); for your enemies howl and arch their heads insolently"—against your people whom they plot to cut off without remainder, "so that the name Israel will not be remembered (*yizakher*) ever more" (vv. 2–5). "Fill their faces with shame . . . and let them be ashamed and bewildered; . . . and know that You alone are exalted over all the earth" (vv. 17–19).

Such a solicitation follows the normal pattern of praises and petitions, never forgetting an erstwhile and omnipresent desolation—intoning in words of appeal a desire for endurance and vengeance—the endurance of the mourner, and the swift doom of the enemy. It shrieks against Divine Silence, hoping to evoke a response from high heaven and clinging to this language of lament as a vestige of what has been lost and the need for restitution. This formulation reverberated for centuries and was the touchstone for one of the most remarkable laments in the near endless repertoire of Jewish lamentations. All that remains for the survivors is language, filled with gasping tears and a sacred protest. Here is a rendition of a nightmarish reality, composed by R. David ben Meshullam, after the rampages and massacres in the Rhineland city of Speier, by rabble hordes in 1090. The elegy (echoing the just mentioned psalm) is called *Elohim al domi le-dami* (God, do not be silent at my blood).[17] The opening stanzas read as follows:

> Elohim, do not be silent at my blood!
> Be not deaf and dumb before my oppressors!

16. Cf. *Minhagot Vermayza'*, collected by R. Yuda Liva Kircheim, with notes and addenda by Y. Peles (Jerusalem: Machon Yerushalayim, 1987), 39 (for recitation on weekdays after the daily psalm) and 342 (in the appendix, for recitation on Yom Kippur eve). The Gaon Ya'avetz (R. Jacob Emden) is cited in the traditional prayer book *Otzar Ha-Tefillot* (Vilna: Rom Press, 1928), 222, to inform worshippers that Ashkenazim recite this Psalm daily (when no *taḥanun* supplications are recited), and he adds that the Polish rite is different). In a note, pp. 219 and 369, the custom of reciting the passage *al tira'* ("Do not fear") after daily prayers is linked to the fear of persecution (*sho'at resha'im*).

17. Published in A. M. Haberman, *Sefer Gezeirot Ashkenaz ve-Tzarfat* (1945; Jerusalem: Sifrei Ophir, 1961), 69–71 (the concluding lines produce the acrostic: David b. Rabbi Shlomoh, *qaṭan ḥazaq*).

Seek and find blood's requital against my enemies;
Let not the earth cover my shedding-site!

May it be revealed to You in its massive flow—
And cover Your garment with its blood-streaked stain!
Judge these perpetrators in an exacting measure,
For the blood of Your sufferers poured out like slain calves.

They gathered together, emptying their draught of poison:
An accursed swarm, overrunning the earth—
To annul Israel forever who bears God's holy Name
Forcing them to follow a faith of vanity and perverse belief!

But the holy seed of Israel, most faithful children,
Exclaimed: "This is my God, and I shall glorify Him!"
And sang: "He is our portion"—to whom they avowed
Allegiance—united as martyrs and bound in eternal life.

Mother and child together in sacrificial perfection—
Like choice lambs selected from sacred domains.
Devoted to the exalted One—though bound and slain
They refused to bow before the contemptible image.

Yearling lambs in holocaust flame—in purity intending
Consumption upon the altar of their perfect faith—
Consoled their mothers: "Have no compassion—for we
Have been summoned to Heaven: a gift-offering to God!"

Stopping here for the moment, nearly midway through the fifteen quatrains, we can offer an initial assessment of this poignant lament. The first notable feature is the opening intensification of its biblical prototype, which calls on God not to remain silent (*domi*) for "my" spilled blood (*dami*)—the speaker hereby giving his personal voice for the murdered community, whose own voice has been eternally silenced save for the citations adduced in this elegy, attesting to the people's firm loyalty and devotion—both the adults who were martyred glorifying God and the children who went as sheep devoted to sacrificial slaughter, urging their mothers to slay them as a burnt offering to Heaven.[18] We thus have a voice and cited voices, silenced speakers and a lament that offers a vocal substitution for their blood and piety. Lamentation is the language of the silenced dead—addressed to a God who is still silent, and solicited in words of utter anguish. The elegy thus remains silent unless recited—a hollow monument on its own terms, a mere vapor of the past. It hovers over the spilled blood of the slain, like a shade. It stands silent, awaiting an exacting retribution. And, like the first speaker, generations thereafter retain their memory of the event through this grieving intonation of heavenly appeal—all the more painful as the centuries wear on. Only communal recitation can fill the void of inattention from year to year. The rupture of the world, evidenced by this tragic lament, leaves no room for similes. It is the void that is omnipresent, and the elegy attests to this. Each stanza spells out an incomparable event. Correlations would be blasphemy and disgrace. If there are resonances, they are primordial patterns of former generations, the archetypes that hold the lamentation intact.

One can perhaps now understand the stereotyped phrases from the past. Many citations of Scripture (Psalm 83:2, but also Exod. 15:3, Deut. 32:9. and Isa. 63: 8) refer to Israel as God's holy seed; others lambaste the enemy as a venomous horde. There are also many references to the sacrificial cult cited from Scripture—the transference of the animal slaughter in antiquity to the human sacrifices of their day. In addition, the lament is marked by acrostics and end rhymes and is replete with allusions to other biblical or rabbinic traditions. Desperately, these

18. This recitation, entered the tradition of commentary by the thirteenth century, as is evidenced by the exegesis in R. Avraham b. Azriel's masterwork, *Sefer 'Arugat Ha-Bosem*, ed. and annotated by E. E. Urbach (Jerusalem: Mekitzei Nirdamim, 1963), 3.36:337–40. I have tried to follow these interpretations in my translation to remain as close to the nuance and allusions of the traditional reception. In certain cases the language is filled with nuanced associations, as in the fifth stanza, where the language alludes to such sacrificial texts as *Babylonian Talmud, Yoma* 15b and *'Arakhin* 2.5 (correcting the printed text), respectively, and the comment reflects how the people's actions was a veritable cultic sacrifice. In the final line of that stanza there is hyperbolic language that alludes to Jesus, as the commentator specifies. The theme of spiritual resistance utilizes numerous canonical texts.

allusions attempt to establish, in words, the sense of obliterated coherence felt by the speaker. They therefore seek patterns from a prior time when the blood of martyrs was requited and when Heaven acted judiciously and with harsh reprisals—when words meant something and petitions betokened hope. Utter incoherence is the disaster that is prescient and palpable on earth. The blood-soaked killing fields on which the corpses lay unburied and the martyr's life blood sank from sight is the blight that shatters the soul. Obliteration and anonymity will soon erase remembrance forever. Laments are desperate acts of language, drawing from the past images of coherence that give form and value to the community. They are a call to witness from a riven heart. Recitation is nearly all that remains. And the speaker goes on to speak about the fluttering, palpitating lungs of the dying young; of pious parents who slaughter their children (repeated from stanza to stanza, like the last gasps of the dying). Though specified in detail, who could believe this recitation and dirge of death, who could rightly honor these memories and their final acts of faithfulness? Whatever shape language takes, it is always a shriek of loss.[19]

The speaker laments, and his words turn to tears, for lamentation is tears and a choking voice. Nothing will wipe away this anguish. Only memory and revenge might substitute for these sacrifices. Listen to the final stanzas, as the poet's words conclude with an agonizing burst of description and appeal.

> Tears from everywhere: pouring out, and streaming—
> Slaughterer and slaughtered groaning, one for the other!
> The blood of fathers and sons, mingled and throbbing:
> Exclaiming their sacrificial benediction: "Hear, O Israel!"

19. Quite remarkable is the use of the vernacular to reinforce this loss of meaning and evoke an erstwhile cultural dimension. See especially the laments for the catastrophe in Troyes, which were also marked by Old French elements, including *chansons* of memorable pathos. Cf. A. Darmsteter, "Deux Élégies du Vatican," *Romania* 3, no. 12 (1874): 443–86; and "L'Autodafé de Troyes (24 Avril 1288)," *Revue des Études Juives* 2 (1881): 237–47. And see now the recent discussion by K. Fudeman, "These Things I Will Remember: The Troyes Martyrdom and Collective Memory, in *Prooftexts* 29 (2009): 1–30.

Behold and see the deeds of the faithful daughters:
Stripped and slaughtered naked in the heat of the day;
Along with noble women, belly-pierced and quartered,
Their new-born babes and afterbirth flung from their loins!

Who has heard such things, and seen their like;
And who could believe such horrendous events?
Parents leading children to slaughter, as to a bridal bower!
At these horrors can You contain Yourself, O most Exalted?

Of yore we were assuaged, believing that Isaac's binding
On Moriah would assure us salvation for future times;
Yet more devotion have we here enacted, beyond words to say!
O living One, their pure hope: protect us and end our sorrow.

This text is a verbal blood stain set before God to see and respond to. It depicts a blood stain of consecration and desecration: the former, the noble death of young and old, faithful to God and Israel; the latter, the perverted brutality of false piety. If the holy seed suppressed their natural emotions to dedicate their lives to Heaven, their oppressors were rotted wormwood, capable of reveling in this bloodlust. The elegist cries and decries; he calls on God, at the end of the penultimate quatrain: *ha-ʿal eleh titʾapeq* (Can you still contain Yourself [at the horror of] these things?). The pronoun *eleh*, "these things," is thus the core term—summing up all of the horrors described and anticipating the near-last line of the lament, which states, *nitosefu eleh vekha-eleh ʿad bilti leiʾmor* (These things and their like, so beyond saying, were added) by the pious, exceeding the act of Abraham on Mount Moriah (whose own singular deed was restrained). In his protest against an absent Divine compassion, echoing Isaiah 64:11, R. David ben Meshullam seeks to induce the silent Heavens to pathos and pain and then respond with acts of protective care. The lament ends with the speaker and listener aghast. Indeed, this is the singular emotion of the lament: it is the strangled breath and heart of the speaker, seeking to elicit the horrors of memory. It is a primal shriek: the breath of life is engorged by a deadly silence.

Otherwise than Words

Words just are; they carry the soul into the world—from inner silence to the shapes of verbal resonance. We get stuck in imagining depictions, thinking about the representation of language; when, in truth, our speaking and language is what creates our lived reality. Language is therefore affective in its first and continued instances. It is the way we plunge into the silence of being and give it effectivity. Lamentation is the truth of this enterprise, arising from the breath of life, vaporous and evanescent, expressive of our limited lung capacity and ultimate finitude. This is the tragedy of our enunciations long before their willed and desired success; or especially before the corruptions of human action. Perhaps the mournful smile of the clown Pagliacci is the true symbol of this sacred grief. He is, for all that, three dimensional and mortal—so much like ourselves. Like Bip, personified by Marcel Marceau, he physically instantiates the inexpressible silence of our condition put into mimetic form through jerks and gestures. Remarkable to say, the character of Bip was invented in tragic times: to entertain young children and keep them silent during dangerous roundups during World War II. His silent melancholy is thus the embodiment of despair—expressing the void in the tragic depths of experience.[20] These actions are lamentations without words.

Paintings are different: each one covering a two-dimensional canvas that conveys the illusions of depth by a lifeworld thick with oils and brush strokes; by lines separating objects on the same plane; and by colors whose sense and impact are affected by their relationships across the plane surface of art. Unlike language, received in sonorities and resonance, one syllable at a time, the painting is from the outset a silent presentation—offering a visual impression long before any thoughts occur to one's mind. It is perhaps also for this reason that the images of sorrow in painting evoke an inconsolable lamentation to the viewing eye. Think of Picasso's *Guernica*, and the event of carnage and horror it portrays of a city bombed to dust in a matter of hours in 1937, when human and animal life were blasted to blood.[21]

20. See the poignant performance clips at YouTube (under "Marcel Marceau").

21. See the penetrating analysis of its painterly composition and meaning, by M. Raphael, *The Demands of Art*, Bollingen Series 78 (Princeton, NJ: Princeton University Press, 1968), chap. 5 ("Discord between Form and Content"), 135–79.

Put the images in your mind: nothing coheres; limbs shoot up and out from all places; mouths open agape in shock and scream—breathing the foul stench of explosions and cadavers: gulping for air or gasping in a death rattled howl of woe. The painter gives us a canvas that is an ensemble of body parts, some in color and other white as bloodless souls. Mothers and babes are here, disembodied heads are there, and animal shapes and terror everywhere. Remember the horse with its gape and glare, teeth wide in frenzy—how it echoes the human faces, unfocused in their wild stupefaction. This is lamentation without sound, the catch of air that creates a soundless cacophony. The facial features are coordinated into collective grief and horrendous solitude. We view silence and horror arising as a moan from the earth, and we know that there is no resonance to this grief that will carry it upward as a prayer of consolation. Here is tragedy without catharsis: it is a raw lamentation.

Isn't this profound silence also palpable in the photographic images taken by Salgado—images of workers in the southern hemisphere of the Americas: ancient Indian faces lined by hunger and emptiness and servitude to the masters of coal; images of their strained muscles and doleful eyes—the mourning of generations, striving, dying, and having children despite the sorrows? The lament is also the inexplicable life urge conveyed to endure cruel fate and the harshest of labor, with bodies lining the hills, lines of mortality converging toward a satanic infinity of death. These images batter the eye, being without words, emitting the cry of life and solitude. There is no expectation of healing or explanation. The bodies and faces portrayed by these images convey an erasure of hope. It is life sunk into the depths of fatality—imponderable despair, stained in sweat. Not even the language of Dante ("The Sacred Face has no place here! / Here we swim differently than in the Serchio") can evoke this horror.[22]

Considering this, you may recall Job's repeated, still life-affirming questions of "Why?" (*mah* and *madu'a*). Such plaintive initiatives resist the suffocations of hopelessness. They retain the potential of lament, when one might still beseech a response. This state is gradually silenced, when lamentation imitates death itself. Its expression is

22. *Inferno*, 21:48–49.

captured by Primo Levi. Near the beginning of his incarceration in a death camp—but for all that the endless evisceration of the soul—he leaned out to take an icicle to quench his thirst, at which moment, a guard patrolling the barracks "brutally snatched it away." Then, in a word from former, human times Levi asked, "Why?" The answer that was returned comes from the poisonous abyss of hell, it is the cruel sucking out of all breath and meaning: "There is no why here"—only Silence and Absence.[23] Suddenly, all breath has evaporated: the abyss is all.

A Final Sounding of the Depths

Only the heart, in the wake of death, can know if verbal similes are possible—or how the world should be seen. Can a song swallow silence and remain song? What is left for a poet who must grieve and lament?

In poems after the Holocaust, Aharon Mirsky lost his universe, and with it the obliteration of people and places. Lost, too, was the very capacity for song, as he says in "Din Ha-Shir" (The Judgment of Poetry):[24]

> *natati peraḥim be-libbi, ve-shiri ke-shiqshuq mei amah,*
> *ve-shiri be-gonei mei zahav, akh libbi bi iymani eiymah,—*

He confesses that the flowers once cultivated in his heart were threshed by a vast, torrential terror, and the colors that had glistened within were now plundered by an abysmal horror, these images marking all the disasters, he says, that cast him into despair and exchanged his song for lament. Throughout, his personal voice cries out in sorrow: "my heart" (*libbi*) was weighted and ruined "my song" (*shiri*). His poetry was submerged by the likes of (*ke-*), a "whirring torrent of water"—such is the double entendre of *shiqshuq* (the simile he uses), and also the double import of the end rhymes *mei amah* and

23. Citing from *If This Is a Man*, in *The Complete Works of Primo Levi*, ed. A. Goldstein (New York: W. W. Norton, 2015), 1:25.

24. See A. Mirsky, *'Alei Siaḥ* (Jerusalem: Mossad Harav Kook, 1966), 7; it was written in 1950.

iymani eiymah (the first meaning a watery pool;[25] the second echoes it by reference to the horrible terror that he experienced). Thus, rhyme intones the poet's inner breakdown, and his simile opens a caesura of pain. His song (*shiri*) is split apart by the simile *shiqshuq*—which only partially mimes the word for poetic sound (*shir*) with the sound *shi-*; for in the end it is the raucous, ruinous cacophony that remains.

Two stanzas in "Reshut Le-Qelalah" (An Invocation for Imprecation) bring out the poet's transformation of natural images into curses and end rhymes into monuments of mourning. The quatrains and style of the poem transform the genre of liturgy, of a cantor's supplicatory invocation to penitence into a brutal testimony of the poet's lament: a broken voice self-proclamation. Here are the first and third stanzas.[26]

> I shall sing a new curse (*qelalah*), like (*ke-*) a new song for this time;
> It shall sweeten my soul as (*ke-*) a lament a mourner's bitter agony.
> I shall adorn my rhymes with curses; entwine my song like (*kemo*) a wreath;
> And all the songs in my heart shall here now, this day, become imprecations.

. . . .

> The birdsongs of my dream have fled, never again to join my song.
> My joyous rhymes have gone silent, like (*ke-*) a barren winter forest.
> My imagery has become desolate: ruined like (*ke-*) my own blank being:
> Each word in my verse is a tombstone, like (*ke-*) the rocks at my city's edge.

In the first stanza, the speaker intones a litany of personal intent—and its result: the curses will be bittersweet, a solace of suffering; and

25. This noun reflects its modern usage (used for irrigation); it is related to the verb *shiqsheq* (*Talmud Yerushalmi, Shabbat* 2.2), used for watering dough before kneading (it was often transposed to *qashqesh*, in related sources).

26. Mirsky, *'Alei Siaḥ*, 88 (it is undated). A *reshut* is a traditional liturgical request of "permission" to chant on behalf of the congregation.

the rhymes ruinous. Thus begins a liturgical stripping of pretense: what will be said is driven by a dark purpose. And just this is the content of the third stanza, which depicts the depletion of the poet. His songs and images are all victims of an unbearable loss. The world has become barren and blind—a cairn of sorrows. The tone of tragedy is like a pounding dirge: *damemu* and *shamemu* both attest to a "silence" and "desolation" that have come to pass, carrying off his verse and its images. These baleful bursts chase the lines to their end, like the shattering curses in Deuteronomy 28:45 that once "chased" the cursed of old to despair.

The lines of the litany are split in two: an initial feature crosses over, by way of comparison, into curse. The link is the repeated adverbs *ke-* and *kemo*—which are bleak pointers to the destitute reality of the poet's soul and song. The images evoked to characterize the transformation of his poetic spirit become the figural specters of bleak suffering. Thus, the terms of comparison do not so much add to the first hemistich in each line as they open a caesura, disclosing an inner landscape of total ruin. The poet knows he can do no more than scream on behalf of his people, for he is himself no more than this. As the concluding line says, "I have forgotten my song altogether: I only know how to curse (*ani raq yada'ti qallel*)." And with that, lament devolves into utter imprecation—one of its primary forms. Just ask Job.

Such sorrow, like all lamentation, comes from the depths: from a desperate longing to be heard. This is the voice of a survivor. We receive these remnants as silent traces of the past, begging to be read. A belated consolation is its imperative for moral memory. But it is meager. The dead cannot be healed.

2

Making "Sense" of Things

SEARCHING HIGH AND LOW

Initial Considerations

The grammar of lamentation extends beyond elegies and dirges of despair and extends into longings for cognitive consolation whereby the many fractures of existence are counterpointed by attempts to formulate some adequate solution or response. But if our search for meaning drives the human spirit forward, the stark undertow of a tragic sense of life impinges on our vaunted constructions. Whether disinherited or simply disoriented, we wobble on a guideless gyre, seeking some insights from personal experience or cultural wisdom. Our very bodies, grounded on the earth, and our eyes, scanning the horizon for significance, cannot escape the world of which we are a part. We live within limited, circumscribed spheres of experience, and we think based on estimations that come to mind within that sphere of occurrences. But that is not all: our upright posture also provides some measure of perspective over things—or simply confirms that we are betwixt heaven and earth, above and below, and buffeted by both. Orientation, position, and perspective are therefore critical components in the ways we negotiate the world and measure its impact. Each of the sections below is predicated on the primacy of our physical stance in the world and the way this condition affects philosophical reflection.

Set within the plenum of experience, we seek ways to negotiate or resolve the travail that confronts us at every turn. Two orders of discourse stand out for their literary intensity and paradigmatic character. They are both essays (in the double sense) in practical and speculative wisdom, derived from a late biblical corpus of thought, on the one hand, and late Hellenistic–early Roman procedures on the other. In the first case, the book of Ecclesiastes, finds its author caught in the web of empirical attempts to figure out some estimable or predictable solution to the recurrent vagaries of life. He looks up and down, seeking a solid and viable standpoint, to little avail—until the end. The meditations of Marcus Aurelius offer a second case, and looking around from within the turmoil of existence, he decides to ascend in mind and mindfulness and thereby become immune (or at least inured) to physical experience. If the author of Ecclesiastes locates the axis of speculation from within the whole, the consul of Rome attempts a view from above, dulling pain by practiced desensitization. I have selected these works because of personal predilections over many years, and having been guided by their poignant counsel in due measure. Subsequent sections will consider how other spatial orientations (notably, the sense of depth) condition different ways of thinking about our being-in-the-world—suggesting alternate estimations of what it means to live and think within the whole circumscription of experience or to locate a spiritual plane of an entirely different order. Taken together, the sequence of examples offers a series of speculative types that still resonate across the ages. A final, personal proposal concludes the chapter.

Hebraic Wisdom Takes a Greek Turn

I begin with the person named Qohelet, who wrote a remarkable book called Ecclesiastes—replete with numerous (and often conflicting) epigrams—that attests to his intense search for orientation among the various queries and proposals of his own devising. Given the self-reference and personal engagement of the discourses, it is possible that this "composition" is a diary of select deliberations served up for himself (alone) or for his disciples. Both the rhetorical sequences and contents are filled with a simultaneous intellectual angst and a striving for intellectual certainty amid the cycles of nature and the ponderable vagaries of experience. His tone is intense and insistent, filled with the frustrations that repeatedly obstruct his quest. Throughout, his investigations are filled with a self-proclaimed determination. For though he was not, in fact, the King Solomon of antiquity, robed in opulence and famous for ingenious legal solutions, he nevertheless laid claim to this character's fame by virtue of his presumptive pseudonym: "I am Qohelet, son of David," he proclaims in the prologue (Eccles. 1:1). Most likely (given the late language and content of his work) he was some philosophic figure of the Axial Age (as Karl Jaspers dubbed it), when in the sixth to third centuries BCE, figures such as Plato and Zoroaster and Gautama Buddha transformed their monumental civilizations with a new spirit of (personal) inquiry and thought.[1] Qohelet (also known as Ecclesiastes, the Greek translation of his name) was just such a person in the closing centuries of ancient Israelite civilization, discontent with the traditional solutions concerning the order of existence, the correlations between action and reward, and the confidence of tradition to ascertain the wisdom of the God of the ancestors. Teetering at the brink of theological anxieties, his sharp questions and spiritual quest resonated with others who similarly felt that their civilization was on a razor's edge that cut the received tradition into splinters, leaving one adrift with more questions than answers. In his strong individualistic temper, Qohelet reflects a similar (contemporary) Stoic style of speculative independence—though he veers into vapid generalizations quite different from their more logical rationality. But we must assume that his critical mood was not unique and struck some resonance in the wider society, as his critiques were included in the canon of Scripture (with the recorded rabbinic demurrals limited to the fact that the collection has internal contradictions). No doubt, the claim of a Solomonic pedigree gave his inquiries a certain aura of authority and legitimacy for others similarly perplexed. In any event, the theological musings in the book of Ecclesiastes provided a paradigm for intellectual independence and critical inquiry during this time.[2]

1. Jaspers published his *Vom Ursprung und Ziel der Geschichte* in 1949 ; trans. Michael Bullock as *The Origin and Goal of History* (London: Routledge & K. Paul, 1953).

2. Despite their brevity, the remarks of J. Guttmann in *Philosophies of Judaism* (New York: Holt, Rinehart and Winston, 1964), 19–22, are precise and pertinent to the Greek atmosphere tangible in the work. Elias Bickerman, in *Four Strange Books of the Bible: Jonah, Daniel, Koheleth, Esther* (New York: Schocken Books, 1968), elaborated on Hellenistic sensibilities, especially the notion of *tyche*. For a comprehensive assessment of the relations between Jewish wisdom and Greek philosophy, see L. Schweinhorst-Schönberger, "*Nicht im Menschen gründet das Glück*," Herders Biblische Studien 2 (Freiberg: Herder, 1996), 232–332.

Caught in the thickness of worldly occurrences, Qohelet tried to sort things out and make evaluative calculations. Both the heavens above and the earth below were part of the evidence. At the center, betwixt and between, was a questioning and interpretative mind. His perplexities reveal a profound rupture of older, settled solutions regarding Divine providence and beneficence (we should not forget that the rabbinic reception of the work stems from a time shortly after the destruction of the Second Temple, late in the first century CE, when questions about theodicy abounded).

Like the Stoics, time (*zeman*) was at the center of Qohelet's attention, albeit in his own distinctive way. His sense of the "folly" (or "vapidity" of "futility") of existence (these alternatives echo the sense of *hevel* in his opening proclamation, wherein he spoke of the "vanity" and "emptiness" of "all things";[3] Eccles. 1:2). Nothing works out; the best laid plans are but mortal contrivances. Moreover, even the natural order and its cycles convey a seemingly blind repetition of events to the human heart hoping to discern something new in the ancient cosmos. This dire perception evoked a mood of despair well beyond the capacity of language to convey. To say that "all things are *yegei'im*," or "tiresome" (as he does in 1:8–9), is to summarize the speaker's sense of ennui and emptiness. What "was" is what "will be," he adds, thereby evoking a world-weariness resigned to the dull round of life without innovation and distinctive qualities. To seek wisdom and put one's mind to this reality leads to the conclusion that it all comes to naught: an *'inyan ra'* (or "nasty business")[4] that *Ha-Elohim* ("the God"—never a personal deity) has imposed on human beings to "torment" their spirit (*la- 'anot bo*; 1:13). The choice of terms, here and elsewhere, captures the sufferance the speaker bears; indeed, the word *'inyan* evokes the "suffering torment" felt at every attempt to assert meaning. This term also conveys an indictment of Deity as perversely insidious

3. See also the précis of meanings assembled by R. Sa'adia Gaon in *Qohelet 'im Peirush Rabbeinu Sa'adya Gaon*, ed. D. Fraenkel (Sziget: A. Kaufmann, 1903), 3a.

4. This explanation follows the commentary of R. Abraham ibn Ezra, who glosses the verse as meaning the "bad" or unfortunate "matter" that humans have to "deal with" in life, since human actions "torment" the soul for having no apparent purpose (*davar shelo' yo'il*). See *Sefer Qohelet 'im Peirush Ibn Ezra*, with added notes by M. S. Gudmann (Jerusalem: Mosad Harav Kook, 2012), 18.

along with the sufferer's excruciating sense of mental and moral limits (the overtone of *'oni*, or "suffering," is not far from the speaker's mind or our ear). He evokes (though he is not wholly resigned to) this state of affairs—deeming the broken order (the lack of apparent coherence in patterns of event and result) something "twisted" or even "perverse" (Qohelet's word for this is *me'uvat*), evidence that things are "beyond repair" (1:15). We have just enough cognitive capacity to perceive the disjunction between longings for meaning and their futility—and God is the butt of a pointed vituperation: "The Deity has put the world into [the human] heart," but without the ability to effectively "discern" what should be done in any circumstance (the plan or "work" of God is called a *ma'aseh* and seems blind and without clear purpose; 3:11).

To put it plainly, humans are at cross-purposes with existence—for no one can add to or detract from what is given and thereby repair or resolve the mental torment of our projects. We can only try to puzzle things out in confusion and, in our darker moods, wonder whether these Divinely determined limitations are part of a design to keep us in reverential travail—to "fear God" in every respect (3:14). Everything results in torment and the fear of results: if one should choose a path of inquiry over physical indulgence, the result would remain mental anguish; and if one should determine to try and safeguard consequences by careful planning, this too would hardly resolve the inscrutable reality that hinders full discrimination or probative discernment. In the end, there is no "advantage" (*yitaron*) to any choice. The benefits of *hokhmah* ("wisdom" as a kind of evaluative knowledge) will only confirm that one is a creature stumbling in the dark. *Yitron da'at* is the idiom used to convey the "benefit of mental awareness" (7:12)—and it comes to folly as well.

The consequence to be drawn from this state of affairs is not to take things too far. Recurrence and rampant redundancy is all ("*Ha-Elohim* seeks repetitions," *yevaqqesh et nirdaf*; 3:15)—and this includes the fact of mortality. Death is the ultimate leveler. It is the inevitable *miqreh* or "occurrence" that befalls all life (and digs a trough of fear before and after every breath). Death is not an occurrence with a purpose. It just is; and it puts the fear of God in our heart. Just look around: death happens to humans and animals alike; it is all one and the same for each and all. The grave swallows hope and achievement, plans and distinction. To think otherwise is blindness to our existential fate and condition, anguish born of false expectations. Qohelet calls this a *re'ut ruaḥ,* or "reaping the wind" (even a "folly of thought" or "hollow desire"). All of these translations are entwined in this insidious phrase (and the author no doubt meant to convey the whole package). In his view, our having good intentions or plans has a limited effect with no certain results—for oneself or for later generations. Hence, a prudent person will duly observe that there is a "time for all things" under heaven, if one knows how to assess the details and their consequences and thereby prepare for them. But even so, this is only a partial knowledge, and it leaves one in the dark, faltering in the morass of insoluble mysteries. Planting or sowing makes sense, of course, but bad things happen, and seeds blow into the wind; building and storing provender are a sensible act, but who knows whether, or when, things may turn to rubble and lead others to ravage the storage. All individual projects run into dead ends, into pitfalls beyond our control. In sum, nothing is for certain except the anguish of being a creature with concerns and hopes or plans for some beneficial outcome. Even a modicum of wisdom realizes that living with anticipations is sheer folly. To assess life in terms of the "benefits" that might accrue, or to engage life based on self-centered calculations (*ḥeshbon* or "computation" is the key term; 7:27, 29) is a ruinous "calculus." It is a *re'ut ruaḥ.* One must draw the implication: *Ha-kol ba'asher la-kol.* It is "all" the same: "what can happen to one person can happen to another" (9:2). There is no exceptionalism when it comes to personal fate or fortune. Thinking otherwise is a narcissistic trick of the mind, an assumption that later Stoics (like Epictetus) derided and counseled against. As he said, "It is not things that trouble us, but our judgments about things" (*Manuel,* sec. 5). To rely on false presumptions, on an "anguished imagination of the future,"[5] is to falter in mindless folly.

The upshot: we live in the midst of things, trapped in a thicket of ignorance; we are left without consolation and predictable hope. Everything closes in unless one can somehow close one's mind to all expectations. But can one live without vision or purpose, without

5. For this expression, see M. Armissen-Marchetti, "*Imagination et meditation chez Sénèque: L'exemple de la* praemeditatio," *Revue des études latines* 64 (1986): 185–95.

intention and hope? What wisdom can be gained from such a contraction of intentions without losing our humanity? Perhaps the first challenge (and this we may even deduce from the end of the book) is to cultivate a reverential sense of the vastness of existence and develop a stoical determination to do one's best in the face of "happenstance." It is toward this conclusion that our author arrives (I believe) at the end: "to fear God (*et ha-Elohim yera'*) and be heedful of each 'command' (*mitzvah*) that claims our attention" (Eccles. 12:13).[6] This remark exhorts one to have a practiced resolve before each occasion of life, before the inconsolable silence of existence. Ecclesiastes's tragic vision is to live intentionally, with a clear and caring eye, but mindful of time and eternity. I suggest that to inculcate just such a consciousness is the chief task of his spiritual realism. It focuses on the panoply of *kol zeh* (all this; 9:1)—the all-exceeding vastness beyond each and every *zeh* (particular) that confronts us here and now. Such a dual modality inculcates a heart of wisdom founded on *yir'ah*—on a great reverence for the ultimate mystery of life conjoined to an attentive obedience to the particular pulse of daily existence. The commandments of God (the events that the world throws in our path) precede the laws of society and may open one's soul and diligence to all the tasks that must be done "with strength" or "capacity" (*be-koḥakha 'aseh*; 9:10).

Qohelet challenges the reader to live in the presence of the world "put into our heart" before all knowing: to live with intentionality and care but without false expectations. This is the task for the spiritual adept, for whom "happenstance," or *miqreh*, must be met with a transcendent mindfulness. How to do so varies by time and tradition. We cannot escape our bodily entwinement and limited perspectives. Reverence and fear are not solutions to the conundrum of ends and means; they are dispositions that measure our commitments to the God-given world without self-centered guarantees.

6. In this work, as in the Book of Proverbs, another collection of sapiential wisdom, *mitzvah* connotes "duty" or a directed "obligation." It has not yet been influenced by the normative usage in the Pentateuch or latter rabbinic legal definitions.

The Stoic Turn on Its Own Terms

In his (or his disciple's) concluding peroration, Qohelet turns his mind both to the Divine Absolute and to specific human responses. It pivots him away from cavil and despair to face the universe in a positive spirit. One may even sense that this is a shift from a weak mode of tragic consciousness to something "more"—this more denoting a stronger tragic sense of life. Such a change requires an uncompromised awareness of living within the mystery of being with resolute attention. Precisely this orientation occurs in the teachings of Marcus Aurelius as recorded in his Stoic *Meditations*.[7] There is much to consider in this collage of personal practices, but two concerns have special significance in this context: the first is the immediacy of the present moment as a sphere of focused discernment and practice; the second is the importance of a radical transcendence that lifts the mind to a view from above. This posture of verticality conveys more than a superior outlook or mastery of life's vicissitudes. It induces a sense of perspectival height, of being above occurrences and their painful realities. Not content with words, Aurelius deploys his vision in vivo. From the thickness of experience, and seeing things from "within" (as per Ecclesiastes), we turn to an orientation that perceives existence from "without"—with many practical consequences (in the *Meditations*). The task that Marcus sets for himself (and those who think in his wake) is to shift consciousness in a twofold manner: to shift one's perspective to a self-conscious disengagement from the flux and incitements of things, and to cultivate actions and thoughts designed to instill this transcendent orientation.[8]

7. Overall, my thinking has been stimulated by the work of P. Hadot, *The Inner Citadel: The* Meditations *of Marcus Aurelius*, trans. M. Chase (Cambridge, MA: Harvard University Press, 1998). I will refer to other works by this author in due course. For the text, see *Marcus Aurelius*, ed. and trans. C. R. Haines, Loeb Classical Library 58 (Cambridge, MA: Harvard University Press, 1930).

8. Marcus considers these practices as "therapies" or "training for character development" (*therapeias tou ēthous*), 1.7. Such practices were thus part of philosophical exercises, and in this regard they influenced the Christian spiritual exercises that developed in late antiquity. See the foundational work of P. Rabbow, *Seelenführung: Methodik der Exerziten in der Antike* (Munich: Kösel, 1954). This orientation has been taken up by P. Hadot, notably in *Philosophy as a Way of Life*, trans. M. Chase (Oxford:

Marcus calls on himself to turn from the external events of happenstance, over which he has no control, to internal states of mind, where he can put "mind over matter."[9] The forms of reality that affect a person in all arenas of life must be replaced by formulations that focus on values—on the priorities required for one to maintain a sense of selfhood or integrity. Thus, he speaks of discerning the "appropriate actions" (*ta kathēkonta*) that bear on implementing one's moral duty toward the good of the world (persons and the universe), ever mindful of the vast interconnectedness of things. This "good," as it pertains to relations that one can foster, requires philosophical training and awareness. By this process, one may be maximally certain regarding the good for a given occasion, especially when all the "consequences" are neither evident nor certain (as both Seneca and Epictetus add, each in their own way).[10] The self must take into account what is both doable and right for the immediate moment (*to paron*)[11]—this being a "duty" deriving from attentiveness to the events and a responsibility to the whole of which one is a part. The present is the only "time" or occurrence that one can control as a moral being insofar as one can bring their mental resources to bear on the event at hand. What is beyond one's control must be discerned or filtered out, says Marcus. One must become "indifferent to indifferent things" and not let externals disturb one's moral will. As part of his own development, Marcus encourages the philosophical trainee to cultivate those types of "inner discourse" that can help one regulate their emotions or recover the tranquility required for some mode of self-mastery.[12] These include an inner discourse regarding the metamorphosis of all things and a cognizance of the transience of material things, so that the reality of death

---

Basil Blackwell, 1995), pt. 2, and in many specialized studies. My use of the phrase "view from above" derives its employment from his work.

9. A major passage occurs in *Meditations*, 6:32, where he counsels himself to be "indifferent" (*adiaphora*) to issues beyond one's control, and to focus on the "activities" that are in one's own "power."

10. See Seneca, *On Benefits*, 4.33.24; and Epictetus, *Discourses*, 2.6.9.

11. Focus on the "present" is a core motif in Marcus's deliberations; see especially *Meditations*, 2.14 and 3.10. Note also that Marcus speaks of drawing a circle around (*perigraphein*) the present (7.29) and finding the present sufficient (*arkein*) (3.12; 9.6).

12. Already in *Meditations*, 2.1 Marcus uses the expression "say to yourself" (*prolegein heautō*).

becomes an inculcated thought—not a shock or disruptive emotion. Similarly, it is crucial that one also be mindful of the interconnectedness of all things and on this basis attempt to consider one's duty at each moment to enhance the "good" of all existence.[13] This requires each person to consider their "allotted" role at each moment and to receive it with a calm resolve. The goal is to hone the mind toward being as coherent and focused as possible, in all circumstances, and not be dispersed by fragmenting emotions.[14]

This meditative practice may require an intentional disengagement from the thickness of life or demand some modes of its disengagement.[15] Accordingly, it is necessary to cultivate a sense of the priorities and ideal good for oneself and for the world. "You must care for the salvation of all human beings, and serve the human community. Nature has fixed as a principle that your particular usefulness should be the common usefulness; and reciprocally, that the common usefulness should be your particular usefulness."[16] To act otherwise is to live without probity and have one's intentions displaced toward realities that are beyond one's control. To build this consciousness into one's awareness is a task for moral readiness—the ideal for the attuned mind.

The same holds for the consciousness of death and finitude—something that Ecclesiastes advocates as a sobriety in the face of frustrated expectations,[17] or that Marcus meditates on as a way to minimize the impact of blind occasions.[18] The contraction of one's focus to the immediate moment is a honing of consciousness, and it is a means of overcoming despair or misguided expectations. To "act" with one's fullest "strength" or "capacity," as Ecclesiastes had tried to

13. Cf. *Meditations*, 6.38.

14. A core image occurs in *Meditations*, 8.48, where Marcus says that "the mind, unmastered by passions, is a very citadel"—a bulwark or "fortress" against sudden impressions and disturbing emotions.

15. On the issue of "delimitation of the self" as a fundamental feature of Stoicism, see Hadot, *Philosophy as a Way of Life*, 120.

16. See Cicero, *On Duties*, 3.12, 51–53. In *Meditations*, 6.38 Marcus stresses the sympathy or shared pathos that breathes through all aspects of the universe and induces a responsibility for the whole.

17. Eccles. 7:1–4, 9:5.

18. See esp. *Meditations*, 4.17, and 36–37; 6.2 stresses that dying is part of life.

counsel himself, requires one to devote oneself wholeheartedly on the task at hand. For Marcus, the philosophical life demands no less. To fail in this task is to succumb to the play of circumstances without a focused center point of consciousness. Death, too, is part of the larger whole with which Marcus was concerned,[19] and this realization could be an inducement for a deliberate training-in-readiness for the lived moment.[20] This appraisal of the role of attentiveness and decision retains the central value of moral action irrespective of events and happenstance. It may also help one to cultivate a disposition of positivity amid the welter of reality and even achieve an attitude of philosophical "joy" when one is able to "accept" every specific situation on its own terms.[21]

The second meditative formulation involves cultivating a consciousness of radical transcendence. In Marcus's terms, this involves a shift in perspective to "open up for yourself a vast space, embracing the entire universe in your mind, by considering unending eternity," to "dwell in your mind upon the changes of the elements into one another . . . [and to] look upon things down below as if from a vantage point above them."[22] Here, too, there is a nullification of the turbulence of daily occurrences by adopting a detached meditative stance. But it is crucial to emphasize that this attitude does not negate one's moral or spiritual responsibility to earthly events. Marcus's concern is to adopt a cosmic perspective (a developed consciousness that we are "assigned" a "tiny

19. Note the expression in *Meditations* 6.47, where the philosopher counsels himself, "all are dead"; nothing lasts.

20. For the notion of "readiness" in the *Meditations*, see 3.5.

21. Cf. *Meditations*, 8.23.

22. See *Meditations*, 9. 2 and 7.47–48, respectively. I have had recourse here to the more idiomatic translations of Hadot in *Philosophy as a Way of Life*, 244. The dual focus on the present moment, and the perspective of eternity characterizes the thinking of Goethe, and these themes are the subject of a rich and stimulating monograph by P. Hadot, *N'oublie pas de vivre: Goethe et la tradition des exercises spirituels* (Paris: Albin Michel, 2008).

part of the gaping abyss of infinite time")[23] in order to act with proper tranquility and probity. This is a position that tries to hold both ultimate transcendence and moral duty in mind for the sake of a disposition of virtue.[24] So doing, Aurelius integrates what are two distinct domains in the concluding counsel of the book of Ecclesiastes. This notwithstanding, the similarity connecting the advice of the philosopher (Marcus) and the observation of the religious sage (Qohelet) must be emphasized. Marcus seeks the nullification of emotions toward "indifferent" things so that he can focus on the moral tasks that are within his power. Qohelet advocates situating oneself within the framework of Divine reverence in order to be spiritually attuned to the command (*mitzvah*) of the moment. The task for the latter is to cultivate a transcendent disposition—one that views existence from beyond our mortal standpoint without denying the cycles of nature or our finitude, ending in death. This involves a different mode of duty and a shift from the desire for rational understanding to a stance of humble alertness to the everyday. He thus replaces his repeated calculations and evaluations for a goal of transcendent wisdom—one that requires an orientation of readiness to heed what each moment brings forth without delimiting presumptions. The Stoic philosopher comes to all this by a different route. The two converge through cultivated acts of metaphysical sobriety.

With these reflections we are brought to the mysterious crossing of cosmic transcendence (the sense of awe) and earthly immanence—the sense of "height" that expands consciousness beyond our worldly horizon, and a sense of "depth" that is embedded in the thickness of reality. Can these two positions be reformulated in contemporary terms? Phenomenological reflection and mystical insight offer some suggestions—and signposts within the labyrinth of our longing. A shift of focus is necessary—away from the vertical or horizontal vectors that are an outgrowth, as it were, of our physical posture. This shift in orientation involves an intuitive sense of inclusion within a spatial totality: it involves a transformed sense of being part of the whole,

23. See *Meditations*, 12.32; and compare Epictetus, 1.12.26: "how tiny a part you are, compared with the All." See also the advice to see things from a "bird's eye view" (i.e., from above) in *Meditations*, 8.48.

24. As noted, this requires a state of nonattachment to things; cf. *Meditations*, 5.19.

but not in terms of linear vectors. Contemporary phenomenologists of perspective have tried to outline the cognitive and experiential differences that are involved—a descriptive task fraught with solecisms (as we shall see), since the alternate viewpoint depends more on epistemic insight than on our ordinary manner of seeing. A succession of notable implications—bearing on art and ritual practice—will follow.

The Phenomena Take Their Turn: Depth Is Primary

Of great importance to the meditations of Marcus Aurelius is the notion of the interconnectedness of being—the cosmos being deemed a vast organism in which the person has a vital role. The role includes the realization that wherever one is, and whatever occurs, occurrences must be received without mental reserve. At all moments one must respond to the given situation and strive to realize the good that is within one's ken and capacity. The interlacing of the threads of being may be in terms of the primary Logos of things (i.e., their inherent or structuring principles, or their supervening reason) and the inherent sympathy of the elements to each other. Knowing these conditions is the first step on the philosophical path of cognitive or emotional self-mastery. This notwithstanding, the Stoic discipline regards the self to be set over against all worldly impingements, thus requiring the adept to attempt to see things "with a view from above." Seeing things in terms of their natural causes or features is one way of beginning to neutralize their impact. Contemporary phenomenology shifts this perspective in a fundamental way. It takes our being "in the midst of things" as primary to our embodied condition—and tries to think from within this manifold: not to draw evaluative conclusions (as does Qohelet) but to describe the nature of our embeddedness in the "depth" of the world.

A profound sense of what is at stake emerges from studies on the nature of perception by the phenomenologist Maurice Merleau-Ponty.[25]

25. Of decisive importance is his masterwork, *Phénoménologie de la perception* (Paris: Gallimard, 1945), whose full impact was felt two decades later upon its English translation as *Phenomenology of Perception* (London: Routledge & Kegan Paul, 1962). The chapters on the body, sense experience, and space are especially significant, and I shall draw on these discussions (note esp. pp. 235–39, 306–11). Among other works of

In his fundamental studies and expositions, we follow the shift from Renaissance and Cartesian notions of perspective and linearity—notions that stressed the thinking mind as looking out on space, which it tries to record (as subject vis-à-vis object)—to the realization that the self is entwined in the totality of existence and stimulated to "think" on the basis of the rhythms or modulations of light waves that affect our nature. Rather than the notion of depth being something added to our conceptions of spatial length (in the natural sense that depth is something spatially farther off or at a far linear remove along the line of sight of the individual with a fixed point of view), depth is now understood as a reality of independent worth (and not classifiable on a mental grid of near-far). For Merleau-Ponty, depth is the first and most primary of dimensions. It is, in his view, the mysterious "abyssal realm" of being where there is no single up-down coordinate or levels of reality. Rather, there is the absolute "fullness of being" that we perceive through our bodily senses. We live and perceive the world from within numerous intersecting planes of reality. Great artists understood this in an intuitive way, and Merleau-Ponty has exemplified his insights via a series of discussions on the art of Cézanne and Rodin.[26] In his view, already at the primary, prereflexive level, a person is plunged into a thick ontology of becoming—since there is nothing fixed for the individual during any given experience of the world. This new notion of depth gives metaphorical expression to such a lived condition along with unsayable experiences of the interpenetrating convergence of diverse lines of sight. All this suggests, also according to Merleau-Ponty, a thick mystic participation in being—deemed an entwinement of the porous and the perceived. In a bold figure the philosopher spoke about this thick global quality of perception as the "eye of God" (wherein all dimensions would be simultaneously convergent and true). Hence, this is not the eye of God from without, as a

importance is the essay "Eye and Mind," published in *The Primacy of Perception*, ed. J. Edie (Evanston, IL: Northwestern University Press, 1968); it is based on the final work produced by the author in his lifetime, *L'oeil et l'esprit* (Paris: Gallimard, 1964).

26. Many artists refer to the sense of depth as *la profondeur*; see the quotations in Merleau-Ponty, *L'oeil et l'esprit*, 64. Also deserving of note, is the stimulating monograph by L. Lavelle, *La perception visuelle de la profondeur* (Strasbourg: Imprimerie Alsacienne, 1921). To the best of my knowledge, Merleau-Ponty does not cite Lavelle.

fixed focal point of perspective, but as the vibrating "container" of all reality. Yet another (now geometric) figure that is employed is that of a cube,[27] which marks the intertwining of the visual and vision in our perception of it. I shall return to the human experience of this figure; but for now, let me add that in the experience of this phenomenon, all egocentricity and subjectivity are preceded by a primary, preverbal sense of "being in the depth" of world-being. At such moments, any distinction between transcendence and immanence collapses: there is only a sense of a great, ineffable totality. For mystics, this is the veritable reality of Divinity—the sacred texture of the Whole: here and now, all at once. How might this orientation comport with the distinctive tasks of life—and also instruct us moderns?

Mystical Resonances: Omnipresence and Depth

For many modes of Jewish mysticism, particularly those medieval and early modern ones influenced by Neoplatonism, Divinity is an absolute, transcendental Reality that suffuses all being (our world and more). Effluences deriving from the hidden depths of this Whole coalesce or interpenetrate infinitely and constitute the reality of God's primordial revelation or "self-exteriorization" into all the myriads of created forms perceivable by humans (who are similarly constituted) through a dimension of consciousness known as the soul and through all the tangible aspects of our natural experience. The latter are brought to sentient awareness through their effect on human bodies; but the inherent Divine reality, at the core of worldly experience, is not perceived "as such"—inasmuch as it is a dimension of what is ultimately spiritual and thus intangible. Whatever humans might sense or know of the "world" is complexly filtered through our mere human nature, and any sense of "Divinity" is only effable on the basis of mystical intuitions whose meanings are then formulated through the interpretations of tradition whose language was believed to contain encoded and symbolic hints ("topical allusions") of all these theosophical references or spiritual directives. On the basis of these traditions and

27. See Merleau-Ponty, *Phenomenology of Perception*, 235–38, 264–65; and also in a late working note from 1959, published in *The Visible and the Invisible* (Evanston, IL: Northwestern University Press, 1968), 202.

subsequent interpretations, masters and disciples were informed that the Absolute Reality of Divinity interpenetrates and effectuates every temporal and spatial dimension of being (and beyond). In the language of medieval Jewish mysticism, this "ultimate totality" has been verbally symbolized as the *'amiqa de-khola* (*Zohar* 3.107a), a pregnant phrase that points to "the (omnipresent) Depth of All-in-All."

The disclosures of this absolute totality, "concealed" in every possible way (*setim mi-kol siṭrin*) in both sacred Scripture and the configurations of the created world, were intended to enable seekers to make partial spiritual contact with the Divinity of All (*kola*). The techniques and types vary. In those cultural types often referred to as modern Ḥasidism (since the mid-eighteenth century), many masters have taught that even the external natural world, tangible and concrete, is suffused with God's immanent transcendence and can provide points of apprehension and connection to it when one realizes that "all is God" and that the experiential world is replete with modalities of Divinity fit for human consciousness. These features are often referred to as the "garments" of an infinitely present Divinity contracted into the worldly forms that humans can cognize. Through a trained focus on these configurations, and consecrating them through the language and rituals of tradition, one can have some human "sense" of this earthly refraction of "Absolute Divinity." Of central significance among these revealed expressions are the twenty-two letters of the Hebrew alphabet, through whose transcendental radiations of energy God created the world and revealed the sacred words of Scripture. Thus, all worldly reality is a refracted embodiment of Divine Speech, and everything that humans experience is a dimension of this godly immanence. Stated otherwise, we are both within and part of its suffusing "depth"; and, insofar as this Divine pulsation takes a humanly communicable form, as in Scripture, one can be informed and transformed by it. Accordingly, Scripture is not a natural language but a veritable code and verbal codification of Divinity. What it "says" about the world transcends all its natural configurations, which together conceal the supernatural reality of God. The mystic consciousness that somehow "senses" the all-subsuming mystery of Divine Reality "finds" that reality disclosed in the symbols of Scripture, and, reciprocally, these verbal hints can direct disciples toward the same transcendent truths. Entering the depth of Scripture is thus a hermeneutic process of gaining access to the Divine depths of reality—which is an energy matrix without syntax and structure, beyond natural language and the space-time dimensions of normal cognition. This reality is the All-in-All as such—to which the letters of the alphabet allude as figures of symbolic truth. And more: like an arcane hologram, even the spatial configurations between the letters constitute a silent, even more esoteric Divine "language." Both intertwine as the Word of God. The rite of entry is a spiritual transformation of consciousness.

So what can an adept do? One expressly developed procedure is to engage Divinity through Scripture by decoding its contents (directed in this wise by the inspired teachers of mystical tradition). By means of their interpretations, seekers of God might break through to a higher awareness—and even sense as a living truth the "depth of God." One of the singular masters whose hermeneutical techniques served this goal was the *Or Ha-Me'ir*—this being the cognomen of R. Ze'ev Wolf of Zhitomer (who, like other masters, was known by the title of his book of sacred instruction).[28] The *Or Ha-Me'ir* flourished in the late eighteenth century and was a disciple of the Great Maggid (R. Dov Ber) of Mezeritch, also known as the *Maggid Devarav le-Ya'akov* (the title of the collection of his mystical homilies and teachings). For both master and disciple, particular emphasis was placed on the manifestations of Divinity in this world—a dimension of immanence often referred to as the realm of the *Shekhinah*. Another term for this realm is "World of *Dibbur* (or Speech)."[29] This connotes the fact that, in the emanated Great Chain of Divine Being (from an absolute concealment to its refracted revelations), *dibbur* is the all-creating "Word of

28. Citations will be taken from *Sefer Or Ha-Me'ir ha-Shalem 'al ha-Torah* (Jerusalem: Even Israel, 1999), 1–2.

29. See the comprehensive study of A. Evan Mayse, *Speaking Infinities: God and Language in the Teachings of Rabbi Dov Ber of Mezritsh* (Philadelphia: University of Pennsylvania Press, 2020).

God"—recorded in the account of creation in Genesis 1)[30]—a Word that remains an active, creative element in this world in its myriad organic and inorganic forms. Humans are also continuous with this verbal helix (having also been created by a Divine fiat). Just this is the ontological basis of the spiritual instructions delivered by the *Or Ha-Me'ir*. His voice, like ours and all creation, is part of the Divine Whole.

The mystical fullness of Divinity is not something that we naturally "see" as such. It must be taught through tradition and its sacred exegesis. For God is not a physical tree on the earth and is not an epistemic construct of human contrivance. Rather, God is revealed throughout reality when the depth of being we experience, through a multitude of interpenetrating vectors, is exegetically translated in terms of the infinite suffusions of Divinity. Merleau-Ponty's phenomenology does not presume the truth of theological interpretations of experience, but it does provide a striking confirmation of the human sense of participating in the ineffable fullness of an absolute Divine totality.

It is from this perspective that we can understand the directives of the *Or Ha-Me'ir*, when he teaches that the true goal of religious consciousness (*da'at*) is to realize that the informing powers of Divinity assume the multiple expressions of worldly reality from top to bottom and, on this basis, seek to ground the essential inwardness of one's thoughts (being the Divine center point of one's soul) in this supernal Reality (*le-dabbeq penimiyut maḥshavto le-rommemuto*). Accordingly, when Scripture states (in Song of Songs 2:9) that *zeh 'omeid le-aḥar kotleinu* ("This [viz., the deer] stands behind our wall," we should understand this phrase as a coded (allegorical) instruction that God is the ultimate reality that "stands (transcendently) beyond" the external constructs, or "wall," of human consciousness. For in the first instance, the word *zeh* (this) serves as a deictic pronoun that points to this Divine reality. Hence, the teacher indicates (via interpretation) that the Divine manifold is potentially manifest to spiritual awareness

30. This is scripturally denoted by the multiple references (ten according to tradition) to the fact that "God spoke (*ve-yidabber*)" and the world was actualized in its multiple forms (there are nine explicit references to this verb act ; the tenth, according to rabbinic tradition, is the opening phrase of Genesis 1:1, "In the beginning God created").

but is blocked from spiritual "insight" because of sin or mental distraction. Thus the deictic term *zeh* does double duty. As noted, it points to everything as a manifestation of God (a referential "this" and "that") concealed in the numerous contractions of external reality. But in addition the term is also an epithet of God (based on Isaiah 25:9), so that we are also instructed that all worldly externalities—every "this" and "that"—not only alludes or refers to God but is a modality of Divinity.[31]

According to this bold hermeneutic, we are informed that everything we point to—each *zeh*—is a Divine reality whose proper realization "stands" just beyond our everyday consciousness. Going even further, the teacher also informs us that the Scriptural phrase (in Numbers 30 2) *zeh ha-davar* ("this is the word [that the Lord commanded]") means that every "thing" (*davar*) that one sees or encounters is a "pointer" (*zeh*) to God. Or, put more radically, that "everything that is commanded *is* the Lord (YHWH)" (since the Tetragram is both the symbol and actuality of all reality that commands or directs our attention).[32] Through such a hermeneutical instruction, the adept is taught to reframe the entirety of world-being as Divinity and to realize that all its manifestations are modal revelations of it. And since human beings participate in this all-suffusing reality, they also participate in the "depth of Divinity" that pervades all "things."

In this way the ineffable realities of God are named in human terms even as they remain wholly transcendent and an absolute mystery. Our acts of naming provide vectors of orientation relative to our human cognitive capacities, and though they are "contractions" that schematize the Divine Reality (the nonspatial "Depth of All"), they are revelations that summon and command our assent. This takes the concluding insight of Qohelet to another plane. Divinity is not the high transcendent Reality, "other" than the things of this world, but Presence as such: the omnipresent manifestation of value within which we participate. To try to gain a "view from above" would be equally distorting, for nothing can be negated or transcended. To do

31. See *Or Ha-Me'ir*, 2:147 a–b. The reference to the "deer" was symbolically (allegorically) understood since rabbinic antiquity (in *Midrash Shir Ha-Shirim Rabba*) as God hastening to Israel for both redemptive and revelatory presence.

32. *Or Ha-Me'ir*, 2:145a–b.

so would be to negate Divinity and value. In truth, the visual *Gestalten* of the world are revelations given by God for our spiritual cognition.

❋

A related aspect of this instruction draws on another passage from the Song of Songs (2:14). According to the traditional, allegorical explication of the verse, God (the beloved) says to Israel (the maiden), "My dove is in the clefts of the rock, in [its] hidden (or secret; *seter*) levels (or cliffs; *ha-madreigah*). Show me your face, let me hear your voice—for your voice is sweet, and your visage is comely." This address was understood as God's appeal to the nation at Sinai that they should respond with positive devotion to the covenant. Such is the historical application of the figure. But for our Ḥasidic master this address is God telling Israel that the *Shekhinah* (the dove, which represents Divine immanence) is hidden "within" the various "levels" (or gradations) of being and beseeches the people to speak in a proper manner regarding this effaced (hidden) presence. What this means is that although Divinity is concealed or refracted in numerous ways among the multiple structures of existence, God appeals to the adept to recognize this truth and rightly construe these forms of appearance. Hence, the task for the spiritual adept is to understand the world as encoding occluded dimensions of Divinity and so to strive to interpret this "verbal prism" as a refracted revelation of God's supernal creativity. Here again, our earthly reality is the "World of Speech" itself, to be received and interpreted as God's Word (or verbalized presence). It is therefore a spiritual duty to cultivate a sustained mindfulness focused on omnipresent Divinity concealed in everything. Recalling Ecclesiastes, we may suggest that each "this" and "that"—each *zeh* that solicits our attention—imposes its own particular imperative and calls on the individual to heed its manifestation and interconnection with "the Whole." Moreover, these verbal events are not seemingly disconnected occasions but flash points that engender reverence for the omnipresent reality of God that permeates all life. Participation *in* this seamless unity is conscious inclusion in *the enfolded Divine depths* of creation. Sacred rituals and their spaces of enactment may bring this spiritual inclusion to active mindfulness (or, at the least, intimate its reality).

Taking a Ritual Turn: The Divine World in Miniature

I referred earlier to Merleau-Ponty's paradigmatic use of the cube. Because of its intersecting lines, angles, and planes, experienced conjointly, the cube evokes the simultaneity of perspectives that constitute both the sense and "phenomenology of depth." This depiction of experience differs from Euclidian notions of surfaces and their conjunctions—notions that continued into medieval studies of architecture and painting, where the "point of view" is stationary and perceives things from the outside. By contrast, the figure of the cube evokes the mysteries of volume and the convergence of vectors. It begs one to think beyond our natural experience of a spatial cube and toward a multidimensional *participation in it*. This description of perception stimulates me to think about the ritual experience of entering into and sitting within a *sukkah*—the improvised ritual "booth" in which the harvest festival called Sukkot, or Tabernacles, has been celebrated since biblical antiquity. All the complex details of this booth—its construction, minimal and maximal height, and even speculations about airspace—were deliberated within rabbinic literature from its earliest discourses.[33] In addition, the ancient sages pondered the very nature of this ritual construct and asked, What is the relation between boards and partitions in the "building"? Was it merely like or actually a temporary home (and therefore requires one to affix a case with Scriptural verses at the entrance—an appurtenance known as a *mezuzah*)? Of related theological interest is the question of how, and in what respects, the *sukkah* is a ritual place of Divine immanence and whether its space is "like" a home or the Temple (albeit as a symbolic replica)? Some of these legal considerations even bear on certain mystical sensibilities—factors that weigh considerably on the ritual sense that, entering into this booth, one has entered into the sacred space of Divine Presence. With respect to the present discussion, each habitation within the ritual space of the *sukkah* would be a veritable experience of Divine "depth"—the "booth" being a theological "cube"

33. The major rabbinic regulations and discussion appear in the tractate *Sukkah* in both the *Mishnah* and *Babylonian Talmud*. For a valuable overall conspectus and analysis, see J. Rubenstein, *The History of Sukkot in the Second Temple and Rabbinic Periods*, Brown Judaic Studies 302 (Atlanta, GA: Scholars Press, 1995).

of Divine immanence. To be sure, this is a mystical-spiritual apperception whereby each individual partakes of the omnipresent Divine manifold (contracted into this sphere), each celebrant being at the vortex of its infinite spatial intersections.

Is there some support for this assertion and its correspondence to Merleau-Ponty's phenomenological deduction regarding spatial "depth" (also something not experienced as such by ordinary consciousness)?

An instructive way to consider this matter is to focus on the initial discourses found in many tractates of the *Babylonian Talmud*. They often contain a concise discussion of themes subsequently developed in the work, and thus serve as a kind of thematic preface to the ensuing discussions (each "discourse unit" is called a *sugya*).[34] In certain instances they convey theological topics as well.

The opening *sugya* of the tractate *Sukkah* (2 a–b) is pertinent in this regard.[35] In this unit, there is a precise consideration of the maximum height of a booth and a comparison of this with the height of entries that separate both public and private domains and the entrances to the Temple. There follows a series of deliberations about the nature of the desert Tabernacle—that is, whether this booth was only a physical object or actually constituted God's supernatural protection of the people in the desert under or within the "clouds of (Divine) Glory" (a topic considered via the alternative opinions of R. Eliezer and R. Akiva in earlier generations).[36] The latter explanation (that the desert booth was a Divine realm of providential care) reflects a mystical view consonant with R. Akiva's theology. In a related manner, the ambiguity in the biblical prescription that booths should be built *le-maʿan*

34. For an overview of prior scholarship and a conceptual approach, see Y. Brandes, "The Conceptual Significance of the Prefatory Sugya in the Babylonian Talmud," *Journal of Jewish Studies* 69 (2018): 22–43. Analytic study of these materials begins with Z. Frankel, "Beiträge zu einer Einleitung in den Talmud," *Monatschrift für Geschichte und Wissenschaft des Judentums* (Berlin: Das Breslauer Seminar; Jüdisch-Theologisches Seminar in Breslau, 1861). Claims of a *Savoraic* dating were based on the tractate *Kiddushin*. Cf. the summary in Brandes, 24–29.

35. See the study of Y. Brandes, "*Ha-Sukkah—Mivneh u-Mashmaʿut: ʿIyyun be-Sugyat ha-Petiḥah shel masekhet Sukkah*," *Asupot* 3 (2013): 251–61.

36. Cf. *Mekhilta de-Rabbi Ishmael*, ed. I. Horowitz and I. Rabin (Jerusalem: Bamberger & Wahrman, 1960), 48.

yeide'u—"*so that* your (future) generations *shall know*" that the Lord brought the people out of Egypt (Leviticus 23:42–43)—stimulated the theological teachings of the ongoing Divine presence in all such celebratory booths (in both historical and eschatological time). On this basis, the ritual dwelling in a *sukkah* on the festival was not only a matter of historical experience but one of active participation in a modality of God's providential presence during the holiday. Thus the *sukkah* came to symbolize (and could be experienced as) the actuality of Divine immanence.[37] On this same basis, entering this ritual space (or "cube") could become a spiritual experience of God's presence. The intersecting vectors that pervade the *sukkah* are deemed further tangible factors in sensing that one is "within" the "Divine Depth"—a locus where there is no single point of view but wherein all viewpoints intersect. To return to the image proposed by Merleau-Ponty, to dwell in the *sukkah* during the festival is, as it were, to be within the "eye of God"—a symbol of the mystery of a total, ineffable, all-providential presence.

In a striking way, the foregoing discussion (about a religious experience) is where a contemporary phenomenology of perception meets ritual consciousness and helps us think productively on its terms. Returning to my initial remarks, it is precisely in the midst of life where cognitive forms achieve their epistemological status—and transcend them, simultaneously. Following Merleau-Ponty's genial work, "depth" is not a dimension within a vertical sense of space or some point on a receding horizon. It is, rather, a primary realm of being—before human thought and manipulation[38]—and of experience through our embodied nature in the world. Put otherwise, the

37. It bears note that even the airspace extending beyond the height of the enclosed ritual walls was legally deemed part of the enclosure. Thus each booth was a tabernacle-like silo that rose vertically to heaven—the horizontal roof being a sacred canopy, symbolic of heaven itself. The worshipper was thus ensconced in a Divine immanence.

38. See Merleau-Ponty*L'oeil*, op. cit., 12. As he repeatedly asserts, painting, among the arts, seeks to engage or bring to presence this primordial quality of reality for the eye; music transcends this visual domain for the auditory and acoustic.

dimension of "depth" offers access to a "primordial knowledge of the 'real'"[39] beyond the separate vectors of normal space-time consciousness. Similarly, the *sukkah*, as a primary symbol of God's "indwelling" in ritual space helps inaugurate the worshipper into a consciousness of the all-suffusing reality of God's omnipresence in the depth or fullness of being.

Within this dimension, there is no reductive delimitation based on one's localized existence. There is only *zeh*, "this here," emergent to human consciousness from the eternal and all-intersecting moments of Divinity. The inducement to be (conceptually) above things and look down from a transcending perspective or point of view, or to be merely within the welter of worldly things, is herewith converted into a ritual readiness to experience whatever just is if and when we live within the veritable "eye of God." For all its profound phenomenological features, the sense of depth is, ultimately, a cultivated consciousness and a lived intuition. Philosophical analysis and theological homily may point us in this direction, but its truth is an experiential truth that is guided by tradition—albeit with exponential significance for a deeper sense of existence and for the value of each moment of consciousness. We are summoned from within the Whole to respond to one thing at a time: for each and every thing is an actual manifestation of the Divine totality in its full axiological significance. Thus, every aspect of our bodily posture is claimed. Repeatedly, our natural positionality may become a reawakened sense of the profound "depth of being"—reclaimed (and reappropriated) from ancestral wisdom.

39. Cf. Merleau-Ponty, *Phenomenology of Perception*, xvii.

3

Correlations and the Imaginal Between

Preliminary Reflections

We open to the primacy of the world as embedded and embodied creatures, from our first morning breath and the numerous pulsations of light that suffuse us. We are life enfolded in life: life-forms within ourselves, suffused by sensations,[1] and extending into realms beyond comprehension. Immersed in the depths of world-being, we partake of the encompassing universe, despite also being self-consciously distinct from the life-forms we confront. These sensate presences are a primary reality that repeatedly impinges on our awareness even when we are benumbed by routine or otherwise distracted. Somehow we still remain aware of being "in the midst of things"—between one thing and another.

One of the vital tasks of consciousness is not only to see and respond to what may suddenly claim attention; but to perceive, by intuition or design, correlations and similarities near and far. Likeness is sometimes an elusive quality but ever a means of unexpected perception—of bringing "things" into a new alignment or new relationship. Suddenly the world is activated by our imagination—and more real for all that. A name of such "likeness" is simile, and through this literary trope the vivid diversity of life comes to mind. With similes, we think betwixt and between the things of this world (as seen or

1. Note especially E. Straus, *The Primary World of the Senses: A Vindication of Sensory Experience* (New York: Free Press of Glencoe, 1963).

remembered) and build imaginal correlations between them in our imagination.[2]

Humility and creative speculation lie at the heart of this mindset. It is as old as the hills—to speak in simile—because it suddenly reveals that the world is more than "this" and "that" and that we are active agents in their potential and instructive correlation. Words are not just words: they are dynamic constructs of thought that can be put in phenomenal interrelation. No doubt many post-Kantian thinkers, such as Hans Vaihinger, would agree that we must swallow the pill of "as if"[3] and realize that we construe and name the world as hypothetical forms—and that we must come to terms with the consequences. Similarly, some post-Wittgensteinian thinkers are convinced (and argue convincingly) that (our naive and natural presumptions notwithstanding) we never see things *as such*—but only "as" this or that.[4] But this assertion notwithstanding, our words do effect real presences,[5] and their extension through description or creative correlation evokes new realities for consideration and understanding. I would even suggest that our consciousness as creators of similes extends our agency and hermeneutic engagement with the world. Existing between thought and world, we create correlations of presence. The phenomenon of simile brings this to mind.

It bears brooding on this connective and imaginal relationship, since it offers an interesting orientation to the powers of the mind to integrate realities of various kinds, and it puts into sharp relief what many moderns have lost and try to retrieve through various attempts at constructing meaningful connections. What has been lost is both the creative world-building consciousness of hermeneutics—the attempt to create new reality through our acts of interpretation—and

2. For a philosophical meditation on comparable entities as perceived and understood, see E. Dupreél, "La similitude et la promotion des étres," *Revue Internationale de Philosophie* 17 (1963): 505–13.

3. See his classic *The Philosophy of "As If": A System of the Theoretical, Practical and Religious Fictions of Mankind* (London: Routledge & Kegan Paul, 1935). The subtitle in the original 1921 German edition is longer.

4. Notable is formulation of G. N. A. Vesey, "Seeing and Seeing As," *Proceedings of the Aristotelian Society* 56 (1955–56): 109–24.

5. I am alluding to the pregnant phrase explicated by George Steiner in his *Real Presences* (Chicago: University of Chicago Press, 1989).

to live in the "between" of every verbal correlation. The following discussion is an attempt to retrieve this mindset. Many examples could have served my purpose; I adduce those chosen here not only because of their inherent merit but also because they allow me to gather a harvest of intellectual or spiritual topics that have interested me over the decades.

First Considerations: Reading the "Ciphers" of Existence

We read the world from within the world, and evaluate it based on intuitions and traditions, the product of instruction and empirical assessment. Being within the stream of life, and part of its manifold parts, may surely draw upon primordial notions of some "*participation mystique*"—as L. Lévi-Bruhl once famously put it;[6] though this sensibility does not preclude more deliberate and deliberated attempts to correlate a survey of things or draw deeper conclusions. I was once entirely and uncritically enamored of similarly construed presentations of the religious mind of ancient Near Eastern antiquity, as presented in *Before Philosophy*[7]—a book based on widespread notions at that time, and which presumed participation in a Divinely animated cosmos—with ancient Egypt and Mesopotamia at the center. On this assessment, ancient Greece marked a rational break with mythopoeic thought, and the inherent interconnections of world-being. The emergence of rational thinking (meaning some mode of objective assessment) was thus deemed to be an emergent phenomenon: like

6. His once highly influential *How Natives Think* (*Les fonctions mentales dans les sociétés inférieures*) (1923; NewYork: Washington Square Press, 1966), is still resonant, as evident in the discussions and revaluations below.

7. The full title was *Before Philosophy, The Intellectual Adventure of Ancient Man: An Essay on the Speculative Thought of the Ancient Near East*, by H. Frankfort, H. A. Groenewegen-Frankfort, J. A. Wilson, T. Jacobsen, and W. A. Irwin (Chicago: University of Chicago Press, 1946). A vigorous critique followed in the review by S. N. Kramer, in the *Journal of Cuneiform Studies* 2 (1948): 39–70. But in fact the opening essay states, "The ancients . . . could reason logically, but they often did not care to do so" (p. 16). This aside, the types of rational or analytic forms of scientific observation were not discussed.

a chicken breaking through its embryonic egg, to evoke imagery of old Phoenician myths. But this is to shortchange the inherent rationalities that could coexist within mythic sensibilities—sensibilities that could also perceive the world as a myriad of Divine phenomena to be studied and correlated, often using complex birth and genealogical phenomena to bring things into new alignment.[8] A significant example of empiricism and rationality in ancient Mesopotamia (and not it alone) is the multimillennial archive of astrology and the divination of terrestrial phenomena.[9] For even if it had its psychic core in a vibrant, Divine universe, this core could include making rational correlations of prognostic value—based on the study of the ciphers of reality and judgment of their correlation. In so doing, the researcher had to have the mental discipline to think in the imaginal 'between' of phenomena.

Perhaps a good place to set the stage for the trajectory to follow is a remark found in an old Babylonian "diviner's manual." that makes explicit what is implied in the huge compendia of celestial and terrestrial signs called *Enuma Anu Enlil* and *Shuma alu*. It states:

> The signs on earth as well as the sky bear signals for us; heaven and earth bring us omens; they are not separate from one another; heaven and earth are interconnected.[10]

This statement reveals the profundity of the mentality involved, which presumes that the entire universe—everything seeable or perceivable—is a matrix or panoply of "signs" that convey "signals" to the human mind for discernment and evaluation. They therefore function in tandem, as an interconnected whole, for the intelligence that strives to perceive (or interpret) their predictive nature. The diviner describes

8. Cf. F. Leichty, *The Omen Series Shumma Izbu*, Texts from Cuneiform Sources 4 (Locust Valley, NY: Augustin, 1969).

9. See the full discussion by J. Bottéro, "Symptômes, signes, écritures en Mésopotamie ancienne," in *Divination et Rationalité*, ed. J. P. Vernant (Paris: Éditions du Seuil, 1974), 70–197. This work is conceptually and factually exceeded by F. Rochberg, *The Heavenly Writing: Divination, Horoscopy, and Astronomy in Mesopotamian Culture* (Cambridge: Cambridge University Press, 2004).

10. Originally published by A. L. Oppenheim, "A Babylonian Diviner's Manual," *Journal of Near Eastern Studies* 33 (1974): 200, lines 38–44. I have followed Rochberg's translation (*The Heavenly Writing*), 166.

this as a beneficence granted by the divinities that manifest these signs (they are "for us"), even as they are merely implicit signals that require human decipherment for actual social knowledge. Mortals are thus not in an alien, otiose universe, but live within a sacred encyclopedia of ciphers that can be made meaningful in earthly terms. We are part of a vast semiotic system, but also betwixt and between its vast series of communications. Thus a worshipper can say to the Divine Moon and Sun: "I . . . keep watch for you; . . . [and] I am (visually) attentive to your appearance."

What this means is pertinent to how a person may go about depicting what is seen; that is, describing what the particular phenomenon is "seen as." For among the many sightings of the moon, in its phases, we are told that when this heavenly body wears a "beard," has a "crown," or rides a "chariot," such and so may be the result on earth (depending on their correlation with events in the past that may be projected into the future); or, correspondingly, the task of divining a sheep's liver may involve estimating features that may be called a "finger" or a "weapon." As is evident, these configurations are personified or presented as figurative tropes of some kind.[11] Clearly, such metaphors are means of depicting the phenomenon in terms of a Divine personality, for the purpose of marking correlations between it and human occurrences (that is, there is not a bow in heaven, but the perception of a certain configuration in the summer or winter sky that may signal something to those who are attentive to it and to earthly events). The point being that there is a 'kind of rationality' that involves metaphoric projections or estimations, and that these latter are 'as if' features that help one to make objective correlations. The diviner is thus both cognitively and imaginatively situated between the earth and the moon, trying to make sense of their interrelations at a certain point in time and space. Hence the 'between' is both a mental and cultural space, and the linkage binds one reality to another. Similitude is thus not identity, but some determined likeness that is perceived to have a hermeneutical or interpretative signification. Derived from a lived matrix

11. Cf. the discussion and evidence in M. Stol, "The Moon as Seen by the Babylonians," *Natural Phenomena: Their Meaning, Depiction and Description in the Ancient Near East*, ed. D. Meijer (North-Holland, Amsterdam: Verhandelingen der Koninkijke Nedelandse Akeademie van Wetenschappen, 1992), 245–77.

of natural realities and possibilities, the correlations perceived therein are deemed Divine intentions that communicate human meanings through the empirical attentiveness of the trained eye. In this sense, contemplation has a predictive purpose, offering a manual for decision and action. It is altogether otherwise for the aesthetic mind.

The Natural Gaze and the Reflexivity of Consciousness

Living in the context of natural correlations for pragmatic purposes is the decoding of ciphers of different types (e.g., astral features with physiological ones), and the attempt to determine the deep syntactic code of an omnipresent (albeit initially inscrutable) Divine reality. Literary creativity similarly senses the great mystery of worldly relations and in the contemplation of their outer forms or inner similarities reveals to the thinking eye something of the depth and dynamics of existence. It is in this vein that Homeric similes provide a primary alternative to the later Pythagorean assertion that "man is the measure of all things" and so guide us to a feature of the creative imagination whose purpose (or at least chief value) is a kind of a revelatory perception: a seeing into the heart of things as compared to an assertion of personal meaning to counter the authority of scientific calibrations or the sensed slippage of a stable point of reference. The long route to our modern condition still has much to teach and, in the process, help shape a spiritual return to the sources of our formation (both natural and literary). It therefore behooves us to adopt the Homeric gaze for starters and from this perspective to try and reach back toward its mode of consciousness.

What, we wonder, is going on when Homer represents the fall and death of Gorgythion with the following simile: "As a poppy in a garden droops its head to the side, being heavy with seeds and the showers of spring; even so he bowed his head to one side, weighted with his helmet" (*Iliad* 8.310–11)? Just what is being conveyed here, and to what effect are these elements correlated? The event is a brief aside, at a point when Teucer attempted to kill Hector with an arrow but misses; and upon striking Gorgythion in the chest, the warrior's head sagged low, earthbound—his demise imminent and implied. What did the poet perceive and wish to convey by correlating these features—a hero in the spring of youth cut down and a plant laden with fructifying water and nourishing seeds? Are we to carry over the image of potential in the poppy to the vanquished youth with all the implied discordance, or is it the drooping poppy that so conveys this mournful and moribund contrast? Further, we ponder, is it just the outer form of a seed-bearing plant bending earthward that struck Homer's mind as he conveyed the collapsing feature of the soldier's head, or is it just the opposite: the pathos of the slain youth, cut down from upright dignity, that calls to mind, somewhat ironically, the death likeness of a storm-infused pregnant plant? Howsoever these all-inducing images were nurtured, they arise as one from the pulse of the poet's heart—alive to the primordial womb of nature and its innate coalescence of generativity and death—both beyond good and evil and "other than" the pathos and complex interface of nature and culture. Or perhaps it is precisely the latter conjunction that the imagination perceives so profoundly and that mirrors through simile the correlation between a human event and its near likeness in nature?

For the poet, I surmise, the terminology of similarity (both "like" or "as" and "so") is not an abstraction, or a reach toward something other, but the actuality of a natural hinge: this death and this laden poppy are primordially one and intertwined. The particles conjoining them make this conjunction both visibly and narratively apparent. The poet's heart lives in the imaginal between of the two, which he perceives with an emotionally engaged eye (and not the differentiating glance of a military memoirist, for whom the blood-soaked bodies and killing fields are not a binocular unity)—and through his inner vision, now made poignant, allows us, the reader-receivers of his formulations, to enter this poignant "between" through the pathos of a sympathetic tremor. With the poet's stimulus, we now, too, perceive with a feeling eye the complex entwinement of human life and nature, and through a *poetry-induced participation* in the manifold of life,[12] we somehow perceive its mythopoeic summons and can never again

12. With great insight, P. Vivante, in his *Homeric Imagination: A Study of Homer's Poetic Perception of Reality* (Bloomington: Indiana University Press, 1970), 83, observed that Homeric similes "stress a natural movement or a mode of being which is essentially the same in man and in any animate object—a parallelism which brings out some

disregard the saturating font of all existence. It is through the magic of similes like this that we may instantaneously sense the primary coexistence of all forms within the mute biosphere of the world, however much or little the great deities that Homer seats high above or behind this phenomenal swirl spin earthly destiny through the webs of immortal fate—even if they are not themselves, already and ineluctably, entwined in its invisible snare and mind-stealing threads.

The poet casts his wand of imaginal similarities across the spaces of the *Iliad* and the *Odyssey* differentially because of their differences (the first a poem of rage and revenge, the second about deception and the longing for *nostos*, or return) but also vibrantly similar in their mythopoeic sensibilities. Think, for example of the correlation of human rage to a "boiling surge" of water and the tears of sorrow to thawed snow that "flows down" from high-ranging mountains; or again, there is the consuming pathos of heartbroken longing or the many feats of shape-changing cleverness that find their similarities within the world of nature—filled with silence and sound. The "between" of these numerous imaginal connections is not a mental space for reflection or analysis so much as the heart-locking realization of some utterly elusive and never completely captured interconnection between all things—whether a primordial force generated within the immortal heart of a silent destiny or an ever-oscillating and pulsing vitality that spawns intention and mating and creative life. All such similes and the stimulating similitudes that they sponsor keep us attuned to the vast underlying (but also visible) enchainment of existence: not through any deliberateness of logical inference but through the unexpected shudder induced by poetic prowess. Image after image leads us into the labyrinth of silence where nothing more needs be said after such breath-catching moments. On these occasions, the participles of *like* and *so* are not suggestions thrown into the void but disclosures of the fusion of external events and their imaginal correlates. What has been joined or enjoined by language is now sutured into one's heart. At such moments, the self becomes, or actualizes, this very "between."

identical dispositions or elemental quality quite apart from the requirements of a particular characterization."

But does such an engaged or transformed consciousness require the reader-listener to be within the same mythopoeic frame as evidenced by Homeric poetry? And if so, would not this situation, for the modern reader, be somewhat akin to the condition of those ancients for whom the *Iliad* remained a "classic" but could no longer instruct directly because of shifts in the perceptions of nature and notions of the hidden Divine. To save the sacred epic, the analytics of the new intellectual constructs became a template for preserving it under the guise of a new rationality and second-order language. This latter refers to the modes of allegory (their very construal and construction) that perceive another cultural logic and signification encoded within a given text. On such occasions, likeness shifts from the horizontal correlation among elements to their vertical depth or deep sense. That is, surface topics or narrative content were not deemed to reveal their "innermost truth" but had to be decoded on the basis of correlations between certain surface cues and some hidden scheme of reference. Among the most famous examples in antiquity are the attempts to read the *Iliad* as dealing with issues of moral virtue, natural science, or Platonic or Stoic philosophy, depending on the concerns of the given interpreter. In the process, these allegorical readings "saved" the ancient classics and allowed them to sustain their canonical and pedagogical status for over a millennium and a half—from ancient Plato to the neo-Platonic philosophers and including Byzantine handbooks for ethical virtue and its pedagogy in the medieval schools.[13]

A similar situation obtained in the rabbinic transformation of the concrete emotional and physical imagery of the Song of Songs into allegorical tropes of the historical relations between God and Israel, and it thereby displaces the erotic tone and focus of the original for something more abstract. Of particular interest here are those occasions where the reader can still have a "cognitive experience" of what is "between" the original imagery and its reformulation. To explore

13. Cf. the influential medieval *Allegories of the Iliad* by John Tzetzes, trans. A. Goldwyn and D. Kokkini, Dumbarton Oaks Medieval Library (Cambridge, MA: Harvard University Press, 2015). For the notion of saving the classics, see O. Barfield, *Saving the Appearances: A Study in Idolatry* (Middletown, CT: Wesleyan University Press, 1988).

this issue, we shall first consider the nature of the similes found in the Song, on its own terms.

Identity and Otherness in the Lover's Eye

In his philosophical musings on rhetoric and poetics, Aristotle often evoked Homer as exemplary with respect to considerations of simile and metaphor. In his account, simile is a developed metaphor in the sense that it makes a statement of identity ("this is that") both specific and explicit ("this is like that") with the crucial term *hos* (meaning "like" or "as") used in all the examples cited in *Rhetoric* 3:4).

Thus the polarity of terms or relations is abridged in a metaphor: "When the poet states that he 'leapt on the foe as a lion,' this is a simile; when he says of him 'the lion leapt,' this is a metaphor—here, since both [subjects] are courageous, [Homer] has transferred to Achilles the name of 'lion'" (Aristotle, *Poetics* 4.1406b.20–23). Elaborating further on the ways the relationship between identified imagery is conveyed, Aristotle says, "The simile, as has been said before, is a metaphor, differing from it only in the way it is put (*prosthesei*); and just because it is longer, is less attractive. Besides, it does not say outright that 'this is that,' and therefore the reader is less interested in the idea. We can see, then, that both speech and reasoning are lively in due proportion—as they make us seize a new idea promptly" (1410b.17–21). This presumption aside, we may well wonder about the difference between a cognitive process that evaluates an explicit analogy and an implicit one, for there remains the need to elucidate what is involved when the poet suddenly "perceives similarity" (1458a.8) and when a receiver of the image is bidden to cognize the correlation. In the latter cases, an interpreter is challenged to re-present the representation (*mimesis*) in their mind's eye and then to interpret its meaning as an aesthetic experience. This is somewhat similar to Aristotle's remark that "Seeing likeness is pleasurable because in contemplating it, people *come to understand* (*manthanein*) through inference what each of its details are" (1448b.15–17, my emphasis). The simile is not "there" as such in reality; it is a product of the creative imagination (a "seeing . . . through inference") and exists as a presence in the mind.

Let us "think with" the imagery of the Song of Songs—at first without any cultural or religious presumptions (allegorical or otherwise) about the nature of the literary figures under consideration. Such a thinking "with" the imagery is a first-order hermeneutical act and brings us close to the voice of desire so redolent in the Song and the expressions of "likeness" repeatedly voiced by the male and female speakers. It is precisely this dialogical dimension of "speaking to" the other that characterizes the discourses of the Song: he speaking directly to her; she speaking similarly to him—or, in his absence, she depicts herself or her beloved to her close companions, intimating her longing and love. In response, these friends also wish to know something of the youth (his appearance and qualities) that make the lass so overcome with rapture and emotion. The similes are thus part of specific speech acts, evocative and expressive of an inner-state that tries to find suitable figures to convey (or to suggest) the nature of one's inner feelings. These linguistic transfers are conveyed either by the particle *ke-* ("like" or "as") or the verbal term *damah* (or *dimmah*) *le-* ("to image as" or "compare to"). Exemplary of the first comparison is the dialogue found in Songs 2:1–3. After the maiden says herself, "I am a rose of Sharon, a lily of the valleys" in verse 1, he says, "Like (*ke-*) a rose among thorns, so (*ken*) is my darling among the maidens" (v. 2). And then she, in turn, adds "Like (*ke-*) an apple among the trees of the forest, so (*ken*) is my beloved among the youths. I desire to dwell in his shade, for his fruit is sweet to my mouth" (v. 3). How can we understand this exchange and (hermeneutically participate in) the passion verbally exchanged between them? To begin, let us first note the opening metaphorical assertions that convey her sense of personal identity: a rose and a lily. This seconding of the figure does not so much provide a synonymous parallelism of terms as suggest the insufficiency of any single descriptive statement. A space is opened between the two terms that undermines the figural sufficiency of self-characterization (both to herself and perhaps also to her listening lover). We are thereby informed that the beloved is far more than a person who can be succinctly portrayed. In response, he picks up the elusive but necessary need to liken her further and does so not in terms of herself but with regard to his exemplary elevation of her among/beyond other women. Speaking in similes, she is to her companions as a rose among thorns—indeed, she is a rose and they are thorns. This supplement provides some added sense of the nature of this correlation: delicacy (yes, he rightly perceives her first remark) versus something prickly—the exact opposite of a flower or natural blossom.

Why is this addition important? Because similes in the Song are terse and without any explication of the "transferred attribute" that links the terms—precisely what is characteristic of the detailed similes found in Homer. And since we are comparing these two types, we may add that in the latter a simile is introduced by the author who suspends the direct action for this correlative aside—a feature that is not the case in the Song, where the simile is a voiced statement of a participant in the action. This said, perhaps some trace of the transferred quality is suggested in the girl's immediate retort. He is not only a tree with edible fruit, among all the trees of the forest, but she boldly confesses her desire to lie beneath it and taste the sweetness of his fruit—a remark that does not so much state the physical attributes of the tree as depict the emotional qualities that so stimulate her erotic fantasies.

In the presence of the beloved, there is always something "more" that needs saying: be it about oneself, to oneself, or oneself to the other. Longing links love to some figure beyond and the need for newly expressed articulations. Thus the eye of the youth looks out at the maiden through the lens of his desire and sees the missing third that palpitates the yearning: for to him her thighs seem like wrought chains, rounded and appealing; or her belly (by euphemistic suggestion) is "like piles of wheat hedged by lilies"; and so on (7:2–3). The eye can't get its full share of the natural world, so erotically alive and vibrant it has become. The similes thus evoke the changing landscape of inner desire: charged by everything that excites it. The eye confesses that it is blinded by rapture ("turn your eyes away from me, for they overwhelm me"; 6:5a), and this then stimulates a kaleidoscopic stream of the "almost-said" (this being the indirection of simile): her "hair is like a flock of goats streaming from the Gilead (hills)" and "her teeth like a herd of ewe lambs coming out of the (bathing) pools—all of them similar and without any blemish: she is like sheep coming up from the water"; 6:5b-6). What is seen is a figural substitute for the blinding sense of desire—a representation of how every element of the external world is correlated with a longing to fill one's eye with an ardor incommensurable to its verbal expression. Hence, the heart is limited to the likeness of a simile; and it is just this that the reader experiences in the flood of imagery that pulsates in the hermeneutical "between" an inner feeling and its forms of literary representation. Mimesis thus includes the participatory imagination of the reader—and with it the acute consciousness of approximation and similitude.

The use of the formula *dimmitikh* ("I have likened you to") and *damah le-* (my beloved is "imagined as") allows the speaker to shift from the immediacy of saying that the other is "like" this or that, to a way of conveying the inward state of their heart. The first example comes quite near the beginning of the Song, when the male states: "To a mare (*le-susati*) among the steeds of Pharaoh, I have likened you (*dimmitikh*)], my fair one" (Songs 1:9). It is a jolting formulation because the initial image (the comparative term is in syntactic suspension before the speaker enunciates the personal imaginative act ("I"-"you") followed by another pronoun ("my") of relation. This construction helps the speaker indicate and confess to a figure of his personal imagination. The marker of connection ("to") provides a deictic or demonstrative aspect that reveals the shape the loved one has taken in the mind of the speaker. This formulation also conveys the immediacy of longing and fantasy. This recurs near the end of the Song, after an extended series of figures (Song 7:2–6). It climaxes when the male speaker is imbued to speak palpably in terms of the personal "desires" (*ta'anugim*) she awakens: "your . . . stately body is like a palm tree (*damtah le-tamar*), and your breasts like (grape) clusters"—"let me climb the palm; let me take hold of the branches; let your breasts be like clusters of grapes; let your breath be like the fragrance of apples" (vv. 8–9). In this instance, the similes (marked by *ke-*, "like") are subordinate to the deeper confession of the imaginative disclosure (*damah le-*) of erotic desire. The evocative quality of the comparisons is concretely communicated to the maiden and thereby to the reader, who is drawn into the likeness of the similes and the emotional connection being formulated. In this hermeneutical sense the latter-day reader, after the fact, so to speak, enters the emotional qualities between the "tenor" (the thing or person being described) and the "vehicle" (the figurative language used to describe it).[14] In this

14. The terms *tenor* and *vehicle* were made famous by I. A. Richards, *Practical Criticism: A Study in Literary Judgment* (New York: Harcourt, Brace; London: Kegan Paul, 1930).

process, the interpreter becomes part of the creative correlation and its meaning.

Reading with Something Else in Mind

Like the charged human emotions in the *Iliad* and the pathos of its dialogues, some later inheritors of the Song of Songs could not readily integrate either its drama or its language into the sacred canon of Scripture, for they deemed its erotic allusions at total odds with the pervasive cultural and religious goals of emotional restraint, legal obedience, and moral edification. Truth to tell, nothing of this kind was suggested by the figures and content of the Song. And so, rabbinical debates and censorship put the text under wraps—until some exegetes were able to save the sequestered material by giving its problematic topics a "transferred sense" (which was the way they reinterpreted the verb *he'etiq* from the book of Proverbs 25:1—a literary term that was remarkably similar to the contemporary Greek use of the verb *metaphērō*, also used to mean an allegorical "transfer," or carrying over, of sense from one cognitive sphere to another).[15] By so boldly injecting covenantal theology into the dialogues of the Song, the work now yielded a series of episodes in which the two new subjects, God (as the male beloved) and Israel (as the fair maiden), recall their former intimacy of religious love and their shared desire for its renewal. The text was now deemed to be redolent with both sublimated love and longing and replete with references that speak of how covenantal obedience could create constancy in the oscillating relationship between these two parties. In the proem that was added to the Midrash on the Song (probably from the fourth or fifth century CE), the authorship of the work was attributed to King Solomon and even considered to be an inspired product of the "Holy Spirit." On this view, the grand master of secular wisdom was a great allegorist who found fitting figures to represent the original language of the Song.

15. The occurrence of the Hebrew verb *he'etiq* with this sense occurs (in a comment by R. Abba Shaul) in *Avot de-Rabbi Natan*, ed. S. Schechter (New York: Feldheim, 1967), version A, I.1, p. 2. For the case for the Greek parallel, see S. Lieberman, "*He'arot le-Fereq alef shel Kohelet Rabba*," in his *Meḥqarim be-Torah Ereṣ Yisrael* (Jerusalem: Magnes Press, 1991), 57–58.

Each of these figures was now called a *mashal* (not a "parable" but a "representative image"). The upshot was that all the central topics and personages of Israel's sacred history were infused with the highly charged religious *eros* in the Song. The similitudes proposed between the figures of this text and the events of the Torah opened a dramatic space wherein the reader was successively instructed, exhorted, and stimulated by degrees.

But this was not the end of the matter, for contemporary with these textual manoeuvers there was another hermeneutical use of term *mashal*—one that aligned a figurative or narrative analogue to the Scriptural text, which was then construed in new terms. This "figural analogue" was introduced by a homilist immediately after the citation of some Pentateuchal verse (notably, one read in the synagogue on a given sacred occasion) via the formula *mashal le-mah ha-davar domeh* ("an analogy: to what may the matter be compared?"). This rhetorical query was then answered by the comment *le-melekh* ("[it may be compared] to a king" or another figure) and followed by a short narrative episode that allowed the biblical passage to be reinterpreted in a new way. The results are dramatically bold theological or ethical reconceptualization of the citation. Formally, the *mashal* stands between the Scriptural verse cited and its figural analogue, mediating between the canonical source text and its secular subject (often using a king or a matron as exempla).

To illustrate this type of hermeneutical transformation, I turn here to one particularly striking example. It is ostensibly concerned to address the reference in Songs 3:9 to Solomon builder of a (marital) pavilion. But this merely provides the occasion to consider features of God's relationship to Israel in terms of the public or private spheres of revelation. Thus a seemingly straightforward passage leads to a bold and altogether unexpected theological discourse. The rhetorical mediation of this discussion comes via an explication introduced by the term *mashal*.[16]

> *King Solomon made for Himself a pavilion* (Song 3:9). By "pavilion" is meant the Tabernacle; "King Solomon (*shelomoh*) made for

16. See in *Pesiqta de-Rav Kahana*, ed. B. Mandelbaum (New York: Jewish Theological Seminary of America, 1962), 1:3–4.

> Himself (*lo*)"; that means: the King [God] whose peace (*shalom*) is His (*she-lo*). R. Judah bar Ilai said: [The verse may be compared] to (*le-*) a king who had a young daughter. Before she grew and showed signs of puberty, whenever he saw her in the market, or in the streets, he would [freely] speak with her; but after she came of age, he said: It is not befitting my daughter's honor that I [continue to] speak with her in public. Thus [he told his servants]: Make a pavilion for My daughter so that I may speak with her therein. It is similarly the case [between God and Israel]. At the beginning, *when Israel was a child I loved him, and from Egypt (on) I called him [publicly] "My son"* (Hosea 11:1). Thus, in Egypt, they [all] saw Me when I said *I will pass through the land of Egypt* (Exodus 12:12); [later,] at the Sea they saw Me, [as it says] *when Israel saw the great Hand* (Exodus14:31); and [thereafter,] at Sinai they saw Me, [as Scripture says]: *Face to Face the Lord spoke with you* (Deuteronomy 5:4). But after they received the Torah, and became [thereby] a complete (*sheleimah*) nation [i.e., had reached mature majority], He said: It is not befitting the honor of My sons that I speak with them in public, so [he said to them]: *Make Me a Tabernacle, and I shall speak from within it.* Thus Scripture says: *When Moses went into the Tent of Meeting he heard the Voice [of God] speaking to him from above the cover of the Ark of Testimony.* (Num. 7:89)

As noted above, the opening citation is taken from Song of Songs 3:9. Its ensuing explication follows the sequence of words in the Scriptural verse, beginning with the term *aperiyon,* taken here to refer to the Tabernacle constructed in the desert. This historical application of the word sets the stage for the allegorical reinterpretation that follows: first by the explanation that the name Solomon, *Shelomoh,* is an epithet for God, the King whose "peace (*shalom*) is His (*she-lo*)." But more is implied (for the preacher) by the fact that the verse in Song 3:9 states that Solomon built this pavilion "for himself" (*lo*), and that the Divine epithet states that God's peace is "His own" or "for Him" (*lo*). And it is just this as yet unexplained congruence of pronouns (in the verse and in the epithet) that charges the homily and stimulates the ensuing theological-historical presentation. In fact, precisely this issue is the basis for the teaching of R. Yehudah bar Ilai, which he introduces as a *mashal* that compares the Scriptural episode "to a king" (*le-melekh*) of flesh and blood. What induced it? Perhaps the sage had in mind the classical statement in the Torah where God is cited as addressing Moses: "Let them (the people) make a Tabernacle (*mishkan*) for Me (*li*)—and [then] I shall dwell (*ve-shakhanti*) in their midst" (Exod. 25:8). That is, the construction of a Tabernacle in the desert was to provide a place "for" Divine dwelling among the people. That is, it was to be built "for" God alone as an earthly abode in the midst of the nation traveling in the desert. Another key passage was likely also in the preacher's mind, and that is Leviticus 1:1. That text stresses both God's dwelling within the Shrine and Moses's exclusive access to it for revelations. How does R. Yehudah's parable bear on these matters and its theological significance?

The homilist begins his explication by introducing a parable about a king who "had (*lo*) a young (*qeṭanah*) daughter" whom he would regularly meet, both publicly and wherever he chose to do so. Referring to the maiden with this term of maidenhood, R. Yehudah evokes the rabbinic understanding that she was still prepubescent (*qeṭanah* is the technical terms for a girl who had not yet shown the requisite signs of her puberty). Hence, the king had no social or other inhibitions to act as he did; for his actions did not contradict propriety. However, when the girl did enter the status of her maturity, decency demanded that the king cease all public contact or communication with her; and so he summoned his servants to build "for him (*lo*)" a pavilion wherein he could both meet and converse with her out of the public eye. Whatever the original status or purport of this narrative, it segues here into a striking correspondence (or similitude) with the history of the nation and its revelatory communications with God. Being a master of Scripture, the homilist adduced a notable sequence of biblical sources to construct a hermeneutical analogue to the *mashal*, beginning with a reference to the fact that Israel was the beloved son of God who, initially, had full and open access to Him in Egypt and at Sinai. During this period, the nation was still in its youth, and had not become *sheleimah*, both physically and spiritually "mature" (use of the female noun here continues the theme of the parable, with its focus on the maiden, even though the proof text refers to Israel in masculine terms). All this changed after the covenant at Sinai. Now only one person could enter the Shrine: Moses, who serves as the symbolic representative of the entire nation.

What is remarkable is the way Scripture is used to demonstrate the historical shift from God's revelation in all places to its delimitation to the sacred Tabernacle. According to the homily, this momentous change was inaugurated after the public appearance of God at Sinai, when Israel received the covenantal law and proclaimed their feality. This "Sinaitic episode" extended from Exodus 19 to chapter 24, after which, in chapter 25 God summoned Moses and directed him to have the people build Him a Shrine (that He might dwell among them). It was only after the completion of the building in Exodus 40 that Moses alone was "called" into its recesses (thus paralleling the beloved maiden of the parable). This being so, it is notable that R. Yehudah's homily concludes with the final dedication of the altar in the Shrine in Numbers 7:89. This verse is significant not only for the subject involved but particularly because it was the climax of the special lectionary unit recited for the holiday of Hanukkah, which commemorates the purification and rededication of the Temple defiled by the Romans. The homily of R. Yehudah was thus liturgically keyed to this event and the hoped for dedication of a New Temple (Shrine) in the future. This reuse of a homily celebrating the desert Tabernacle exemplifies how the terms of an old *mashal* could be put in the service of later rabbinic theology and its messianic hopes. What more can be said about the imagery of the parable?

It is evident that the sage's use of the topos of a young maiden and a king would have special resonance with the language of the Song, since the maiden in this text had long since been allegorically identified with Israel just as the male personality had been interpreted as God. Hence R. Yehudah's homily evokes the special relationship between the people Israel (the beloved maiden-daughter) and its God (the King of kings). The imagery of the parable thus both highlights the *eros* and special intimacy between the king and maiden even as it shifts attention from this valence to the themes of Israelite history and theology. By this means, this rabbinic sage (like his colleagues) performed a significant hermeneutical feat: he preserved the charged (nuptial) language of the Song of Songs while transforming it into the argot of (normative) biblical topics. The use of earthly tableaux to explain Divine behaviors (feelings and acts) and Scriptural developments (the selective delimitation of direct access to God) is also remarkable and has a notable effect. The similitudes of the *mashal* and its allegorical applications invite the receiver to engage exegetically the correspondences that lie "between" the two and thereby participate in their cultural reception. Indeed, the homilist's *mashal* becomes the means of mediating new teachings to the people, and it discloses (by figural substitution) the deeper import of a culturally difficult (even disturbing) Scriptural passage. Later Jewish sources take the allegorical potential of the Song to further interpretative levels. It is to this enterprise that we now turn.

Quest for Meaning and the Question of Purpose

What might it mean to take the Song of Songs to heart and be transformed by its imagery? By this query I do not ask how one may interpret those formulations or types of depictions that do not make sense to latter-day readers. I mean it as a reader who would be inspired by the Song's profound longing for interpersonal connection and as a religious person who would hope to engage the allegorical readings of the Song in terms of a quest for spiritual significance. This being so, the epistemological task of taking the images to heart involves a double jeopardy: to reallegorize the allegories in terms that may speak to one's epistemic situation and spiritual desire. Traditional spiritual interpreters might tend to override such a transfer of meaning—whereby the text is read as a living instruction for one's inner life—given their inherited beliefs in certain types (and limits) of reinterpretation. Modern readers will have a more complicated and self-conscious struggle to achieve this same result. Both types—the traditional and the contemporary—are the subject of this section.

To exemplify these considerations, I shall first convey the gist and concerns of a remarkable collection of spiritual teachings on the Song of Songs and then offer a reconceptualization of is mystical theosophy in a quite different key. The texts cited are drawn from the Ḥasidic teachings of R. Ze'ev Wolf of Zhitomer and found in his multivolume collection *Or Ha-Me'ir*.[17] In his homilies the master

17. The book was originally published in Koretz in 1798, immediately after his death. The text and pagination used here is from a reprint edition (Jerusalem: Machon Even Israel, 1999). The Songs commentary is found in 1.249a–284b.

emphasizes that a spiritual adept should interpret the words of Scripture on a personal level so that it can influence their soul and direct it toward God. This is especially the task for a reader of the Song. At the outset of his comments on this work (based on a formulation in the *Book of Zohar*), the master states that King David and his son, Solomon, represent two types of spirituality. The former devoted his life to purifying his spiritual service to the *Shekhinah* (viz., the Divine Immanence) through devoted ritual and ethical practice (simultaneously purifying desires and virtues); whereas the latter, blessed with a more transcendent wisdom, looked beyond his own somatic and mental structure to its transcendental Divine "Image" or "Form" in the supernal realm. Thus, if the task of King David (and those who follow his path) was to cultivate one's religious devotion through the Torah and its ritual practices, the concern of a more advanced adept, modeled by King Solomon, was to restore the letters and teachings of the Torah to their primordial origin (which requires connecting the words and the tasks of Scripture to their ultimate Divine dimension before the supernal mysteries were transformed to accommodate our human consciousness and capacity).[18] Thus, if the first religious task (modeled by King David) is to focus on one's mortal being (the particular *tzorekh*, or "need" of the individual person), the Song also points to a higher goal, which is to focus on restoring the letters and teachings of the Torah to their original provenance in Divinity (so that the aim of human action and consciousness is on the *tzorekh gavohah*, or transcendental Divine "need," as it were—for which human actions are essential).[19] Disclosing this spiritual task is the chief hermeneutical concern of R. Ze'ev Wolf's explication of the two central figures that make up the Song. In the process, he employs the terms *dugma* and *dimyon* to indicate metaphorical "analogy." (These terms were also used by Rashi in his eleventh-century commentary

18. This accommodation is theologically referred to as a "contraction" of the spiritual realities to a more mundane form. Such a Divine delimitation marks the widespread mystical notion of *tzimtzum* in Ḥasidic sources.

19. See R. Ze'ev Wolf of Zhitomer, *Or Ha-Me'ir*, 258b–260a. This task is ultimately unitive, a restoring of the manifest material world to its spiritual source in Divinity.

on the Song, and both words are akin to Latin *similitudo* and *figura* in Christian typological exegesis).[20]

Now the mysteries of Torah are one thing; their encoded reality or manifest appearance within the world is another. To get beyond such appearances, the natural eye requires the cultivation of a spiritual awareness: only then will one be able to perceive the presence and reality of God within and through the totality of existence and be able to recognize how Divinity "appears" or "seems" (*nidmeh*) to the individual amid the multiple forms of life (whose diversity repeatedly "confuses" or "impedes" (*mone'im*) the mind from perceiving the ultimate Divine dimension).[21] According to R. Ze'ev Wolf, every worldly element has its supernal dimension, and so if one can focus on their spiritual center, it is possible to recognize Divinity concealed in the world of appearances. An instructive verse to which the master makes use is Song 2:14, "My dove, in the cranny of the rock, in the hiddenness of the cliff (*be-seter ha-madreigah*)—Let me see your face, let me hear your voice." According to his explication, this passage is the voice of the spiritual seeker—informed by tradition that Divinity is obscured or concealed in the depth of reality (by the multiple forms of creation)—and beseeches God to allow this concealment to be spiritually recognized and thus transcended. Accordingly, the term *seter* is understood to be a mystical term that connotes the "obscured" or "hidden" aspects of Divinity, and it is conjoined to the word *madreigah*, which is now taken to refer to the various "gradations" of this obfuscation to our natural eye.[22] Commenting on this passage, the teacher remarks that there is nothing (i.e., nothing in existence) where Divine reality is absent—no matter how much it is concealed in the various garments or "modalities" (*middot*) of external reality. He then adds that one must learn and "know" precisely how the Creator is revealed

20. Cf. S. Kamin, *Bein Yehudim le-Noṣrim be-Farshanut ha-Miqra* (Jerusalem: Magnes Press, 1992), 13–30 (Hebrew section). For the changing sense of *figura*, from Latin rhetoric to medieval Christian typological uses, see E. Auerbach, *Time, History, and Literature: Selected Essays of Erich Auerbach*, ed. J. I. Porter, trans. J. O. Newman, (Princeton: Princeton University Press, 2014), chap. 7.

21. See R. Ze'ev Wolf of Zhitomer, *Or Ha-Me'ir*, 258b.

22. I referred to this remarkable citation in the preceding chapter on "Depth" and return to it here for its added value to a discussion of appearances.

or "appears" (*nidmeh*; "is likened") to human consciousness through the forms of the world. We perceive the manifestations of existence as merely natural events or occurrences, whereas in truth they variously conceal and convey God's judgment or mercy, power or stability, and creativity or receptivity. The world is therefore a vast prism of God's providential presence, and it is precisely this that the attuned spiritual mind must attend to in order to recognize the revelation of Divinity in all things (and thus link all things to their transcendent Source in God). Appearances must therefore all be deciphered (allegorically, as it were) to get behind the literal appearance of things and their seeming multiplicity to their more inherent (and unified) Divine truth. In His essence, God is utterly beyond these manifestations and transcendent to every imaginable *dimyon*. Correspondingly, the spiritual adept must become aware that God "seems and appears (*nidmeh ve-nir'eh*) to his creatures in a concealed manner (*be-hastarat panim*)." But all appearances to the contrary notwithstanding, God is actively present and revealed through all things (the construction *hastarat panim* being a theological gloss on the phrase *seter ha-madreigah*).[23]

Hence, the human interpretative task is crucial. Developing a proper vision of existence (a consciousness of God's infinite manifestations) will yield a proper spiritual perspective—the first step in serving the "needs of Divinity" in this world (this being the restoration of the manifestations of Divinity in the world of nature to their transcendent Source). For the spiritually awakened and informed person, consciousness of God's myriad appearances results in recognizing that "all is God"—infinitely present in multiple modes of worldly presence. Restoration of Divine unity is thus conjoined to the cultivation of a total monotheistic focus (this being a mode of nondual, "theological monism"—God being the All-in-All). And since God contracted His Being into all the forms of existence for the sake of the ordinary human mind, the appearance of differences must be reversed. Precisely this is the life task of the spiritually perfected human being. The natural world is therefore a conflation of figure and reality, of tenor and its vehicle. Hence, if the key hermeneutical task of allegorical interpretation is to perceive the difference between each manifestation and

23. See R. Ze'ev Wolf of Zhitomer, *Or Ha-Me'ir*, 258b–260a.

its *hyponoia* (or deep sense), the task of spiritual hermeneutics is to recognize the reality of Divinity within all its concealments. Exactly this is the spiritual-cognitive labor practiced by Solomon and retaught by the *Or Ha-Me'ir* to his disciples. In this master's view, there is truly nothing between the human and God. Consciousness is all. The "glass darkly" through which one sees the world under natural (normal) circumstances is a refraction of the light of God as it passes through the prisms of created (worldly) existence and the structures of (normal) perception.

Is it possible for us to salvage something of this spiritual instruction, and take its teaching to heart? I would propose the following appropriation of Ze'ev Wolf's teaching for moderns who might hope to discern ciphers of Divinity in the depths of world-being—and do so with integrity.

Like the seekers in the Song of Songs, the contemporary soul still retains a longing to make contact with the unfathomable Source of creativity and to perceive "unity in difference" and "difference in unity." But on the way, we are (self-consciously or otherwise) constrained both by our cognitive structures and the limits of language. For many, this aborts the search from the outset. But perhaps the problem conceals the solution (if we follow Ze'ev Wolf's advice), through our cognitive awareness that every verbal formulation is a shaping of the ultimate mystery in human terms. For then we may realize that each word with which we hope to mediate meaning is not so much a reduction of infinity to human proportions as one of the many ciphers of our yearning to go beyond the self-referential goals of a King David toward the transcendent purpose exemplified by King Solomon. Along this spiritual path, which acknowledges but seeks to transcend our concern to cultivate a life of probity, there remains an impulse that propels us toward the "Infinite Other"—the reality that ultimately informs our daily tasks. This is not a yearning for one specific thing or another but a longing for a reality that is "wholly other" than anything imaginable through the limited vector of our embodied minds. Viewed thus, all our formulations may have the ethical purpose advocated by David—but also the anthropomorphic forms of the absolute mystery as allegorized by King Solomon. Precisely this may serve as a contemporary spiritual challenge: to remain fully mindful of the restraints on our spiritual intentions and desires but nevertheless somehow to transform the limits of language by becoming part of its spiritual intentions of attaining modalities of consciousness of the Divine mystery. So considered, our words may carry our spiritual impulses toward a higher, inscrutable unity—toward perceptions of likeness in difference and being shaped by their creative conjunctions. This is not a minimal achievement for our all-too-human embodiment in the world. We cannot transcend our mortal limits; but perhaps this suggestion offers human fallibility a transcendent task.

4

The World, Numina, and the Challenge of Theology

We are creatures of the earth, first and foremost: it is our primary existential ground, and the multitude of appearances, both major and minor, make up the first-order moments of our everyday reality. This panoply of experience affects our sense of its external diversity—as both visible manifestations and modalities of creative power. Whether out of fascination or fear, both factors (manifestation and power) profoundly influence our perceptions of reality. The archetypes of our soul confirm this primary truth—by absorbing these external forms at the deepest psychic level and then by reconfiguring them through the many expressions of our creative imagination.[1] It is therefore through its phenomenal bounty—both durative and momentary—that the world speaks to us and comes alive. Over time, tradition and individual talent give these "modes of presence" names and epithets and characterize them in diverse ways. This interpretative process emerges quite naturally and is part of our primordial endowment as people who belong to the earth and have thought and language. In addition, our reactions to these various seen and unseen realities constitute our natural religiosity—and inspire more speculative estimations. In what sense or to what degree, one wonders, are these natural manifestations expressive of physical or even transcendent powers;

1. For reflections on the fragmentation and personalization of archetypal aggregates, see E. Neumann, *The Origins and History of Consciousness* (1949; Princeton, NJ: Princeton University Press, 1970), 320–41.

and how (if at all) are these diverse occasions related?[2] Polytheists focus on the multitude of forms and the primal forces that engender them, whereas monotheists center on the whole, believing diversity to be an inclusive or integral unity, empowered by one supreme Divinity. Equally important are speculations regarding the character (personal or impersonal) of these forms and the most effective ways of soliciting their powers of protection or sustenance. Such matters have life consequences, and understandably religions give them ideological and institutional priority.

As is evident from a history-of-religions perspective, sacred scriptures and religious hermeneutics are primary means of encoding these issues. Through their authoritative genres, normative topics are featured and evaluated, and cultural and conceptual boundaries are established and sustained. These include programmatic and pedagogical ideals—both theological and ideological—that provide the regulative measures by which religious conformity or deviance is assessed and by which cultural challenges can be authoritatively integrated or rejected. In addition to such positive expressions of identity, polemical juxtaposition and ideological polarization may also have a negative dimension, providing the primary means of constituting forms of "normative inversion."[3] This phrase refers to the practice of identifying those groups that represent the negative cultural antitype (or rejected "other"), whose activities are often portrayed with verbal and emotional animus. Such a dual process of identifying and segregating the "other" remains significant in our time as well—in proportion to the felt need of religious groups for strong boundaries. Indeed, precisely because conceptual and institutional boundaries are porous and repeatedly challenged by contemporary social realities (through the easy spread of information and physical proximity), some groups dogmatize their differences and turn normative inversion into a way of life. This often results in a hardening of the ideological issues regarding

2. Still unsurpassed, and of major import, is G. van der Leeuw, *Religion in Essence and Manifestation: A Study in Phenomenology* (London: George Allen & Unwin, 1938). Also of enduring value is the penetrating study by W. Otto, *The Homeric Gods: The Spiritual Significance of Greek Religion* (New York: Pantheon Books, 1954).

3. For the term, see J. Assmann, *Moses the Egyptian: The Memory of Egypt in Western Monotheism* (Cambridge, MA: Harvard University Press, 1997), 216.

rejected practices as well as the reuse of this terminology long after authorities reclassified these or related theologies as nonidolatrous—even monotheistic, in certain cases. By striking contrast, many tropes originally formulated against idolatrous practices were reappropriated as internal critiques of normative practices deemed to have lost their spiritual vitality. In such instances, warnings against external idolatry were reinterpreted as cautions against certain ways of performing normative worship. As a result, routinization or formalistic practices were included among such exhortations (diverse examples shall be considered below).

❋

Because of the complex dynamics of idolatry, each generation must take up the issues anew in terms of its perceived normative constraints or values; and because the latter considerations evoke spiritual boundaries and distinctions, subcommunities within any particular religion regularly disagree on such matters. The diversity of social solutions past and present therefore provides an index of each community's assessment of the contemporary situation and their sense of what constitutes religious or cultural integrity. The ensuing discussion does the same for Judaism, being an index of my sifting and sorting of the issues. Given the complexity of the subject, the initial task will be to consider the issue of idolatry with an eye to the historical past and the ways it has been portrayed or invoked in classical texts and traditions. This will provide a conceptual prelude to my attempt to engage these matters for myself and this time—which is at once postmodern in its openness to multiple challenges and influences but also necessarily must assess what can be appropriated with integrity and what bears the imprint of idolatry and should be rejected as such. Even though the strong opprobrium once attached to "idolatry" has diminished in modern life, it is a premise of this inquiry that it remains a significant category for spiritual and cultural reflection. A crucial aspect of modern Jewish thought and theology will be the beneficiary.

How may we proceed? To develop a contemporary Jewish theological approach to the topic, grounded in traditional sources and their interpretation, I shall take the long route through historical texts. This will prevent a conceptual leap to the situation of modernity and allow me to consider both programmatic and polemic portrayals of idolatry on their own terms. Then, through a more contemporary formulation of the issues, I will evaluate their import for modern theology. In the process, the challenge to monotheism will be reformulated and rethought.

An Overview

Because the presentation will develop in several stages, I wish to provide a brief overview of my argument. I take up three topics, each highlighting a particular position in the process, with examples offered to illustrate their specific modality but not trying to account for every nuance or historical variation. The movement of the discussion is both linear (in the sense of an emergent sequence) and dialectical (in the sense of internal dynamics). In each instance, one modality of religious consciousness is highlighted, alongside the type of false consciousness related to it—this latter being the particular mode of idolatry involved. Part 1 begins by introducing the sharp radical difference between biblical monotheistic transcendence and the mythic plenum of the surrounding ancient world in terms of the exalted supremacy of one Divinity (deemed creator of heaven and earth and totally "other" than them and their elements) and the strong derogation of all types of physical (or featured) cultic representation, including their presumptive Divine aspects. This distinction is repeatedly stressed in the biblical sources as an absolute and foundational distinction whose blatant disregard (specified in terms of turning to "other gods" and their forms of worship) is trenchantly denounced in polemics of many kinds. Part 2 takes up the religious consequences of this difference, insofar as "radical transcendence" opens a space of absolute theological differentiation between God and the visible powers of the natural world, with two primary consequences: the dangers of repeated misrepresentation of the features of the world and a misapprehension of their inherent validity or efficacy (with a consequent backsliding to idolatrous practices). Thinking through these two issues will allow us to consider their conceptual correlates in modern terms. This will prepare the basis for a new theological turn. Accordingly, Part 3 attempts to close the theological space between transcendence and immanence through a mystical move—one that shifts from a radical theistic difference between these two aspects to a recovery of Divine plenitude. This turn reconceptualizes the older mythic plenum in monotheistic terms and introduces new theological engagements with the transcendent mystery of God. In the process, the tasks of the religious life undergo a fundamental epistemological shift, and the meaning of idolatry is reinterpreted.[4] It is toward this fundamental reconsideration that my presentation aims. The preceding generalities provide the overall framework; I now spell out the details.

The Mythic Plenum and Monotheistic Aniconism

Cultures often come to self-definition through deliberate contrasts—as do their individual adherents—and over the generations these cultural countertypes (as perceived and as inculcated) provide primary layers of identity. The frequently marked differences between Egypt and Israel are a striking example of this phenomenon both in the canonical articulation of the differences in Scripture and in their ongoing explication throughout Jewish literature. To rethink the issues involved requires one to conceptualize the cultural-ideological factors at stake. Not being able to transcend ourselves, the ensuing evaluation inevitably constitutes a contemporary variant of a multimillenial process based on our modern reading of the sources.

Two primary Scriptural moments will set our discussion in motion. The first involves the theomachy (or Divine battle) of the plagues; the other concerns the second commandment. They are inherently correlated.

Among the notable features of the Divinely wrought plagues is that they are presented as counterpoints to the sources of life: blood—as death and the pollution of water (the source of irrigation, arising from the earth itself); pestilence—as the destruction of crops and herds (the natural and animal sources of food); and utter darkness—as the eclipse of the solar luminaries (and the capacity to see by day and

4. Upon completion, I realize that this typology (which moves from a monotheistic rejection of mythic potencies to their mystical retrieval) parallels the dialectic proposed by G. Scholem in his *Major Trends in Jewish Mysticism* (New York: Schocken Books, 1941), 7–10. This factor notwithstanding, the two typological dynamics serve quite different cultural purposes. Thus my dialectic must be assessed on its own terms.

navigate by the evening stars). Indeed, more than primary inversions, the plagues constituted a veritable assault on the Egyptian deified powers of sustenance and survival by an unknown god of vagrant slaves on whose backs the stones of the immortal pyramids were carried and through whose labor wheat was threshed and baked. As the Scriptural source stresses, the plagues were horrendous events "the likes of which had never happened in Egypt" (Exod. 9:18, 10:10)—occurrences that signified the defeat of the local deities, high and low. Such in fact was the pronouncement of the perpetrating God, who said, "I shall wreak judgments against all the gods of the Egyptians" (Exod. 12:12), and as repeated in retrospect by the wandering people years later (Num. 33:4).[5] For these gods were the named embodiments of the mysteries of sky and water, seeds and flocks—all teeming, spontaneously, from the sun-body of Atum and emitting and begetting the gods of air (Shu) and fire (Tefnut), and then Geb-earth and Nut-heaven, even unto the fourth generation. Out of this primordial, all-generating cosmogonic power (deemed and called *khefer-djesef*, or "the self-generated one") emerged all the biomorphic forms of life and energy.

Like the scarab with which Atum was identified, all things emanated or were somehow secreted from his being. If there is any deeper principle here it is the inherent unity and correlation of things despite their external forms and the sense that they communicate an "immediate signification" of meaning.[6] Shapes are what they are, as primary expressions of Divinity; and yet, within this mythic plenum they are but sacred portions of a "single essential substance."[7] Whether you turn to the (just-noted) Helepolitan cosmogonies or those from Memphis[8]—or you read the so-called Coffin texts—similar

5. This polemical motif appears as a *theologoumenon* in the mouth of Jethro in Exodus 18:11.

6. The term recurs in A. Assmann, *Die Legitimität der Fiktion: Eine Beitrag der literarischen Kommunikation* (Munich: W. Fink, 1980).

7. This is the formulation of J. A. Wilson, in *The Intellectual Adventure of Ancient Man* (Chicago: University of Chicago Press, 1946), chap. 3, p. 68. He also speaks of "consubstantiality" (68, 70).

8. For a host of the texts annotated here, see especially S. Sauneron and J. Yoyette, "La naissance du monde selon L'Égypte ancienne," in *La Naissance du monde: Égypte, Akkad, Hourrites et Hittites, Canaan, Israel, Islam, Turcs and Mongols, Iran préislamique, Inde, Siam, Laos, Tibet, Chine*, Sources Orientales 1 (Paris: Éditions du Seuil, 1959),

theogonies (or the mythic accounts of the genesis of the gods) about self-created emergence recur. Listen, for example, to the following hymn to Amon-re from about 1400 BCE, and thus shortly before the Exodus: "He came forth self-generated, all his limbs speaking to him," and then more directly, "You have taken on your first form as Re. . . . You created all that has come into existence and all that exists."

Given the Divine inherency presumed in all things, in the Egyptian belief system, and the direct correlation between the forms of Divine representation and their innate reality, is it any wonder that the initial self-presentation of Israel's God at Sinai pronounces, "I am YHWH who took you out of the land of Egypt" (Exod. 20:2), and immediately thereafter the commandment, "you shall have no other gods (*elohim aḥerim*) besides Me" (v. 3)? Surely not. For with this conjunction, it is clear that the epithet ("who took you out of . . . Egypt") is more than a proclamation of political theology[9] (YHWH as the supreme Lord) and is inextricably coupled to its fundamental corollary: the absolute prohibition of worship of "other gods" *and* all modes of representation—be they in the heavens or on the earth (v. 4). Aniconism is thus a primary polemic and cuts far deeper than theological loyalty.[10] It is, in fact, the cultic corollary of a new mode of religious consciousness, one that we may label "radical transcendence." God is "other" than the world, and there is no inherent or objective correlative between the two—in whole or in part.[11] Hence, figurative representations are

---

17–91. For other citations, see also J. Assmann, "Creation through Hieroglyphs: The Cosmic Grammatology of Ancient Egypt," in *The Poetics of Grammar and the Metaphysics of Sound and Sign*, ed. D. Shulman and S. La Porta (Leiden: E. J. Brill, 2007), 17–34. See also the summary assessment in Wilson, *Intellectual Adventure*, 50–61.

9. For a fully developed analysis, see J. Assmann, *Politische Theologie zwischen Ägypten und Israel* (Munich: C. F. von Siemans Stiftung, 1992).

10. It bears emphasis that the crucial issue in the prohibition of images is the cultic representation of God, *not* the reported figural appearances in prophetic vision *or* the imaginal expressions and depictions of God (in terms of volition, mood, or activity) in poetry and prayer. This distinction is often disregarded or variously obscured.

11. I stress the word *inherent* since there is, of course, one significant exception: the human being was created in the "form and likeness" of God. Certainly, the issue of creation is the distinctive element; though it must be emphasized that the human creature is the only "creation" not brought into existence by the Divine word. Indeed, with respect to this event, the Scriptural account has strong mythic overtones (thus, in

absolutely prohibited. To drive this point home, a later homily expanded on the brief statement in Exodus 20:4 that only refers to the things in heaven and earth in general terms, filling in the polemical space with a specification of the entire order of creation. In this extended polemic, Moses alludes to all the elements of Divine creation in Genesis 1—starting with human forms and moving through the creatures of earth and sky to the heavenly bodies in what is manifestly a deliberate reversal of the latter sequence. Thus, using the teaching of Genesis 1 as a blueprint of potential images and powers, the result is a vigorous prohibition of all forms related to the visible or sensate world (Deut. 4:16–19).[12] And why are they so vigorously prohibited? Because, it is stressed, when God appeared to the people at Sinai, the people saw no image but only heard a voice (vv. 12, 15). In contrast to the eye, and the earthbound imagination, the ear has no spatial correlate. Hearing occurs in time, as something received—and not as something perceived in spatial terms.

Radical theological transcendence thus introduces a revolutionary moment that marks a fundamental cognitive break with the mythic plenum and its principle of correlation or partial representation of divinities or Divine powers. The new mindset is disjoined from seeing within the forms of the world potential figurations or representations of God. Even more, there is no permitted embodiment of God's acts of creation in the phenomenal world. The cognitive disjunction between what is perceived and what (or "Who") one is dependent on is absolute. To accede to this kind of monotheism imposes a new mode of religious consciousness, one that takes a preeminent role in the hierarchy of Divine commandments. Indeed, the fundamental significance of this theological demand is signaled not only by its primary position among the norms that follow *but also* by its address to one's personal religious life. The imperative, "You shall not have (*lo yiheyeh lekha*) other gods besides Me" (v. 3) means that one must not have other gods "for yourself (*lekha*)." And with this strong emphasis on

Gen. 1:26, the formulation is "let us make, *na'aseh*, man," and in Gen. 2:7 it states, "[The Lord God] formed (*va-yitzer*) the man from the dust of the earth").

12. See already my comments in *Biblical Interpretation in Ancient Israel* (Oxford: Clarendon Press, 1985), 321–22, and the initial formulation in "Varia Deuteronomica," *Zeitschrift für die alttestamentliche Wissenschaft* 84 (1972): 349.

the spiritual life of the worshipper, the onus of false worship is focused both on ritual behavior and (on an incorrect or false) theological consciousness.

The worshipper is warned to be vigilant regarding the appeal of the mythic plenum and not be drawn into any seduction to the arresting vitalities of the world. This theological position regarding absolute transcendence, focusing on both its cognitive recognition and its ritual preservation, is the center of the new religion. It is also, I believe, the ideological core for all those who would receive Scripture as a religious document addressed to their theological life (and not solely to their social solidarity). Hence, this issue is also the pivot of the present discussion. To state my point somewhat differently: *the initial theological command against idolatry is concerned with making the spiritual-cognitive event of liberation* (from nature and the mythic plenum) *into a permanent epistemic endowment.* The need to negate any and all forms of representation is a foremost necessity of the positive apprehension of transcendent monotheism. Self-monitoring is therefore crucial; the imperative of *lo yihyeh lekha* is addressed to one's theological integrity. I consider this to be a consideration of foundational value with central bearing on any modern Jewish religious psychology—one that will require an equally radical rethinking of the nature and limits of human expression. Eventually the theological point will be asserted: "To whom (*miy*) will you liken (*tidamyun*) God, and what (*mah*) form (*demut*) compare to Him?" (Isa. 40:18).[13] The spiritual challenge is formidable.

The Dialectics of Difference and the Problematics for Monotheism

Let us think further about the spiritual dangers of having "other gods" from this conceptual and theological perspective; for the radical disjunction between the perceptual (or phenomenal) world and the imperceptible (and transphenomenal) otherness of God is not easily

13. There is no doubt that this, too, is a polemical challenge to Genesis 1—in this case, v. 26. Cf. Isaiah 40:25.

maintained or sustained—as a significant amount of biblical evidence indicates.[14] There is repeated evidence of an ongoing fascination with and stimulation by the powers latent and manifest in the forms of the world—in trees and wind, in thunder and rainclouds, in animal life and vegetal growth. The expressions of the world stimulated a natural sense of dependence on the manifestations of life and the Divine powers inherent therein—and certainly on the Divine powers that were traditionally worshipped throughout ancient Canaan. From the beginning, as the prophet Hosea laments, the people's "mouth" was filled with "the names of the Baalim"—calling them "My Baal" (2:19) and asserting, "I will go after my lovers, who supply my bread and my water, my wood and my linen, my oil and my drink" (v. 7), not knowing who was the true source of vitality and efficacy (v. 10). Accused of a false religious consciousness, the people followed natural instincts and needs—the tangible expressions of their tangible needs. Jeremiah continues this polemic, accusing the people of defiling the land through lusting after the local gods of the land, lying in worship under sacred trees, and saying, "I love foreign gods (*zarim*) and shall follow them (*aḥareihem*)" (Jer. 2:25)[15]—not realizing, beyond their apostasy, that such gods were ultimately futile forces that could not "save" them in times of need (v. 28). This heated invective of ignorance and folly (ignorance of the transcendent source of beneficence and folly in following their physical instincts) was repeatedly conjoined with others, filled to the brim with irony and sarcasm. It is to these polemics especially that we now turn to help us think further about idolatry and its bearing on contemporary theology.

The first text to consider is Isaiah 44—certainly one of the most provocative polemics in Scripture and the product of the late, postexilic prophet Isaiah, who proclaims a theology of a pure monotheistic universalism (virtually for the first time). After making his primary proclamation that the Lord God is the "first" and the "last" and veritably

14. I presented a full spectrum of evidence in my essay, "Israel and the Mothers," in *The Other Side of God*, ed. P. Berger (Garden City, NY: Anchor Press/Doubleday, 1981), 28–47.

15. These terms blatantly refer to false gods, specifically the so-called *elohim aḥeirim* (other gods).

the "only God" (Isa. 44:6, 8),[16] he proceeds to mock those who create or "form" idols and their product: those who make these objects are "wastrels" (*tohu*) and the upshot "without benefit" (*lo yo'il*)—for they do not realize the folly of their labor and are not ashamed (v. 9). What they "do" is spiritually ludicrous: they forge iron implements to cut trees, measure their girth, and frame an idol from this mass; and then, with double folly, they use the wood as fuel to heat their food and warm their bodies, and with the remainder they make a "god" and bow down in worship, saying, "Save me, for you are my god" (v. 17)—never thinking to say, "Surely my right hand acts falsely" (v. 20). Vitriolic mockery aside, two profound theological matters are involved. One is the "nature" of the cultic object; the other is the "act" of attribution and interpretation. They are both expressions of folly and hubris.

What is particularly striking in this polemic is the misprision of what it means to be a creature who tries to "act" on one's behalf with a theological intervention—in this instance, the construction of an idol from the world itself with the irony of its double usage (that the wood both gives creaturely warmth and is deemed viable for salvation). If the first act is merely utilitarian, using the wood of a tree, the second attributes Divine agency through another portion of that same earthly object. What the idol maker does not realize is the category mistake of believing that the ritual image is more than a figure of the human imagination—that attributions and representations are not the "thing itself" (whatever that may be). In contemporary terms, the cognitive error involved in making physical images of God is one of misattribution and the failure to be properly mindful of one's role in such acts of signification. The idolater fabricates (in the double sense) constructs of the world without taking responsibility for their misappropriation or self-contradictory nature. That is, as a homo faber (a maker or fabricator) he forgets that he is constituted by the same reality he is recomposing. The principle of transcendence (as I now appropriate it) requires a person to live within the cognitive space of delimitation with theological cognizance of the creative limitations of all human acts of signification. To disregard this issue is to mistake (or

16. This theological formulation is also found in Deuteronomy 4:39, toward the conclusion of an apparently postexilic supplement.

misconceive) the nature of human transcendence (when one falsely thinks they are somehow more than "mere nature"), and thus reify elements constructed from the world, of which we are a natural part.[17] In this double sense, modern idolatry is a willful or ignorant misuse of the work of one's mind. I would therefore suggest that what is involved is both a *forgetting of the Divine principle of transcendence* and *not giving proper regard to human limitations*. I shall return to this matter below.

To deepen the cognitive folly ridiculed by Isaiah, we now turn to the second conceptual error of our passage. It is one of hermeneutical hubris: an assertive act of theological attribution and misrepresentation. When the idol maker says "You are my god," he is "doing" what Austin would call "something with words"—he is engaged in a performative act that transfers reality to an object through speech,[18] all the more problematic for it being an assertion of theological sense and significance and for having no inner reflexivity wherewith to critique one's action (i.e., the maker doesn't have sufficient wisdom to reflect and say "I have burnt half for fuel . . . and with the remainder have acted abominably, bowing down to a tree trunk"(Isa. 44: 20). From this perspective, the folly of idolatry includes a lack of hermeneutical distance between thought and language, between meaning and its implication. Hence, the presumption of the idolater even lacks the sense of shame that such a cognitive perspective brings (v. 9). Acts of idolatrous representation thus attribute a "false concretion" to the object signified and presume that this very act of linguistic signification actualizes a transcendent reality. Jeremiah voices the cultic drama of this act when he fulminates against his contemporaries who "say to the tree, 'you are my father (*avi attah*),' and to the stone, 'you have given birth to me (*at yeliditani*)'" (Jer. 2: 27).[19] Only a fundamental change

17. For a profound philosophical consideration of the issue of the human laboring animal as a *homo faber* and the dangers of reification, see H. Arendt, *The Human Condition* (Chicago: University of Chicago Press, 1958), chap. 19. (On the related issue of "makers" who have conceptual images in mind, see further below.)

18. See J. L. Austin, *How to Do Things with Words*, ed. J. O. Urmson and M. Sbisa (Cambridge, MA: Harvard University Press, 1962).

19. I am reading the Masoretic text with the *ketiv*. The theological counterpoint for the future is when the people will say, "You are my father (*avi attah*), the companion of my youth" (Jer. 4:4).

of consciousness would result in the retraction, "We shall no longer say '*eloheinu*' ('our gods') to the work of our hands" (Hosea 14:4).[20]

A related polemic drives the preceding issues deeper; for like these texts, which link the folly of the idol maker with his fallacious results (each being empty and worthless), Psalm 115 also specifies the inconsequence of the idols but then makes a more telling critique of such worshippers. Referring to the non-Israelite "others" who make idols in the image of themselves—with mouth and eyes and ears and nose, and with arms and legs to boot—the psalmist poignantly adds that not only are these figures incapable of speech or hearing or touch or movement but also that "their makers"—who trust in them—"are just like them" (vv. 4–8). The external acts thus transform the actor reciprocally: false theological presumptions produce correlative mentalities. Instead of producing living gods, they themselves become mindless "things." This is a hermeneutical critique of a false religious consciousness taken to the extreme: the idolater becomes like the work of his hands, an impotent object. Hence, idol making is both transformative and constitutive of their makers in equal measure. The hermeneutical act is ineluctably entwined with its physical labor. You are what you make (or what you don't think about when you make it)—as Gershom Scholem adroitly implied, with profound modern concern, when he inaugurated a new computer at the Weitzman Institute of Science in 1965, dubbing it a Golem consigned to deadly possibilities if it merely served as an extension of pure ingenuity and not humane principles of life.[21]

I wish to turn at this point to a related reflection on the conjunction of radical transcendence and aniconism, deepening my discussion of the

20. The prophet Hosea is replete with idolatrous acts. The acts of divination by means of a "staff" are of particular note in this context (4:12), and ritual offering under sacred trees (v. 13). In the latter case, one may wonder whether the two poplars mentioned there, *elon* and *elah*, do not refer to male and female deities manifest in these entities.

21. See "The Golem of Prague and the Golem of Rehovot," in G. Scholem, *The Messianic Idea in Judaism* (New York: Schocken Books, 1971), 335–40.

connection between language and attribution, and thereby bringing into play some other considerations bearing on theology and idolatry.

The worship of the Golden Calf at the foot of Mount Sinai marks a paradigmatic event of collective idolatry. At the surface and factual level, the narrative reports that with Moses's ascension to God on Mount Sinai and continued absence, the people were distraught, and they asked Aaron to "make gods for us, who will go before us—because we don't know what has happened to Moses, the person Moses who took us up from the land of Egypt" (Exod. 32:1). And if this contrast with the Divine self-proclamation at the beginning of the Decalogue, which states, "I am the Lord, your God, who took you out of the land of Egypt" (Exod. 20:2), were not sufficiently striking, then also note what the people assert after the idol is made: "These are your gods, O Israel, who took you out of the land of Egypt" (Exod. 32:4). Two substitutions are involved, which effect the inversion of the principles of Divine transcendence and aniconism. The first is the substitution of Moses for God; the second of molten idols for Moses, now called gods (in the plural, thereby activating the inherent multiplicity of the polytheistic term *elohim*). Such displacements—from God to human to physical image—mark the religious (and natural) need for concrete presence. Thus, invisible Divine transcendence devolved into a human representation, and the occlusion of the latter resulted in a cultic image. Idolatry therefore takes diverse forms because of the problematics of presence resulting in cases of faulty attribution (or, as Whitehead would say, of "misplaced concretion"), topped off by the performative enunciation: "These (*eleh*) are your gods (*eloheykha*)" at the conclusion of the fashioning of the idol. We thus have a striking parallel to what was noted earlier in Isaiah 44, where the act of constructing an image (vv. 12–16) was followed by its proclamation as a god (v. 17). In both instances Divine transcendence was compromised to the detriment of human cognition.

Going beyond the primary narrative, let us think about this act of designation in contemporary terms—which raises the stakes for modern theology. As exemplified above, unthinking acts of linguistic designation blend both sign and signification with the result that there is no conceptual interval perceived between the thing named and its denomination. The thing named is deemed the thing itself, as it were, and as a result there is a disregard (or, in Isaiah's locution, a misunderstanding) of the creative interval between the act of speech and the world that it creatively indicates or refers to. Such an elision obscures cognizance (and thus responsibility) for the locutions and their effect. These epistemological consequences are even more significant in a theological context to the extent that these cases of "naming God" (as an assertion or characterization) are presumptive acts of human attribution, and they border on the idolatrous when they go beyond individual acts of testimony (naming a moment or event of Divine manifestation) and purport to be substantive indices of Divinity. In such circumstances, idolatry is the counterfeit coin of the worldly realm, falsely presuming that one's mind and language can purchase an ultimate theological truth and meaning. And thus, instead of a person realizing the impossibility of naming or signifying the transcendent "Divine Other"—so utterly beyond imaginal representation (figural or figurative)—one is blinded by hermeneutical hubris. The unnamable horizon of infinitude collapses into the channels of cognitive presumption. Linguistic and cognitive idolatry are the result.

For its part, medieval Jewish philosophy has worn the mantel of radical transcendence and conjured positive assertions about God or theology into themes of new or transformed significance. Thus, the noble path of philosophical theology was deemed a way of negation; that is, its goal was to unsay or negate the natural idols of the mind (or also the anthropomorphic images of tradition) and through this process to purify and redirect the mind toward an absolutely imageless account of God and Divine Reality. This process of purification of Scriptural images and terms emerged with particular vigor with R. Saadia Gaon[22] and achieved its classic expression in Maimonides's celebrated opening seventy chapters of part 1 of *The Guide of the Perplexed*—where the images of God mentioned in Scripture find their allegorical recalibration in hyper-rational terms. Certainly this is an intellectual achievement of monumental proportions, and it has continued unabated to our age, when a philosopher of the stature of Hermann Cohen substituted rational cognitions and mental structures of God for immediate

22. See the essay by S. Rawidowicz, "Saadia's Purification of the Idea of God," in his *Studies in Jewish Thought*, ed. N. N. Glatzer (Philadelphia: Jewish Publication Society of America, 1974), 246–68.

theological experience and expression.[23] Emptying the mind with legerdemain, the bounty of the world is thereby rationalized and conceptualized—and the modern dangers of instrumental rationality and scientism fill this void. Max Weber famously understood this form of cognitive transcendence to be a first cousin to the "disenchantment" of the world and the death knell to the mystery of Divine presence.[24] Worship of the technological work of one's hands, based on the reification of mental images, takes place in the desanctified canopy of quantitative time and space. These factors raise the following theological question: Can a viable version of Divine transcendence (radical and ultimate) be formulated that doesn't dilute (or disenchant) the wonder and mystery of worldly plenitude but that may actually envelop it or even deepen its dimensions? And if so, how might that formulation recalibrate both monotheism and idolatry? I take these questions as a spiritual provocation and intellectual challenge. The ensuing final part will try to respond in a positive way.

Transcendence and Divine Plenitude

We yearn to close the gap between ourselves and the Divine. Can we do so without falling prey to idolatrous mentalities? The concluding movement of our dialectic aims to reinstall the mystery of transcendence as an expression of Divine plenitude. This means constructing a new theological epistemology—a three-step process based on three striking instances of mystical hermeneutics.

I begin with a consideration of the people's proclamation in Exodus 32:4, at the completion of the molten calf: "These (*eleh*) are your gods"—as interpreted in the *Zohar* (1.2a). The significance of the passage lies in its central position near the beginning of the "Introduction" to the *Book of Zohar*, thus joining the mystery of creation and idolatry as a primary concern. Just before this unit, we are informed of

23. Note, in this regard, M. Buber's critique of Hermann Cohen, in his "The Love of God and the Idea of the Deity," fin *Eclipse of God: Studies in the Relation between Religion and Philosophy* (New York: Harper & Row, 1952), 52–62.

24. See his famous essay "Science as a Vocation" (1919) for the term *Entzauberung*, republished in *From Max Weber: Essays in Sociology*, ed. H. H. Gertz and C. Wright Mills (Oxford: Oxford University Press, 1946), 148.

two spiritual realities originating in the most hidden, transcendental realm of Divinity but that can also be experienced or perceived here below in our worldly existence. Both elements are hinted at in Isaiah 40:26: "Raise your eyes on high and see who (*mi*) created these (*eleh*)?" In its Scriptural context this exhortation is addressed to the individual to look upward to heaven and realize "Who" (God) created this cosmic spectacle and its heavenly bodies. But for the mystics of the *Zohar* more is at stake, since they say, first, that the word *eleh* designates the lowest part (or final "rung") of the Divine emanation that extends earthward and is mirrored in the creation of our universe and whose concluding statement is "These *(eleh)* are the generations or the heavens and the earth" in Genesis 2:4. Hence, *Eleh* symbolizes the perceptual world emanating from hidden recesses of wonder, which is beyond understanding, at the absolute border of the imaginable. For that reason it is called *Mi*. "Who?" is thus a limit term for absolute Mystery.[25] To look upward to the heights is to bring one's mind to the hidden wonder of being. The evocative "Who?" is thus the symbolic indication of the Divine "Beyond."[26]

We are now in a position to read the following.

> Seeking to be revealed, to be named, it [the theological symbol *Mi*] covered itself in a marvelously radiant garment and created *Eleh*. *Eleh* attained the [Divine] Name "*Elohim*" by joining its letters with those of *Mi* [thus: *e-l-h* + *im*]. Until it [*Mi*] created *Eleh*, it did not attain the Name *Elohim*. Because of this mystery [of the conjoined Names], those who transgressed with the Golden Calf [only] said "*Eleh* (these) are your gods, O Israel" [Exod. 32:8]. Just as *Mi* is combined (primordially) with *Eleh*, so the Name *Elohim*

25. *Zohar* 2.231b stresses the essentiality of this question and comments on its irreducible nature when it states that the question—the perception of a supernal Divine gradation as *Mi*—"ever remains a question (*qayyema tadir le-she'ela*)." Commenting on the radical formulation of this principle in *Zohar* 1.1b, the sixteenth-century kabbalist R. Shimon Lavi made this striking statement: "Regarding whatever cannot be grasped: its question is its answer!" See *Ketem Paz* (Djerba: J. Haddad, 1940), 1.91a. Elsewhere in *Zohar* 1.1b *mi* is deemed a "healing" dimension "that concealed, supernal rung in which all exists"—through the deferment of all limit and delimitation (it is thus positivity of an absolute negative theology).

26. This summation occurs in *Zohar* 1.1b.

is forever undergoing [creative] combinations. On the basis of this mystery [of the recombinant Names] the universe exists.

How can we understand this passage? One major thrust is that the mystery of existence, indeed of all being, is the infusion of "mystery" with "things." The actuality of perception here on earth is grounded in the multiple things that God created, setting them out in different forms and orders and relationships. This is the external world of reference and comparison—the world to which we point and name. *Eleh* is thus a deictic or referential term for things knowable or capable of indication. By contrast, *Mi* opens the eyes to wonder and mystery in the way that only a question unsettles some formulation. Such attention to the marvel of reality does not (and cannot) name this reality as such, for *Mi* is but a mark of speculative awe. What *Mi* adds to *Eleh* is the transcendent dimension of "otherness" ever latent in all perception, as well as the realization that this combination of two elements is the mystery of the Divine Name *Elohim*. And what is more, since our worldly perceptions (the domain of *eleh*) are constantly changing, the terms of this sacred name are also constantly mystically recombinant. Thus, although the name *Elohim* is externally one in appearance and sound, it spiritually actualizes every transformation existent in our world. To reduce the world to *eleh* (devoid of *mi*) is therefore to truncate and traduce its all-embracing Divine mystery. It is to see things as just "this" and "that"—secularities without God. This is idolatry plain and simple, says the *Zohar*: the evident achievement of all those for whom the world is reduced to thingness—to be used and manipulated. The mind of idolatry makes attributions but has lost any sense of transcendent magnitude. The counterpoint is spiritual humility. Such a disposition is a first step toward the restoration of existence as a bountiful Divine plenitude.

We may now take the next step in the epistemological process. To do so, I would like to begin the discussion with the word *anokhi*, it being the opening Divine assertion of the Decalogue ("I am"). According to one line of Ḥasidic thought, preserved through a question the "Holy Jew" (R. Ya'akov Yitzḥak Rabinowitz) asked his student

(R. Simḥah Bunem Bonhardt of Przysucha), What biblical passage marks its theological core? The latter suggested that it was Isaiah 40:26, cited above, which lauds God the creator of nature. But the master demurred and said that such a proposition might hold for humankind as a whole, but the core of Jewish theology is the word *anokhi* (the Divine "I," expressed at Sinai), since it marks the beginning of a unique spiritual connection between God and humans—this being fundamentally different from a starting point in the world of nature.[27] In terms of our earlier discussions, this insight suggests that the monotheistic breakthrough is marked by a Divine self-proclamation that demands exclusive worship together with the rejection of "other gods" and addresses itself to human subjects. Such a new theological moment catalyzes a strong sense of human transcendence (spiritual and cognitive responsibility) inspired by a supervening transcendent Subject.[28] This insight granted, a later disciple of R. Simḥah Bunem, R. Mordechai Yosef Leiner of Izhbitz (known as the "Izhbitzer"), gave further import to the word *anokhi* by capitalizing on a minor lexical variation. Pondering why the word *a-no-kh-i* was employed at this juncture rather than the more common first-person pronoun *a-n-i*, the Ishbitzer remarked that the letter *kaf* (*k/kh*) was inserted into the latter word to highlight that all our human conceptions of Divinity are fundamentally limited by our mortal mind and imagination. As mortal creatures we perceive the world and theological realities by linguistic indirection, by comparison and similitude—and this epistemological approach is symbolized by the letter *kaf*, which serves (here and elsewhere) as a stand-in for *ke-* or *kemo* (in the sense of "like").[29] Given the limits of our human capacity, nothing transcends this mode of thinking, not even the phenomenon of language itself—insofar as words name things by means of conventional attribution and do not constitute the designated object "as such." By inserting this letter *k* into the Divine self-proclamation (*ano<u>kh</u>i* not *ani*), we

27. The Holy Jew reports this in *Siftei Tzaddik* (s.v. "bereishit"), collected in *Sefer Kedushat Ha-Yedudi* (Bnai Brak, 1997), 130a.

28. Thinking along the same lines, and concerned with the character of a social-legal covenant, R. Scruton has termed this a *transcendent bond*; see his *The Soul of the World* (Princeton, NJ: Princeton University Press, 2014), 94.

29. See *Mei Ha-Shiloaḥ* (Brooklyn, 1984), pt. 1, 25a, col. 2 (*Yitro*, s.v. "anokhi").

are told that all theological statements (even interpretation itself) are qualified. Put differently, the signifier *k* highlights (for cognition and for theology) that the transcendent truths of Divine reality must pass through the limited constructs of the sign-making human mind to be formulated and comprehended. The world we "know" lies in the shadow of mortal cognition, which filters and mediates the transcendent light of God's creation. Indeed, according to the Izhbitzer, all our theological cognitions and interpretations are "merely a *demut* and *dimyon*" (an "image" and "imaginal figure") of ultimate Divine reality and truth. And to underscore this fact, we are also told, Scripture appends the Divine injunction: "Don't make *lekha,* for yourself, any idol" (Exod. 20:4)—this being an incisive warning to resist the temptations of theological hubris and presumption. Awareness of our epistemological limits is therefore a hedge against idolatries of the imagination. This is a primary consideration for developing a spiritual perspective. The letter *k,* inserted into our deepest subjectivity, thus functions as a marker of mystery—of all that transcends our limited hermeneutical abilities.

Having briefly considered the relation between transcendent mystery and the constructs of our worldly perceptions, we are in a position to suggest a more robust theological presentation of the issue. With it comes a new formulation of the plenitude of Divine reality in the universe and our epistemological delimitations of it. The result will be a reconception of both monotheism and idolatry. The former (monotheism) no longer articulates an absolute theistic difference between Divine transcendence and the world but a nondualist panentheism wherein God fills the totality of worldly existence though not limited by this omnipresent manifestation. The latter (idolatry) ignores or diminishes this Divine dimension and reduces the world to its all-too-human mental constructs. I believe that this monotheistic alternative is a spiritual transformation of the mythic plenum (and its multitude of Divine powers) into a dynamic mystical reality. On this view, a comprehensive Divine plenitude is the truth (both manifest and concealed) of perception and existence.

A paradigmatic enunciation of this position is found in a hermeneutical teaching by the Maggid of Mezeritch, R. Dov Ber Friedman.[30] I present it here in line with the overall thrust of the present discussion. It builds on a dynamic correlation between his mystical ontology and the conditions of human epistemology.

According to the Great Maggid, Divine reality is absolute transcendence—infinite and beyond human comprehension (an Infinite Absolute, in philosophical terms). The primary symbol for this reality is absolute light, because such luminosity is deemed a "pure substance" without variation, gradation, or particulars. This being so, and because of God's beneficent desire that humans have some degree of God consciousness, this radiance was delimited or compressed for the sake of cognition (for otherwise mortals could not "bear" it, as he was wont to stress). This willful "contraction," says the Maggid, is the decisive creative principle of *tzimtzum*. It is the spiritual investment (so to speak) of Divinity into the garment of the physical world—this Divine dimension being a component of every particle of existence: their necessary ontological core.[31] Hence, "The whole world is filled with His Glory" (or more concretely, "The fullness of the world *is* His Glory"), and "there is no place devoid of God."[32] However (and this is decisive), this transcendental Divine component is spiritually concealed *within* the natural world. The result is the paradox that there is a hidden, radical transcendence to Divine immanence.

The natural mind only sees and knows things in terms of their external particulars and therefore does not realize that everything perceived is (in actuality) an expression of God. However, this is not something one could naturally know. Hence initiation into the truth of reality requires spiritual instruction and the faithful determination to have spiritual cognizance of the Godhood within being through a

30. The teaching to be discussed below is found in *Maggid Devarav Le-Ya'akov*, ed. R. Shatz-Uffenheimer (Jerusalem: Magnes Press, 1976), no. 142, pp. 239–42. Other references are keyed to this edition.

31. See the opening teaching in *Maggid Devarav Le-Ya'akov*, no. 1, pp. 9–13 (hereafter *MDL*).

32. The first phrase is from Isaiah 6:3; the second is an Aramaic formulation ubiquitous in Lurianic and Ḥasidic theosophical literature (and see already in *Pesikta de-Rav Kahana* 1.2). In our passage, see *MDL*, p. 240, and cf. elsewhere (nos. 26, 52, 87, 145–46, 200, 207).

proper mental disposition (inculcated while performing the Divine commandments, especially). The theological ideal is to know that the "outer" world of nature and the "inner" dimension of spirit are two correlative aspects of one Divine disclosure. Or, to put the matter otherwise, the creation is fundamentally a revelation *of* God (understood as both an objective and subjective genitive—that is, a revelation of God, Godself, and a revelation of existence through Divine agency).

We shall first consider how the Maggid presents this difference between Divine ontology and human epistemology and then suggest how his understanding of the monotheistic difference—that God's transcendent otherness is within the world and not radically distinct from it—might be reinterpreted for a contemporary theology.

The Maggid begins his homily by stating the principle that all created reality is made up of two simultaneous aspects: the aspects of "front" and "back," or *panim* and *aḥor,* respectively. In rabbinic parlance (and Lurianic Kabbalah), this "bimodal-" reality is called *du-partzufin,*[33] and it even has a scriptural formulation in Psalm 139:5, which states that human beings were created *aḥor va-qedem,* both "back and front." This correlation between world reality and human beings allows the Maggid to discuss the dynamic relationship between mystical ontology and human cognition. Presuming both the creative principle of *tzimtzum* noted above, and the spiritual result that the entire world is filled with God's Glory, we are instructed about the inner and outer aspects of God's "transcendent immanence" through the bimodal factor of reality. Thus we learn that the spiritual dimension of Divine presence (denoted as its *panim* or "face") is concealed under the cover of the physical nature of existence (denoted as its *aḥor,* "back" or "other"). The result is the paradoxical fact that God's worldly "omnipresence" is "hidden" from view—the result being a radically transformed sense of the rabbinic locution *hastarat panim* (literally, "concealment of the face"). Whereas earlier rabbinic theology used this expression to convey the mysterious absence of God's guiding providence during times of strife or difficulty, it now specifies God's actual (but concealed) presence in the world. And since there is nothing in existence that is not an expression of Divinity, this reality

33. *Babylonian Talmud, Berakhot* 60a.

"fills" the mind in every possible way—though the ignorant perceive the world in the most superficial and naturalistic terms.[34] They do not know or understand that the outer husk of existence conceals an inner-Divine transcendence. For them, worldly reality is just what it seems, and human predications are based on the apparent sum and substance of life. Only a right-minded hermeneutic can pierce the veil of appearances.

How might we appropriate this teaching in contemporary terms? Beginning with an acknowledgment of the Maggid's teaching that we are creatures suffused within an omnipresent mystery of existence, I would propose a shift from mystic theosophy to hermeneutic theology. This conceptual move bypasses his strong metaphysical ontology (which asserts that Divine qualities are supratemporal entities present within existence in a derivative mode) while retaining the importance of spiritual cognition.[35] Toward this end, I shall reformulate the key terms *panim* and *aḥor*. Accordingly, the word *panim* now designates the plenitude of worldly appearances that confront consciousness at every turn.[36] These are the "facets" of phenomenal reality that are both manifest and inferred on the basis of perception or memory (taking *panim* to indicate all that Husserl meant when he investigated how things "show themselves" to consciousness based on our complex embeddedness in the phenomena of experience *and* our analytically transcendent overview of them). Thus, as located creatures with finite minds, perspective is a fundamental symbolic form of our limited understanding and interpretation.[37] It is, moreover, a primary factor

34. See *MDL*, p. 240, where we find several striking formulations of this (both positive and negative). The principle is already enunciated in no. 1, p. 10, in even stronger terms. It is a vital component of the Maggid's theology.

35. This conceptual shift reflects my personal (postmodern) predilection, which acknowledges (with Kant) the conceptual problematics of medieval notions of ontological entities.

36. For a phenomenology of this primary sensibility, see E. Minkowski, "La plenitude de la vie—image première," *Tijdschrift voor Filosofie* 24, no. 3 (1962): 507–23.

37. Exemplary is the classic work of E. Panofsky, *Perspective as Symbolic Form* (New York: Zone Books, 1997). But as M. Merleau-Ponty rightly emphasized, "classical perspective is not a law of perceptual behavior. It derives from the cultural order, one of the ways man has invented for projecting before himself the perceived world, *and is not a copy of this world*" (my emphasis). See M. Merleau-Ponty, *The Prose of the World*, edited

in our corresponding recognition that what we perceive is exceeded by an inestimable surplus—a "fullness that utterly transcends human comprehension." This realization, and the dimensions of the unknown that we infer, point to a transcendent otherness that we shall label (based on the Maggid's terminology) *aḥor*. The word now designates the transcendent mystery of reality present in the depths of world-being (the *mysterium tremendum et fascinans*—the awesome wonder of things, inspiring both reverence and humility). Human estimations of it constitute the *panim* of conceptual reality. Put differently, *aḥor* is the omnipresent mystery of *panim*—its transcendent dimension.[38]

Reformulating this in theological terms, we may state that the plenitude of reality is the multimodal manifestation of God's transcendent creativity to which we give finite expressions through our lived perceptions and interpretations. As a result, human beings constitute a crossing-point, or nexus, between the suffusing bounty of Divinity and all hermeneutical predications of the Divine.[39] Our minds are filled with God's Glory but are limited by our mental structures and traditions; and these provide our (contracted) epistemological expressions of it. God as such is ineffable and absolutely transcendental to all cognition, yet we try to articulate the manifestations of Divine immanence for human meaning and signification. Being conscious of our intermediation of God's omnipresent manifestations (recall the cipher *k*), our mental predications are reflexively qualified, and having Divine transcendence actively in mind, the infinite mystery of reality (recall the word *mi*) may provide a counterpoint to epistemological hubris. Disregard of these matters can result in a reification of our perceptions and an idolatrous bondage to the constructs of our mind—a spiritual danger repeatedly asserted through citations of a teaching of the Ba'al Shem Tov (the vaunted "founder" of modern Ḥasidism). One striking formulation was given by his grandson, R. Moshe Ḥayyim Ephraim of Sudilkov. Building on the Talmudic teaching that

---

by C. Lefort (Evanston, IL: Northwestern University Press, 1973), 51, and the ensuing discussion of representation and style.

38. This is, of course, quite different from the "transcendent otherness" of worldly phenomena—over against human cognition.

39. I first began to think about the "crossing-point" or "nexus" in my book *Sacred Attunement: A Jewish Theology* (Chicago: University of Chicago Press, 2008).

when Scripture admonishes, "Do not turn (*tifnu*) to idols" (Lev. 19:4), R. Ephraim first interprets this to mean that persons should not "turn to" or rely on their own "mind" (*da'atkhem*).[40] He then cites the warning of his grandfather, who interpreted the injunction that one should not "turn away (*ve-sartem*) and serve (*ve-'avadetem*) other gods" (Deut. 11:16) to mean that "Whenever one turns (*ve-sar*) their thought from cleaving (*mi-deveikuto*) to God . . . one immediately worships (*oved*) other gods (*elohim aḥerim*)."[41] On this radical view, the structure and content of one's theological consciousness (or religious epistemology) are crucial.

The import of these reflections brings me back to my opening remarks, when I spoke about our primary embeddedness within the world and its perceptual forms. The revolution of spiritual-religious awareness that I have presented can now be understood to have the following (bimodal) epistemological structure. As distinct from a radical theistic position that cleaves theological reality into two separate planes (the absolutely transcendent dimension of God and the concrete worldly realm of creation), the present panentheistic position experiences the omnipresent Divine reality within the world as a humanly "mediated immediacy." That is, from this nondualist perspective, God's transcendent mystery is the depth dimension of all phenomenal immanence—never perceived as such but intuited as the infinite surplus within and beyond cognition.[42] Stated with respect to our "subjective perception," the infinite plenitude of God-given reality is mediated through one's participatory imagination (and therefore affected by human capacities, limitations, and values).[43] Whereas stated with respect to the "objective data" of the

40. See *Babylonian Talumd, Shabbat* 149a.

41. See in *Degel Maḥaneh Ephraim* (Jerusalem: Mir, 1995), 162b (*Kedoshim*, s.v. "al").

42. Hence it is fundamentally different from the perceptions of a "mystical ontology" rooted in medieval kabbalah.

43. Speaking from a different but related mystical stance, see the reflections of R. Pannikar, *L'Expérience de dieu: Icôns du mystère* (Paris: Albin Michel, 2002), chap. 1.

world, the phenomena of lived experience (the manifest perceptions of *panim*) are the finite testimonies of an inestimable Divine actuality (the primordial dimensions of *aḥor*). The infinite occurrences of existence are thus manifestations of the absolutely transcendent reality of all being—derived from God, "the Life of life" (*ḥei ha-ḥayyim*)—as processed through our mortal minds. Accordingly, the emergent images of human thought and imagination are the epistemic (all-too-human) constructs of the God-given mystery of existence.[44] In a related manner, the anthropomorphic depictions of Divinity throughout Scripture (forms of literary "presence") should not be denigrated as "false images"—to be rejected or reconfigured through allegorical explication. They should rather be deemed *testimonies* of concrete, momentary meetings with God (thus, textual renditions of the "events" or *Geschehen* of this encounter; or "mediated immediacies," using the phrase just proposed).[45] These literary refractions may even, in turn, engage one's religious consciousness, and, by means of these hermeneutical mediations, evoke new (personal) engagements with the Divine revelations that elicited the original formulations. To forget this overarching consideration (of God's unknowable transcendence *and* the spiritual dimensions of all discernible reality) is to constrict human thought to the surface plane of worldly perception. We are left with the "work of our minds" and the potential reification of our predications—where nothing qualifies our assertions except the stimulus to find new or more effective cognitive models.[46] This is

44. The great counterpoint to Weber's notion of *Entzauberung* (noted above) is Rilke's verse, "But for us existence still can enchant (*verzaubert*); in a hundred / places it's still Origin. A play of pure forces, / which no one sees who doesn't kneel in wonder (*bewundert*)." See Rainer Maria Rilke, *Sonnets to Orpheus*, trans. E. Snow (New York: North Point Press, 2002), 78–79 (sonnet 2.10).

45. I am obviously indebted to F. Rosenzweig, "A Note on Anthropomorphisms in Response to the *Encyclopedia Judaica*'s Article," in *God, Man, and the World. Lectures and Essays*, ed. and trans. B. Galli (Syracuse, NY: Syracuse University Press, 1998), 135–45. For the original essay, see *Der Morgen* 4, no. 5 (1928); it was subsequently reprinted in *Kleinere Shriften* (Berlin: Schocken, 1937), 525–33.

46. See Max Weber, "Objective Sociology and Social Science and Social Policy" (1904), in *The Methodology of the Social Sciences*, ed. E. A. Shils and H. H. Finch (New York: Free Press, 1949), 86 (where he refers to the "*Götterdämmerung* of all evaluative

epistemological idolatry by any other name.[47] The spiritual challenge is therefore to hold in mind the infinite mystery of God along with our mediations of the God-given occasions of existence,[48] inherently limited by and subject to cognitive limitations.[49] Hermeneutic humility is crucial. The alternative has consequences for our soul and our culture.

---

perspectives"), and cf. Max Weber, "Science as a Vocation," 138, on the endless search for ends.

47. Note also the language of Psalm 81:10, "You shall have no strange god *bakh* in you," as interpreted in the *Babylonian Talmud, Shabbat* 105b (not a "strange god" in your midst, but within you—personally!).

48. I mean "occasions" in the rich sense employed by A. N. Whitehead in *Process and Reality* (New York: Free Press, 1978).

49. Thus both poles (the antinomies of intuited mystery and perceived manifestation) are the products of our always embodied longing for meaning. We cannot escape this this hermeneutical circle. Integrity requires living in the dialectical "middle"—between the wonder of (absolute) unknowability and the utility of our cognitive constructs.

5

The Inner Point

SPIRITUAL CONSCIOUSNESS AND ATTENTIVE REGARD

Some Preliminaries

It is hard to imagine that one's upright posture is not of primary significance both for one's standing in the world and for one's orientation to it. By "standing in the world" I do not simply mean our human preeminence among primates in terms of mere physical and mental development. I mean it in the more concrete sense of our ability to have a superior perspective over quadrupeds and the earth generally by virtue of our elevated positionality, since our eyes in our heads are cast forward with a peripheral expanse to encompass much of what is "before" us (straight ahead and down below) as we move forward into lived situations. Standing upright and moving ahead, our gaze alights on conditions of value or danger, perceiving what is here and now, within available reach, and registering what is concealed or obscure. Our posture also influences how we see or envision persons (near and far) and of course how we respond to the environment in which we are embedded. In sum, the two valences of our "standing in the world" (having height and being directed forward) connect our mortal physiology with a phenomenology of personhood in the world.

It is the abiding significance of Erwin Straus to have devoted detailed studies to both aspects.[1] In a particularly notable contribution, he indicated how the gaze of the eye binds diverse planes of light, and therefore he emphasized that the "phenomenology of vision is

1. See E. Straus, "The Upright Posture," *Psychiatric Quarterly* 26 (1952): 529–61.

no mere addendum to physiological optics." It helps account for our mode of living. Moreover, we gradually, with maturation, develop a "contemplative gaze" that can peruse things at a distance without our going over to the "thing" seen[2]—and this, he adds, begins a process whereby the "suchness" is not simply viewed but is subject to abstractions. By this process, we may construe a figural eidos (or mental image) that remains connected to the primary suchness until this figure is reconstituted or reconfigured into an object (be it a physical utensil or some object d'art).[3] Such visual developments thus enhance our human situation in the world and all that we may achieve on this basis. There is no doubt, then, that our physical axis and positionality has many ramified dimensions. In a word, we are embodied beings with eyes on the lookout.

Another innovative thinker, Eugène Minkowski, combined the same skills and interests as Straus. In his last article (in 1970) he gave exuberant reference to the latter's essay on perception and formulated a phenomenological account of the world that appears "before" one's frontal gaze in contrast to the obscure unknown that is ever "behind" one's back.[4] These reflections emphasize the significance of the world that opens up in front of one's face, projecting a person's perspective in a forward direction—directed both toward the future and its becoming. With these meditations, Minkowski circled back to his earlier profound interpretation of Henri Bergson's notion of lived vitality, or élan vital, and his stress on the importance of "lived time" for humans—this being a world-forming process of creativity, always unfolding and all-pulsating.[5] In his most singular way, Minkowski transformed the evolutionary and metaphysical emphases of Bergson. Without denying their value, he focused on how this élan expresses itself in a typology of ways the human being is oriented to time by virtue of their

2. Straus, "Born to See, Bound to Behold: Reflections on the Function of Upright Posture in the Esthetic Attitude," *Tijdschrift voor Filosofie* 27 (1965): 659–88, esp. 668.

3. Straus, "Born to See."

4. E. Minkowski, "Le monde derrière nous," *Tidschrift voor Philosopie* 33 (1970): 86–94.

5. Minkowski, *Lived Time: Phenomenological and Psychopathological Studies* (Evanston, IL: Northwestern University Press, 1979). This work originally appeared in 1933 under the title *Le temps vécu*.

sense of expectation and hope (in the future) or feeling of diminishment and loss (due to a contracted sense of horizon induced by illness or a sense of death). Inevitably, these intrapsychic dimensions have a crucial impact on external relationships with persons or projects. His chapters on psychopathology build on these phenomenological descriptions and demonstrate how clinical impairments and the sense of lived time are related (e.g., how brain lesions affect the modalities of communication). Throughout these studies, Minkowski followed Bergson's focus on concrete experience: how we live from moment to moment (in time) is directly related to our physical being-in-the-world—both how we see it and our capacities to relate to it in some measure.

In a notable formulation about "lived time," Minkowski referred to what he called a "lived synchronism" between the particular time sense of an individual ego—who moves through successive temporal zones, self-aware and active—and the way we are sometimes totally absorbed in the "flow of existence" with no sense of time passing. The first relationship to time is personal and marked by discrete and separate events whereas the second is (so to say) an impersonal engagement with the primordial, creative vitality of existence.[6] No doubt our acts in the first case are also part of this "flow," but we carve it up into pragmatic segments. It is just here that we touch ground zero of Bergson's theory of "creative evolution." For this philosopher (and his followers), time is the quintessential reality, ever actual, alive, and in the process of constant transformations. This continuous process (in which world-matter is subjected to creative transformations) is called the *durée* (or duration), and it constitutes the process of attentive regard for the living, evolving expansion of an organism. We humans similarly participate in this organic process and may attain an immediate, intuitive contact with it. By contrast, our intellectual knowledge is of a secondary, constructed, and retrospective order; and it therefore divides the flow of time into conceptual segments of one kind or another. We may then overlook the fundamental temporal dimension of existence at our peril, succumbing to repetitions and fixed behavior and not attending to the possibilities of vibrant creativity that

6. See Minkowski, *Lived Time,* chap. 3.

encompass us. Characterized as a divine force, the vitality of time has a near-mystical omnipresence; or, in the depiction of one thinker: time is a "purposeful cosmic energy . . . [that] penetrates the world and coincides with the spirit of the Creator."[7] By assimilating ourselves to this all-creative principle, we may tap into the spiritual force that energizes nature and allows it to evolve into ever-new forms—forms that not only have organic benefits for a species but have ethical and spiritual benefits for human beings. At its most sublime, this spiritual life force might culminate in a cognitive state marked by moral and loving actions. Such was Bergson's vision, and his intellectual trajectory spanned the spectrum of physical and spiritual life: from the biology of *Creative Evolution* (one of his first books) to the sociology of religious forms in his *The Two Sources of Religion and Morality* (his last work).[8] Living in time is therefore our fate and freedom; it draws force from encounters with contentious entities, but also offers occasions for great beneficence.

I have opened this discussion with the preceding reflections because they provide a double vector into the subject. The abovementioned paragraphs provide an empirically based phenomenology of the standing structure of the human and their relationship to vision and perspective; the second group is also empirically based but emphasizes the creative evolution or adaptations of organisms in the course of time—temporality being a primary reality that marks the ways entities constantly seek solutions over the course of their life process. A student interested in the history of religions will be struck by these features (both practical and theoretical) and ponder similar structures in this universal phenomenon (particularly their speculations of different notions of time and how a spiritual adept should relate

7. This citation is from L. Kolakowski, *Bergson* (New York: Oxford University Press, 1985), 69, 73.

8. The original French edition of the first appeared in 1907; the last work appeared in 1932. The study by V. Jankélévitch, *Henri Bergson* (Durham, NC: Duke University Press, 2015), gives full analytic expression to the arc of Bergson's creativity and coherence. The first edition was published in 1930 and updated in 1959.

to them). In one striking case there is an uncanny resemblance between the cluster of topics in Bergson's and Minkowski's work and those found in the homilies of a late nineteenth-century Ḥasidic master, Rabbi Yehudah Aryeh Leib Alter of Ger (Gora Kalwaria), Poland (near Warsaw).

One can hardly imagine any possible influence or contact between these resemblances, but they nevertheless serve to stimulate a trove of reflections on this Ḥasidic teacher's phenomenology of religious ideas and practices—particularly with respect to the values given to a worshipper's attentive regard to the world and its temporality, since this is the realm wherein a person of flesh and blood (but also spirit) may connect with the "creative energy" of Divinity omnipresent in time and space. To anticipate the topics, I shall briefly encapsulate the most salient and evident similarities. These include (i) the designation of the all-creative and all-effectuating Divine vitality as *ḥiyyut* (or creative "life force")—which echoes the term élan vital; (ii) the spiritual value inherent in the ceaseless course of time in the unfolding of reality, as against the segmented character of temporal units; and finally, (iii) the repeated emphasis on universal creative energy as a Divine force that suffuses all world-being and its processes—such that there is nothing that is separate from and not vitalized by it. For R. Yehudah Aryeh Leib, this Divine immanence constitutes the monistic "Whole" of all earthly reality, its truly Real and omnipresent quality (this near-pantheistic feature being in tension with the normative theistic conceptions in Judaism in general and many types of Jewish mysticism in particular).[9]

Naturally, the spiritual core of existence is not self-evident, and it cannot be empirically confirmed, being encumbered by physicality and by our natural minds. Religious instruction is therefore required both to evoke and to elucidate it. It will therefore be one of the main goals of the ensuing discussion to clarify this double dimension (of a spiritual core to the natural world) and the spiritual education that is presented to respond to this situation. Toward this end, I shall supplement my philological explication of the teachings with

9. Perhaps a better formulation for the public expressions of his thought is "panentheism"; but it is hard to deny the resonance of the other term in many of the author's formulations.

a phenomenological apprehension of the spiritual ideals involved. How might a person cultivate an attentive regard for the Divine life-principle concealed in external reality (a particular modality of what Straus called the "contemplative gaze") and conjoin this to its enactment? Might Minkowski's notion of a "lived synchrony" (of the external world of segmented time versus the deeper flow of eternal Divine vitality) be in play here too? And, if so, what is the religious consciousness that is fostered?

My chief concern in the following discussion is to consider the issues of "lived time" within a traditional mystical framework and to examine the emphases formulated by a great spiritual master. How did he strive to transform natural sight into spiritual insight? On the basis of his teachings, we shall then seek to evaluate the notion of "attentive regard" as a contemporary spiritual value.

Divine Vitality and Its Expressions

R. Yehudah Aryeh Leib was the second master of the Ḥasidic dynasty of Gur, leading this community of disciples from 1870–1905, during which time he delivered numerous homilies on Sabbaths and festivals that were collected in his master work, *Sefas Emes*—whose title became his own personal sobriquet.[10] These sacred occasions provided the Scriptural lectionary sources through which he proclaimed his great spiritual vision of a creative Divine vitality, called *ḥiyyut*, that courses unceasingly through all existence.[11] Elucidating these texts through a multifaceted spiritual hermeneutic was the means by which his evocative insights were conveyed to a wide audience of disciples. As shall be seen, this process of exegesis (of recovering the Divine instructions latent in Scripture and tradition) runs parallel to the

10. All citations are taken from *Sefer Sefas Emes 'al ha-Torah u-Mo'adim* (Jerusalem, 1971), in 5 volumes.

11. For a concise review of background and influences, and a conspectus of themes, see A. Green, "Three Warsaw Mystics," in *Jerusalem Studies in Jewish Thought* 13 (1996), 6–21 (English pagination).

necessity for each individual to recover, through their attention to worldly phenomena, the hidden Divine vitality that sustains all existence. Thus, each person was tasked with the spiritual-hermeneutical challenge of perceiving God in all things: God, the All-in-All.

The formal structure of creation taught by the *Sefas Emes* is grounded in a complex medieval theological metaphysic based on a neo-Platonic tradition. In the opening homilies of the Book of Genesis, the master first discloses a major esoteric truth; namely, that the creation of the world expresses the Divine desire to emanate a primordial light from the Ultimate Source of Unity—to both effect and to sustain the myriad forms of existence. This primal force of creativity is known as the *koaḥ ha-po'el* (or power of actualization), and it is eternally present in the *nif'al*, this being the created reality "effectuated" by it.[12] This process is marked in Scripture by the successive events of Divine speech recorded in Genesis 1—a process that is renewed every day and that gives the bounty of life to all creation. Accordingly, each of the primordial six days of creation constitute the foundational, temporal "structures" of worldly reality; and these days, in their diurnal rotation, contain the multiform variety of life that we see from moment to moment in the natural world. Temporality and its duration are thus an essential aspect of the created world and derive from the inner pulse of Divine light within each element. External reality is therefore not an illusion; but it is not the whole truth.

The Torah of Moses, or sacred Scripture, is thus a cosmic blueprint for all existence. Not only does it specify the Divine source of this mundane reality but all worldly matters derive from its own transcendental blueprint: the supernal Torah in Heaven. This ultimate reality is entirely spiritual; accordingly, its transmutation into physical worldly realities required a series of condensations and refigurations. In this process, the pure spiritual vibrations of Divine speech took on the vocal and literary forms that made them communicable to earthlings and emanated (through a continuous act of Divine creativity) all the natural forms of existence. Nature, as we see it, is the worldly manifestation of this condensation of God's all-vitalizing Word, which is its innermost spiritual core. Accordingly, Divinity is essentially immanent

12. See *Sefer Sefas Emes*, 1:3a–b.

within the creation, from the beginning and evermore (the primordial power, or *koaḥ ha-po'el*) being effective in everything)—all external appearances to the contrary notwithstanding. This (esoteric wisdom) is the essential sine qua non of religious knowledge and practice. Not knowing the inner reality of world formation, a person can be blindsided by the material world and its manifestations; but knowing this may induce one to shed the visual scales of surface sensation and begin to perceive the invisible truth of God's omnipresence. And since the Torah of Moses is derived from Divinity, it is the formative guide in this process of realization. As R. Yehudah Leib states, the Torah of Moses provides instruction and "advice" for the clarification of human consciousness as it strives to discern Divinity within the manifest world.[13] It is therefore a human task to devote oneself to the Divine Will, the vitalizing inner point of God's creative activity.

The inner core of vitality, emanated by God, is the Divine quality referred to by the *Sefas Emes* as the *nequdah ha-penimiyyut*—the spiritual "point" of "innermost being," or the "point" of Divine "interiority."[14] It conceals (but inwardly manifests) the vitality of all the created formations evident in existence. Indeed, this vitality and all its individual distinctions are precisely what we experience as the volatility and diversity of lived temporality. But this is not its primordial truth, which is both wholeness (*shalom*) and harmony (*shleimut*).[15] And thanks to God's grace, a symbolic manifestation of this truth is "given" on the Sabbath day: a day of rest in which the flux and ferment of existence is spiritually integrated. According to the master, when Scripture states, after six days of creative vitality, *va-yekhulu ha-shamayim veha-aretz ve-khol tzeva'am* (the heavens and earth and all their host were

13. Cf. *Sefer Sefas Emes*, 1:4b: *le-khol davar yesh aḥizah ba-torah* (Everything has its connective source in the Torah); and the aid for the Divine clarification is via the Oral Torah (3a). And also: *kol ha-ma'asim she-ha-adam 'oseh mukhan lo ve-'iqqar ha-'avodah le-khavven ha-sha'ah ha-re'uyah lahem* (Every deed that a person does is prepared for him, and the essence of Divine worship is properly to orient oneself to its right [or appropriate] time). See, ibid., IV, 83c. Note the temporal coordinates of *mukhan* (from God's side) and *le-khavven* (from the human side).

14. Cf. *Sefer Sefas Emes*, 1:3c.

15. Notably, in *Sefer Sefas Emes*, 2:3b, we have the formulations *nequdah ha-meyuḥedet* and *nequdah ha-aḥdut*, "the point of uniqueness" and "the point of unity," respectively. Significantly, the noun *nequdah* is not part of a construct chain.

completed; Gen. 2:1), the verb *yekhulu* (were completed) encodes the more profound truth that on the seventh day all phenomenal multiplicity was, as it were, unified within the temporal *keli* (vessel) of the Sabbath—every element suborned to the primordial Divine point (its inner harmony and integral structure) such that the climactic seventh day was the "inclusion" (*hitkallelut*) of each and all into a One-and-All.[16] This integrating or integral day is distinguished by a mode of spiritual "stasis" that allows the inherent Divine illumination, vibrant at its innermost core, to break through and affect the consciousness of all persons who cease their labors in the daily world of multiplicity and partake of the God's "gift" of the Sabbath. This day constitutes a resting point of time—a modality of transcendental harmony, and it helps manifest to its celebrants the immanent Divine creativity that pulses everywhere and always.[17] What is latent or obscure during the ordinary week days becomes more fully disclosed (as a Divine "gift") on the Sabbath. Quintessentially, this day is beyond time, since the primordial Sabbath was not a created entity. It therefore radiates a primordial reality. Hence, the master refers to it (in the traditional idiom) as *mei-ein 'olam ha-ba*, "a hint of the world to come."

What does our existence in "time" demand so that we may grow in spiritual awareness and cultivate a Sabbath consciousness?

For the spiritual adept, according to the *Sefas Emes*, the task of the workday week is the mental focalizing on the fragmented phenomena of Divine unity that vitalizes the plenitude of existence, moment by moment, by turning consciousness to the hidden point that animates it. This process is guided by the content of Torah and Tradition. How so? We are repeatedly told that one must cultivate a sustained intentionality directed toward the ever-hidden inner point and a correspondingly recurrent act of self-nullification to it. For this inner point is nothing less than the hidden God in all being.[18] The first (the issue

16. See *Sefer Sefas Emes*, 2:3a. The terminology will be further discussed below.

17. Particularly notable is the formulation in *Sefer Sefas Emes*, 4:46b: "Truly, whenever a mitzvah is performed it partakes of the quality of the Sabbath (*Shabbat*), with the [fundamental] caveat that it is the most comprehensive 'stasis' (*shevitah*) of all, and involves the return [or restoration] of the entire creation to its Source (*shoresh*)."

18. Cf. *Sefer Sefas Emes*, 2:2a, and the articulation there: "the *penimiyyut* [innermost interiority] of the *ḥiyyut* in every 'thing' [*shebe-khol davar*] is from God." In a more

of intention) is guided by faith and trust in tradition; the second (the negation of one's will) by an inner subordination to it. This means that one must initially suspend one's experiential sense that the material world is all that there is and that its appearance is the ultimate reality; and then, on the basis of a "belief" (*emunah*) that there is a Divine core (the innermost *nequdah*) at the creative center of all existence, one must subordinate one's natural will to the Divine Will that addresses the individual throughout all the phenomenal features of the natural world. Subordination means trust (or "faith") in the teachings of Torah and Tradition, first and foremost, but it also refers to one's devotional desire to execute every commandment (or unspecified task) in a God-focused way. Attentiveness to the lived situations at hand is therefore crucial, and it is precisely this primary spiritual disposition that one must cultivate. For through this "belief" in the hidden reality of God in all things one may attain the ultimate "truth" (*emet*): a realization of the Divine element in all existence.[19] "To the degree that one knows (or spiritually apprehends) this *nequdah*, all (of experienced reality) is blessed and attached (*nidbaq*) to the source of (all) life."[20] And not only this: precisely because this *nequdah* is part of the vitality of life, it is eternally renewed from its Divine Source[21] together with every creature that is able to make contact with this supernal reality ("for the *penimiyyut* is the actual vitality of God").[22]

Cultivating Consciousness

The six days of the week mark the flow of the Divine *ḥiyyut* repeatedly, ever since the creation, into the ordinary time of human existence. This vitality is ever-generating but is hidden from a normal consciousness. Accordingly, the religious adept must try to inculcate a religious perception of this reality by spiritual labor at every moment

radical formulation, we read that "even the power of the concealment [*ha-hester*] is from God—even though it appears to be contradictory [*le-hitnagged*] to holiness."

19. For a concise (instructional) statement of these matters (specifically the relationship between *emunah* and *emet*), see the homily at *Sefer Sefas Emes*, 1:133a.

20. See *Sefer Sefas Emes*, 1:133b.

21. See *Sefer Sefas Emes*, 2:2b.

22. Cf. *Sefer Sefas Emes*, 1:132a.

during the week. The central commandment of these days is stated in the Decalogue: *sheishet yamim ta'avod ve-'asita kol mela'khtekha, ve-yom ha-shevi'i shabbat la-YHWH eloheykha* (You shall labor for six days; but the seventh day is the Sabbath for the Lord) (Exod. 20:9–10). According to the *Sefas Emes*, the initial phrase, regarding work on the weekdays, was interpreted as a hortatory call to each person to strive to discern the inner-spiritual actuality within nature in all that one does, so that, through this spiritual labor, one's soul will be repeatedly renewed, aroused, and enhanced (for the fullest Divine bliss on the Sabbath).[23] To embark on this devotion, which is not self-evident, it is necessary to have "faith" or "trust" (*emunah*) in the truth of the teaching that everything is a gracious *matanah* (or gift) of God's overflowing bounty (*shefa'*). Accordingly, a "person of faith" (*ish emunot*; Prov. 28:20) is one deemed to be "drawn to the [transcendental] source (*shoresh*), and even though he performs his daily physical deeds (*ma'asim gashmiyyim*) in the external world nevertheless knows [by spiritual instruction] and remembers [by ritual reflection] that everything (*ha-kol*) derives from the blessed Lord."[24] Such acts of knowing and remembering therefore provide two operative considerations whereby an individual may attain a spiritual state and transcend every temporal or spatial "division" (*peirud*). The ideal of religiosity is a monotheistic consciousness in the fullest sense: awareness of God in all things. This is belief in the Oneness of God. To keep this truth in mind (to both know it and remember it) is thus an ongoing act of meditative focus. The human will is an enticement that can lead to folly; hence, every person truly engaged in a God-centered devotional life must "annul" [or subordinate] their personal desires or will to God's Will (*retzono*) alone. Here is one of many exhortations: "A person who has [spiritual] consciousness (*da'at*) must exert himself in his mind to know the right and righteous deed. However, in truth, no human being is able, by themselves (*be-'atzmo*), to find the proper path. Hence it is necessary [for this person] to annul (*baṭṭel*) his entire mind to the Torah and commandments of the Lord, and by that act of annulment (*biṭṭul*) he may succeed to raise all his thoughts to

23. See, for example, *Sefer Sefas Emes*, 2:44d, 47d.

24. Ibid., *Sefer Sefas Emes*, 2:116a.

God."[25] Only in this way can one "discern God's Will" in the world and suspend their individual mind and natural wisdom. This directive is nothing less than an intensification of the ancient rabbinic instruction preserved in the collection *Pirkei Avot* (Ethics of the Fathers, at 2.4): "You must annul (*baṭṭel*) your will before His Will (*retzono*) so that His Will may become your will." This bold formulation is directed to a radical transformation of religious consciousness. The spiritual ideal is that one's "personal will must be annulled to the (Divine) principle and directed to enact the Will of God" (*ve-ratzon ʿatzmuto yitbaṭṭel le-ʿiqqar ha-mekhuvan la-ʿasot retzon ha-Maqom*).[26]

A striking explication of Proverbs 1:20 gives further insight into the personal task required. That verse states, "Wisdom [*ḥokhmot*] cries aloud in the street [*ḥutz*], she raises her voice in the broadways [*reḥovot*]." Similar to the situation considered above, which emphasized the need to be constantly concerned that all actions become Torah acts, the master stresses that "there is a holy [Divine] spark that vitalizes everything, but it is concealed in [material] nature and [physical] externality (*ḥitzoniyut*) . . . [accordingly] a person must know and clarify that every occurrence is from the *ḥiyyut* of God."[27] The relationship between the homiletical teaching and the biblical proof text is exegetically evident: the Divine wisdom, concealed in the external world (*ḥutz*), makes itself known to those who can discern its call and respond to its reality through an expanded consciousness (*reḥovot*)—this latter term being the way the *Sefas Emes* explains one of the wells dug by Isaac and named *reḥovot* (Gen. 26:22), since it symbolizes the "expansion" (*hitraḥavut*) of the sparks of holiness in the mind of each person as they increasingly perceive the "vitality" of God and cleave to Divinity inherent in all things.[28] This intense striving (also called *hishtadlut*) results in the multiplication of spiritual points of holiness

25. See in R. Yehudah Aryeh Leib's commentary on Psalm 1, *Sefer Tehilim ʿim Shnei Peirushim Yeqarim ve-Ḥashuvim* (Jerusalem, 1998), 2d. I prefer the sense of "annulment," but "negation" is roughly synonymous.

26. See *Sefer Sefas Emes*, 4:35b; cf. also 36c.

27. *Sefer Sefas Emes*, 1:51a–b.

28. *Sefer Sefas Emes*, 1:51a–b.

in the seeker's soul during the days of the week—conjoining in a mystic fusion on the Sabbath.[29]

The effort of human spiritual growth detailed in the foregoing teachings sheds new light on the Ḥasidic concept of *ʿavodah be-gashmiyyut.* Usually, this term was applied to those life practices such as eating or doing business that do not fall explicitly within the norms of Halakhic practice. As these actions were necessary but involved mundane physical acts and thoughts, considerable effort was expended to stress that they, too, could be sanctified and serve God. Nothing was beyond the pale of spiritual consciousness in mind and deed, and thus the term came to mean the "service" (*ʿavodah*) of God even through one's physical needs (*gashmiyyut*).[30] But R. Yehudah Aryeh's homilies put a new spin on this term. Since all actions require the worshipper to "strive" to find the spark of Divine vitality concealed in external reality, there is ultimately no distinction between the normative practices of religious worship and the diverse worldly acts that must be purified of self-interest and invested with spiritual value. So considered, every action requires *ʿavodah be-gashmiyyut,* since the central spiritual task is to discern the vital core of Divinity hidden within the interiority (*penimiyyut*) of the natural world. Subordinating one's private will to these phenomena transforms every thought and gesture into an act of wholehearted devotion to God.

These devoted spiritual acts may accumulate over the course of the week, or one can remain mired in materiality and its external diversity. But if the latter, one will come to God at week's end, on the Sabbath day, fragmented or empty handed. Only an *ish emunot* (a person who strives continuously to perceive the mystery of God's presence in all things) will be rewarded with some perceptions of the ultimate truth of transcendental harmony. Inevitably, our embodied nature limits our spiritual achievement such that we strive for some illumination

29. Another key term for this striving is a constant yearning for Divine contact: "A person should constantly long (*le-hishtoqqeq tamid*) to conjoin (*lidvoq*) with the source of life (*be-shoresh ha-ḥayyim*) and not be separated from the root of his soul in the one God." See *Sefer Sefas Emes,* 5:28a; he earlier emphasized the need for the release of one's "hidden" soul from material bondage and to "expand it" (*le-harḥivah*), 27d.

30. For a rich and nuanced discussion of the sources, see T. Kaufman, *Be-Khol Derakhekha De-ʿehu* (Ramat-Gan: Bar-Ilan University Press, 2009), chaps. 4–6.

through the refracted mirror of consciousness whereby the phenomena of existence may reveal prismatic indications of the Divine reality reverberating within. The task, therefore, is to polish one's spiritual lens in order to perceive the inherent providential dimensions of all reality. Such a way of seeing (or attending to reality) parallels God's own acts at the creation. We are told that when Scripture states that "the Lord saw (*va-yar'*) that [the act of creation] was good"; this seeing (*re'iyah*) is in fact a "perpetual giving of vitality and permanence to every created entity."[31] This life-giving process is also symbolized by the "well" (*be'er*) named *la-ḥay ro'i* (Gen. 25:11), near which Isaac dwelled (was spiritually conjoined).[32] Its meaning therefore refers to God (the Living One) as the life force whose providential beneficence is an ongoing "seeing" or "giving" of spiritual vitality to all creation. This "living well" is also a symbol of the Sabbath day, the "vessel" (noted above) into which the streams of Divine *ḥiyyut* gather as one integral whole.

This brings us to the second sentence of the Decalogue (cited earlier): "But the seventh day is a Sabbath for the Lord (do not do any labor)." What does this language mean within the auspices of the *Sefas Emes*'s spiritual instructions and directed practice?

The Mystery of the Sabbath

According to R. Yehudah Aryeh Leib, "lived time" has two modalities: for ordinary consciousness, time is experienced as a series of separate oscillations, marked by the quality or quantity of events that affect one's life; for religious consciousness, these latter are moments of secularity (or *ḥol*) as distinct from the fixed occasions of the ritual year, which are sacred (or *qodesh*) and marked by special actions that bring

31. Cf. *Sefer Sefas Emes*, 1:52b.

32. The Scriptural reference that Isaac dwelled "near" (*'im*) this well would have suggested an added spiritual sense to seekers; namely, the preposition would connote a conjunction "with" the Divinity revealed at that place. A full exposition of the sense of "seeing" as creativity occurs in *Sefer Sefas Emes*, 1:31c: "'And God saw that it was good' is written for all the created beings; and this seeing (*re'iyah*) exists forever and gives subsistence (*qiyyum ve-ha'amadah*) to the work of creation. It is especially joined to those who know that the vitality of all the worlds is due to the providence of God." This formulation may be influenced by the comment of Naḥmanides at Genesis 1:4.

the sanctity of the day to mind. Among these occasions the Sabbath is the paradigm, because on it the worshipper must be totally divested of secular behaviors—and rest from all one's workday labors. But because the creative Divine vitality flows ceaselessly since the creation through the temporal structures of the week, there is a Sabbath dimension to the *ḥiyyut*—a modality that derives from God's Absolute Reality and becomes manifest within the world to the degree that a person cultivates a Sabbath consciousness. This notwithstanding, the Sabbath day is special, for on it "the innermost point [*nequdah ha-penimiyyut*]—which is called *shabbat* [Sabbath], and is the essence of the *ḥiyyut*" that sustains all existence—"returns (*shavah*) and restores all things to their [supernal] source; and thereby the essence of the [Divine] Will at the creation is perfected."[33] Thus, on the Sabbath, the hidden reality of Divine vitality becomes manifest and unified as it was at the primordial occasion of the creation. This transformative integration of all spiritual points "in the mystery of unity" enables every created entity to come to "the integral-totality (*kelal*) of the creation." In its inner truth the Sabbath marks the "integration" (*hitkallelut*) of all existences into a spiritual totality of all-encompassing unity.[34]

How does this affect human consciousness? The teacher states, "On the Sabbath there was no event of creation (*beri'ah*) other than rest (*shevitah*); and this *shevitah* is what sustains (*qiyyum*)all created entities . . . [on the principle that] every [entity] that receives must be totally suborned [literally, *baṭṭel*] to their giver—hence, in proportion to the attachment (*devequt*) that any being has to the [Divine] Source of [the all-effecting] efflux (*mashpi'a*), its receptive capacity is sustained. Thus on the Sabbath, when human creatures (*ha-nivra'im*) ascend [spiritually] to their Source, inasmuch as by virtue of this Sabbath rest (*menuḥah*) they become certain (*nitbarrer 'aleihem*) that there is a Lord who rules . . . each creature can approach their Source; and . . . by means of their spiritual desire can be annulled (*baṭṭel*) and integrated (*hikkalel*) into the Life of life. Accordingly, the [subordination or] annulment (*biṭṭulo*) of something results in its sustenance

33. *Sefer Sefas Emes*, 1:3c.

34. See *Sefer Sefas Emes*, 1:3d. In another significant formulation, *Sefer Sefas Emes*, 2:117a, the Sabbath is deemed *kelalut ha-aḥdut*, "the integrality [or totality] of the Unity [of Divinity]."

(*qiyyumo*)."[35] This passage is of axial significance, for in it we are informed that the quintessence of a "Sabbath consciousness" is the annulment of one's will to the Source of all existence. It is a mystic attainment of the quality of rest or supernal quiescence. This raises the question of a religious seeker's task during the week, wherein the ideal is self-annulment to the Divine Will manifest in the Torah. The answer lies in that fact that the essence of the Divine *ḥiyyut* is the Sabbath; hence, every spiritual act of *biṭṭul* taps into the primordial Sabbath "quality" that vivifies existence. The result is that its reality may become part of an individual's religious consciousness in the course of their life of Divine service. The "Sabbath" is the inner principle of a transcendental consciousness, and this sublime state reality may be accessed in some measure through acts of spiritual annulment at all times.

A more radical formulation of this ideal may now be noted. On its terms, the seeker's goal is to move from being an *ish emunot*—one who is fully aware "that a human knows nothing" (*she-ein ha-adam yodei'a kelum*) and must strive to find God concealed in all existence—to an ultimate spiritual state. Such a person strives to annul their "intellect and knowledge" (*ha-da'at veha-sekhel*) in the hope that a transcendent Divine light will break through the forms of the world and God will become immediate and actual to consciousness.[36] At this level of spiritual realization, a person ascends from their state of not knowing to one of absolute or total silence (*shetiqah*).[37] Now the seeker has plumbed the ultimate depth (*'omeq*) of being, where all is quiescence (the pure integrality of the Sabbath). Such a state is the culmination of a life devoted to the spiritual hints in the everyday and their integration

35. See *Sefer Sefas Emes*, 1:4a. The spiritual goal of *hitkallelut* is one of total "inclusion" in the Divine reality. For examples and a discussion, see M. Idel, "Mystical Union in Jewish Mysticism," in *Mystical Union and Monotheistic Faith: An Ecumenical Dialogue*, ed. M. Idel and B. McGinn (New York: Macmillan, 1989), 39–46.

36. Cf. *Sefer Sefas Emes*, 2:34b.

37. In *Sefer Sefas Emes*, 2:34c-d, the *Sefas Emes* discusses two kinds of "silence" (*shetiqah*).

into one's consciousness. Stimulated by the teachings of the master, a spiritual adept strives to bring to mind (and actively internalize) the spiritual truth latent in Scripture. Indeed, the forms of spiritual pedagogy seek to shape a form of life that conforms (in some mortal measure) to the transcendent (but omnipresent) Divine Reality.

Congruent with this teaching is another remarkable statement by R. Yehudah Leib (it is presumably an autobiographical testimony, not a theoretical statement). He remarks that one who achieves the supreme condition of *menuḥah* (of rest or quietude) on the Sabbath has their soul elevated beyond time into eternity, and then "everything that occurs to him [for weal or woe] is one [*eḥad be-ʿeinav*]."[38] This extraordinary spiritual state is one of supreme psychic indifference to external realities: a state of transcendental nondifferentiation that, like the Sabbath, "is a measure of *ayin* [or ultimate "Nothingness"] beyond time . . . [and] conjoined to the 'Divine unity' itself (*davuq be-aḥdut Elohut*)."[39] This is an event of mystical bliss before the emergence of cognitive states of "difference": good and evil being their paramount human reality. It points to a "pinnacle point" wherein the absolute plurality of Divine realities has been condensed at the supreme, undifferentiated apex of emanation. The holy *Book of Zohar*, in its opening portrayal of creation (1.15a), refers to this as: a *nequdah ḥada' setimah ʿila'ah* (a single point, concealed and supernal). As this account goes on to say (with highly esoteric allusions), this "point" is itself illuminated from an even more primordial "flash" that breaks forth from the Divine *ayin* (or transcendental Nothing) at the very onset of emanation. This ultimate *nequdah* is unknowable in itself,

38. See *Sefer Sefas Emes*, 2:7b. At this pinnacle of rest, absorbed in "his communion with the Divine source (*deveiquto ba-shoresh ha-Elohi*), there is no striving (*yegiʿah*) whatsoever."

39. Cf. *Sefer Sefas Emes*, 2:9a. The phrase "is a measure of *ayin*" translates *bi-vehinat ayin*. The word *beḥinah* is a hermeneutical term in Ḥasidism that connotes the sense that some given feature has the "quality" of a certain Divine dimension or modality. In another, even more radical formulation, at its spiritual apex, the human mind approximates an edenic state—before the difference between "good and evil," when one drew directly from the Divine source of sustenance (regarding Adam, it therefore stated that he was *bi-deveiqut ha-aḥdut mamash*, "actually conjoined to the [Divine] unity"); see 7c. That *aḥdut* refers to Divinity is also evident in the idiom *nequdah ha-aḥdut* in 3b.

and beyond it "nothing is known *kelal* [whatsoever]." Being the axial point of all emergence from absolute Divine unity (*aḥdut*), and known as "the *nequdah* of *aḥdut*,"[40] this point has not yet differentiated into the successive stages of the primordial emanation of being. It is (and remains) Pure Unity. For R. Yehudah Leib, this most supernal point is the ultimate harmony of the Whole. As remarked earlier, a mystic might access this supreme state through focused contemplation and worship on the Sabbath day but might also do so by seeking the Divine core (*ḥiyyut*) that is vitally present in every created entity. Spiritual transcendence is thus a lived possibility for those who annul their will and attach themselves to the *nequdah* that has "spread out" (emanated) from God.[41] As this "point" is beyond time or temporality, those who connect to it may similarly transcend the vagaries of existence and attain a state of silent indifference (beyond difference and pathos).

Presence in Plain Sight

The theological consideration presented earlier, which asserted that Divine "seeing" is both a discrete act of creation and one that marks a sustained attentiveness to (or providential regard for) existence, is both remarkable and stimulating. It is remarkable, since it calls attention to the way our eyes give us the presence of the world as an organ of world awareness. And it is stimulating for the way it evokes a range of meditations on how our human situation is guided by the eye and its capacities to help focus attention. This interrelationship between "eye" and "mind" is a crucial factor in our experience of the world. Through vision we sense the immediacy of the world and experience it as a "prolongation of [our psychophysical] structure."[42]

40. See in *Sefer Sefas Emes*, 2:3b (cited above several times).

41. There is no doubt that R. Yehudah Leib had this *Zohar* passage in mind, for when it refers to the impact of the primordial *nequdah* on the subsequent stages of emanation, it states that its light "spread out" (*itpasheiṭ*) into these realms. Precisely this verb is used by the master in *Sefer Sefas Emes*, 2:3b, where the following formulations occur in close succession: *she-nequdah ha-aḥdut titpasheiṭ*; *nequdah ha-mitpasheṭet*, and *hitpashṭut ha-nequdah*.

42. Cf. J. Brun, "Le regard et l'existence," *Revue de métaphysique et de morale* 62 (1957): 287.

Where do we begin if not with the opening of our eyes to daylight and its situations? This is a condition induced by an inner physiological readiness—in different degrees—and by the external impositions of natural forces—also to different degrees, depending on circumstances. The opening of our eyes in the morning is thus not simply a reflex, like the blinking we do daily without intention, when adjusting our retinas to light and distance. It is response to the empirical call of the world. If, however, we choose to lie in bed with an awakened consciousness, perhaps to complete some image or sensation that preceded the summons to return to the external world, we then intentionally keep our eyes closed in order to retain something of the lingering inwardness that somnolence bestows. By contrast, there are events so disturbing that we may choose to shut our eyes to their reality (sometimes this is even an instinctive response). Out of sight is thus not out of mind. Closing our eyes in such cases does not make us blind to the world—it is rather a sign of its inalienable omnipresence.

Given the variable occasions of vision, we may first consider of how things are brought to our attention by some "presentational force." This metaphor stands for a variety of experiences, and these require exposition. Returning to the event of awakening in the morning, we readily acknowledge that light and sight open us to a prolixity of presentations, signs of externality and the ways they induce a mood of receptivity. Soon, without realizing it, "things" fall into their "worldly" place (like they were before sleep), and we connect them to our lived lives and its memories. Once again, the world has returned in its habitual patterns as we begin to move about spatially with only the dimmest sense of time. Each moment becomes a zone of near instinctive occurrence. We are now (in some still-somnolent stupor) on automatic pilot, and only with the memory of tasks to be done does actual intention intrude. And then, for the first time in the day, we sense a double reality: the levels of mind and its focus along with our emotions and their palpable dispositions.

It goes without saying that these levels of mind are also porous and interpenetrating, as diverse thoughts intrude on each other. What we may see at any moment is not merely some object but something laden with a certain value or significance. We feel the world as we see it. Inside and outside interpenetrate, and we may choose to respond to the given values and tasks that they impose. Based on their "presentational force" we make decisions based on what we perceive and our capacity for discernment. Who would deny that sight "gives" us the world, that it is engaged in "making" it a creation, and that it "supervises" the concurrence of events with a providential regard for the best results. Sight and insight have a dominant (often overwhelming) primacy in our lives.

It bears noting that in addition to our lived duration in time, there are special instants that have a qualitative impact. Precisely this was the point that Gaston Bachelard wished to levy against Bergson's emphasis on the flow of existence. His contention was titled *L'intuition de l'instant* (Intuition of the Instant) and highlighted the significance of moments (and elements) that suddenly capture our attention.[43] Such happenings seize our consciousness and jerk us out of the routine of our lives. On this basis, Bachelard later composed his great work, *The Poetics of Space*, in which he emphasized such life-arresting illuminations as the stimuli of human creativity.[44] The poet annotates these revelations in his verse. The "thing" that reverberates or suddenly shines forth is a phenomenon seen in a new way and becomes the chief focal point of consciousness, whose radiating center in experience is the revelatory center of the poem. A later reader must somehow locate this center in order to rotate on its evocative axis. In this way it may, in turn, inspire a new mode of awareness beyond that of the original writer. If so, reading such works may serve as a spiritual exercise of a certain kind—training the mind to see anew and the soul to locate the spiritual center of a work of art.

In addition to being stimulated by some object that imposes itself on our attention,[45] there is what may be called a more "reflective regard."

43. The original French text was published in 1932; the English version is titled *Intuition of the Instant*, trans. E. Rizo-Patron (Evanston, IL: Northwestern University Press, 2013).

44. See *The Poetics of Space*, trans. M. Jolas (New York: Orion Press, 1964). The French original, *La poétique de l'espace*, was published in 1958.

45. A. Steinbock brings this (and various topics from Husserl) to mind is his "Affection and Attention: On the Phenomenology of Becoming Aware," *Continental Philosophy Review* 37 (2004): 21–43.

This involves an act of "seeing" that is not induced from outside the self but that has a more intentional or meditative character. This does not mean that the event is "other" than the experiential sense of it or that it is self-standing or distinct from an individual. The studies on the phenomenology of perception produced by Merleau-Ponty belie this depiction. He contended, based on empirical evidence, that one is actively engaged in the act of perception, and that we are intertwined with the modality we "sense"' (accordingly, sense has the double meaning of feeling and thought). His insights on the way the eye and mind co-inhere in the process of perceiving space or depth were considered earlier.[46] In this context I would stress that one cannot discount the importance of reflective intention—what I shall label "the pause." This indicates the distinct moment that may open a mental space for considered engagement. Two modalities of time are involved. The first involves profane or ordinary time; the second has a more spiritual dimension.

We are not determined or conditioned simply to "go with the flow": we both learn and appropriate many reasons for acts of restraint based on what we see and evaluate in the outside world and when we determinately pause or hesitate on the basis of some internal consideration. For what we see are not only "things" but conditions of value (be it for benefit or not, or for generosity or self-interest). We look and listen; we see and intend; we regard and consider matters with due regard for their consequences.[47] Certainly, acquired learning and emotional intelligence have a lot to do with these assessments, for we do not come to experience tabula rasa. A lifetime of prior events influences our vision as we look out on the world and scan it for context and sense. Thoughtful discrimination therefore plays a crucial role.

46. See my reflections toward the end of chapter 2, above. For a powerful expression of such "entwinement," see especially Merleau-Ponty's essay, "Eye and Mind," published in his *The Primacy of Perception*, ed. J. Edie (Evanston, IL: Northwestern University Press, 1964), 159–90. It originally appeared in *Art de France* 1 (January 1961).

47. The fundamental issue of the way we look, or are looked at—the angle and composition of the gaze, and more, are indicated by J. Gibson and A. Pick, in "Perception of Another Person's Looking Behavior," *The American Journal of Psychology* 76 (1976): 386–87.

In the flow of events, it is also not just bright colors that make us turn our heads and attend to some fandango. The whir of events is not so swift that it may override the stimulus to focus on one thing in particular. It is our considered preference for it or its novelty that induces this redirection of attention. This contraction of regard brings distant events into nearer focus or allows the somewhat near at hand to move away into a safe or considered cognitive distance. Thus, in the best of scenarios, a pause helps contract the panoply of stimuli and allows one to take stock of events.[48] It is just here that we may rejoin the counsel of spiritual masters, albeit from our modern situation. How so?

The immediacy of events addresses our attention from their radiating center, wherein the happening seems to have a focal point of immanent force. This force is not factually "in" the object. Rather, an event that captures attention or regard strikes some center point "in" us. We perceive some coordinate that conjoins or aligns our self to what stimulates it. On such occasions, our senses are condensed to a specific point of stimulation. Looking into someone's eyes may partake of this magnetic conjunction of centering and create an interpersonal communion of great significance. When we say, "I see you," this testimony conveys the fullness of relational presence. "I see you" thus refers to a suddenly centered mutuality between two persons. And what is more, this phrase articulates a meditative reciprocity that centers one individual to another. In these cases the event of mutuality has a sacred aura that evokes the mystery of shared personhood. Who would deny such vital points of interhuman connection?

Going beyond personal relations, we may also encounter the double face of artistic mediation. At special moments, an individual somehow sees a worldly presence that bewitches the senses and draws the self into its force field until some center point is perceived. This may be a tonal chord, a vibrating color, or some synesthetic union between the two. However it happens, the artist feels a corresponding vibration in their inner being, inducing a creative metamorphosis of the experienced phenomenon. This moment is both a settling of focus and incitement of creative energy—one that tries to elicit the suddenly

48. The sense and spiritual immediacy of "duration" notwithstanding, Bergson gave repeated emphasis to the "attention to life." Cf. the striking range of sources assembled by Jankélévitch, *Henri Bergson*, 275n29.

perceived center point of the external "thing," albeit in a new form. It is the coordination of this inner and outer center point that conveys the true import of their creation and, correspondingly, induces the conviction in a receiver of the work that the product is authentic and rings true. This shared temper is a great mystery and altogether invisible. For what do we see when we see "into" the canvases of Klee (or follow Kandinsky's interior tone of colors); and what do we perceive, when we are drawn "through" the notes of Mahler to something beyond death, even as this is conveyed through a melodic parody of a death dance? What do we see when we see like Rilke, whose meditative concentrations penetrate the visible world and reveal a reality he calls the (ontological) "open"? On such occasions we perceive nothing but a modality of the force field that transformed the artist. And somehow, if we can share their centering point of insight, we, too, may be transformed.

Bearing this in mind, we may wonder, can we coordinate these multiple spiritual points in our soul—like some integral influx of creative energies, with each element manifesting its unique difference within the imponderable panoply of existence? Some sense of this awareness is our limited intimation of the heavenly whole, irradiated with unique particularities at every moment. It is a gift: revealed to our attentive heart.

PART II

6

Tears and Testimony

A LITERARY MEDITATION

An Initial Consideration

Tears flow from primary moments in life: from the dark well of loss and abandonment—or the poignancy of an emergent memory; from the emotional release of pent-up feelings—or the sudden reconciliation with persons long absent in mind and heart. During such moments, the self becomes present to its inner magnitude as diverse layers of sensibility resurface before one's inner eye with an unnerving force, shaking the foundations of one's seemingly settled emotional life. The upsurge of early but still primary emotions fuse past and present in a bifocal way, marking the unresolved experiences of one's life. Similarly unnerving is the encounter with old traumas, still stored in one's soul—venomous serpents kept at bay. Sometimes, these emotional events emerge as language: not the verbal stuttering of raw pain but the settled refinement of later creativity. When they do, these expressions may be transmitted across generations—especially when they have entered the canon of culture and offer testimony to our human condition. We acknowledge the truth of tears precisely when they attest to a personal chasm at the preverbal core of speech. And it is as testimonies to human crisis that we receive them in our own lives. Tears are silent ciphers of our mortal nature.

The great Hebrew poet Chaim Nachman Bialik put it more decisively at the conclusion of his essay "Gilluy ve-Khisui ba-Lashon" (Revealment and Concealment in Language)—for there, after brooding on the power of words and their evanescence or trivialization, he speaks of something more primary and more fundamental than social verbiage or even the desire to put experience into words and retain a trace of its reverberating import. This something more is at the taproot of our humanity; it is at the primordial core of any rebirth of language. This something rises from the naked abyss.

> So much for the language of words; but God has still other languages without words: songs, tears, and laughter. And the human speaker is capable of them all. These languages begin where words cease—not as barriers to words but for their renewal. They emerge as tremors from the primordial depths—manifestations of this primal void. Therefore these "languages" rise and sweep us away in their turbulence against all attempts to hold firm; and likewise they may swirl up and drive us mad, casting us beyond the social order. Every creative act that is not resonant of any of these three languages is stillborn, and would be best had it never been made.[1]

I regard this paragraph of inestimable significance in its recognition of the foundational core of sound, of joy—and tears. Sound is surely the murmuring mystery of the world as heard and expressed by vocal tones and song; laughter is the expressive joy before sheer beauty or even paradox. But tears, for me, are the most primordial—witness to our sorrow and fragility, evanescence and memory. They are silent and before all language and therefore provide a witness to our primary emotions—before the witness of language. We cry as children for loss and abandonment or pain; we cry as older youth for silent isolation or the longing for care and compassion. And we cry as we age—for losses and diminishment and failed hopes. Our tears mourn the mysteries of absence, of God's presence or human consolation. And if a poet yearns for inspiration the mourner cries for absence itself. Human time is a vale of sorrow: it leaves us with the specter of silent words, traces of inconsolable endings, and sheer evil. Sometimes we cry simply to stay sane.

The following discussions will try to exemplify these matters. Each tableau of texts has merit in its own right. Collectively, the ensemble represents my personal attempt to construct a spectrum of sources

1. The essay appears in *Kol Kitvei Ḥ. N. Bialik* (Tel Aviv: Dvir, 1938), 207–9; the citation is at the conclusion (my translation).

and emotions with tears at the core—at the verge of the unsaid. I deem the following an essay in literary phenomenology.

Mimesis and Memory

The way memory (and its emergence through tears) is represented is distinctive for each culture. In his stunning use of Aristotle's term for literary representation, *mimesis,* Erich Auerbach produced a much-acclaimed comparison between two epic styles. The first is a narrative mode of concrete and immediate presence (or foregrounding) of individuals and actions and is best exemplified in Homer, with particular reference to the episode of Odysseus's scar.[2] This event is depicted toward the end of the *Odyssey,* when the hero returns home, unrecognized save for the housekeeper Euryclea, who, upon washing the stranger and touching his scar, realizes his identity—recalling with pathos how he was gored in his youth (bk. 19). The second narrative is the unnerving episode in the Book of Genesis wherein Abraham conducts his son Isaac to an altar where he intended to sacrifice him in obedience to a Divine command. Their nearly silent journey to the place of slaughter is conveyed with minimal description; indeed, the literary depiction is "fraught" with background, given its ellipses of style and dialogue (chap. 22). If the Homeric episode charms the audience with its thick presentation of events and dialogue, the Hebraic case conveys an event of spiritual submission in the starkest of terms. Furthermore, if Odysseus is a hero and a bard who can supplement the court singers with the detailed accuracy of his deeds, Abraham is a "knight of faith" (to evoke Kierkegaard's epithet) whose awesome task is portrayed with a reverential distance. In such formal ways these two narratives convey their central character's personality to two diverse audiences for their cultural edification.

Based on the terms of this contrast there is no denying Auerbach's argument. Following a frequent stereotype, Greece and Israel (Athens and Jerusalem) appear in counterpoint. However, there are other stylistic features in these two epical sources that bring them into a quite

2. See E. Auerbach, "Odysseus's Scar," in *Mimesis: The Representation of Reality in Western Literature,* ed. E. Auerbach (Princeton, NJ: Princeton University Press, 1953), chap. 1.

different alignment—one that centers primarily on the psychic processes of memory and self-disclosure. What I have in mind are two episodes of tears and testimony portrayed in the *Odyssey* and Scripture. In the Greek epic, the notable event occurs when Odysseus hears the bard Demodocus declaim his heroic deeds at Troy while he was incognito among the Phaecians (bk. 8),[3] whereas the notable event in Scripture occurs in the course of Joseph's dialogues with his brothers after he (incognito and unbeknown) heard them recount the episode and near murder (for which they were complicit) that resulted in his sale and descent to Egypt (cf. Gen. 42–45). Ostensibly cultural worlds apart, these narratives share poignant particulars of cagey dissimulation, emotional drama, and psychological ingenuity. Upon hearing others narrate episodes of their past life (in the *Odyssey* in a typically detailed, poetic style; and in Scripture, in thickly wrought episodes and speech acts), the two heroes listen silently to these reports until they are overcome with emotion and disclose their hidden identity. Accordingly, a "literary mimesis" (the retelling of the past events) evokes a mimetic experience for the characters, even as it simultaneously stimulates emotions in the reader, based on their aroused life experience and capacity for empathy. Such testimonies serve as a mode of cultural pedagogy binding later generations into a narrative stream of shared memory. Altogether, we have striking cases of literary modeling: the hero first participates in the disclosure of emotional events (by listening to an account of his life that tallies with his own memory), and then later recipients also participate in this decisive event of the past. But more must be said about these narratives and their testimonies of self-disclosure.

The critic Gerard Genette once pondered the "oblique relationship" between the *Iliad* and the *Odyssey*;[4] and his telling phrase helps us

3. See *Homer: Odyssey I–XII*, introduction and notes by W. W. Merry (Oxford: Clarendon Press, 1895), bk. 8, lines 585–89. Tears also figure prominently when the hero rejoins his sons and wife in books 16 and 19 (see *Homer: Odyssey XII–XXIV*). The various discussions of tears in H. Monsacré, *The Tears of Achilles* (Cambridge, MA: Harvard University Press, Center for Hellenic Studies, 2017), are most illuminating.

4. G. Genette, *Palimsettes: La littérature au seconde degré* (Paris: Seuil, 1982), 200.

ponder the relationship between event and the evocation of tears. Achilles, of course, appears throughout as a person of brute passion—whose emotions are violent and his psychic transitions abrupt and without restraint. By contrast, the Odysseus of the *Odyssey* has left the blood of battle and is on his journey home. The dreams of hearth and wife that bolstered his resolve in Troy are now transformed into visions of longing for the fields of Ithaca. The need to restrain his emotions is the constant inner strife he endures as the trip takes twists and turns. Sitting alone on rocky isles, only the waves see his sorrow as his tears meld with the sea that separates him still from his family. Or later, listening to the bard sing about the strife in Troy and his heroic exploits there, Odysseus is overcome with pathos and conceals himself in his mantle—fighting his "fiercest battle" within as he attempts to contain his emotions while shedding tears of grief for the heroic deaths now recited.[5] Shortly thereafter, he requests an account of the Trojan horse and his own cunning ruse. Once again, stunned with emotion, Odysseus "melted" profusely into "tears" of sorrow, though now the bard's song was interrupted, and he was asked to recite his own exploits.[6] Having become a singer of his own *kleos*, or "glory," he recovered and so revealed his identity. "I am (*eim'*) Odysseus," he cried, "son of Laertes, known to the world for every kind of ruse—my fame (*meu kleos*) has reached the heaven. Sun-lit Ithaca is my homeland." Therewith the revived hero launched into an extended series of references to his home and to Calypso and Circe and then the "bewitching queen of Aeaea"—retrieving through this recitation his memories and his nostalgia and his personal destiny.[7]

Who is this "I am" that speaks? Who testifies? It is no longer the Odysseus of war and wiles at Ilion, nor is he yet the husband of Penelope, grieving in Ithaca, united with her in their fields near Mount Neriton. He is rather a recovered version of his former self and yet himself all the same. Odysseus's outflowing tears were a visible expression of this complex person, one who recovered his selfhood through a mimetic hearing of his life and then through his own narrative voice.

5. P. Pucci, in "The Song of the Sirens," *Arethusa* 12 (1979): 126, has emphasized how the song of heroic exploits "brings forth irresistible tears."

6. See *Homer: Odyssey I–XII*, bk. 8, lines 521–49.

7. In *Homer: Odyssey I–XII*, bk. 9, lines 1–38; the disclosure is at lines 19–20.

Between the one and the other, he stated, "I am." We can only imagine all that was bottled up in his heart in this cry of self-identification: memories of his heroic comrades, his strife with Achilles, thoughts of his son and wife, and his own lamenting self cast on foreign shores by shipwreck and siren song. All this opened his heart and voice. The "I" that testifies in public is now revealed to himself most of all, beyond all former restraint. Now Odysseus can sail again and be restored to his family; he can now carry memories of death toward a new, restored life. His voice picks up the thread of epic articulation—alternating "me" and "we" and a host of descriptive details. Such is his testimony born of tears.

To whom and what may this be compared, if comparisons can be drawn—is it not to the biblical narrative about Joseph and his emotional reconciliation with his brothers? Joseph, too, was a survivor—twice over, in fact: once, for his having been rescued from the pit where his brothers cast him in enmity; and later, after his release from a dungeon, where he had been sentenced after a contrived accusation. All these events (so different from the terse episode about Abraham) are depicted in a settled narrative style characterized by pungent dialogues or repartee (sufficient in kind to get a sense of the personalities involved and how these words recur and regenerate the plot). The reflective dialogues open up when Joseph's father, Jacob, sends his sons to Egypt to purchase food because of the famine in Canaan, and in the course of their journeys to Egypt and back, due to the ruses of Joseph (to engender their memory and responsibility for his plight), the brothers recount their family history and tell Joseph (the apparent vizier) that one brother (Joseph) "is no more (*einennu*)"—though he was standing before them all the while, repeatedly overcome with emotion and hidden tears.[8] The emotional climax follows the poignant speech of Judah (who had just returned from a visit to their elder father and pledged himself as surety for the safety of their young brother Benjamin). Upon hearing this representation of old events, Joseph is overwhelmed and "raised his voice" in a tumultuous "cry" (*bivkhi*; Gen. 45:2). Thereupon, there is a double self-identification of

8. Note especially the formulation when Joseph, unrecognized by his brothers who recount his sale and near death, "turned aside from them and cried (*va-yeivk*)" (Gen. 42:24).

Joseph to his brothers: "I am (*ani*) Joseph," he exclaims—in the first instance (v. 2), and asks, "Is *my* father still alive?" since this was primary in his consciousness. Immediately thereafter, Joseph also links his disclosure with a direct statement to these attendees: "I am . . . *your* brother whom you sold" (v. 5).[9] Having heard Judah's poignant account of his family history, Joseph recovers his past and his will for self-disclosure. Hence, perhaps even involuntarily, he responds to this moment with a corresponding act of self-identification. He affirms his older self: he is Joseph, the long-lost bearer of dreams of personal prowess and power—and the reality of their fulfillment. This sense that "the God" has meant it for good may more directly account for his lack of recrimination toward his kin. Saying "I am" is thus a personal assertion of his many layered self and pronounces his sense that his life has now achieved sudden coherence. Yes, he is surely the youth who had been sold to the Ishmaelite traders; and he is equally an Egyptian vizier, the trusty aid to Pharaoh. But he is especially the son of Jacob, and a brother, and the bearer of God's promise. All that had been repressed is now revealed. The confession "I am Joseph" is thus the language of tears that bursts the constraints of self-control. The phrase "I am" is the language of this survivor's identity—for no more needed to be said. In the directness of this psychological event, elaborate rhetoric would be out of place.

What a striking obliquity binds this biblical narrative to that of Odysseus! In both accounts, the reports of past events defer the narrative climax and build a personal tension in the hero. And in both episodes, tears testify to living memory, evidence of the psychic distress that so pained each hero before the language of disclosure. Tears and testimony thus close a gap in the psychic structure of each account even as they do likewise in the heart of each hero and between the hero and his audience. Mimesis is doubled and tripled by the dominant narrative voice, by the voice of participants (including the bard who recites the deeds of Odysseus and the various recollections

9. The direct object pronoun *oti* (me!) conveys his self-reference in an emphatic way, as also in verse 8, when he states that "you sent me (*oti*) here." At the disclosure, Joseph told his bothers, *geshu-na eilay* (come near me), and they did so (*va-yiggashu*; v. 6). The verb echoes the preceding narrative, when Judah "approached" (*va-yiggash*) Joseph at the climactic onset of the reconciliation (Gen. 44:18).

of Joseph's brothers), and by the individual heroes. For the latter, their unrestrained tears elicit their poignant and self-disclosing "I." The reader participates in all this in their corresponding mimetic fashion—and, by this process, a thick layer of cultural identity is engendered.

❋

Before turning to other literary types, let us evoke another, related epic. It also commands attention in its own right, but I mention it here for its capacity to put us in mind of the soliloquy of tears whereby great poets may reclaim their identity. I am alluding, of course, to Virgil's *Aeneid,* and its song about another hero seeking his homeland after the bloody toils of war. Having landed in Carthage, Aeneas is confronted by Venus, who poses to him her questions. And so he began his disclosure with clear confidence: "I am (*summo*) . . . Aeneas"; and then, echoing that earlier wanderer, Odysseus, says, "my fame goes beyond the skies" (bk. 1, lines 378–79). With this introduction, he began a tale of woe; but Venus interrupted his lament. Quite soon thereafter, this hero and his companion come to a grove and behold a stunning artistic scene of the events in Troy, with the Greeks in full flight and even portraying Achilles's most gruesome treatment of Hector. Aeneas is overwhelmed by this representation and exhorts his friend, Achates, to behold this rendition of fame and glory—even in this faraway place. "Even here," he then exudes, meritorious deeds are lauded—"even here the world is full of tears (*sunt lacrimae rerum*), and the burdens of mortality touch the heart."[10] The raw sweeping sorrow of existence is thus graphically memorialized and given testimony by an artistic depiction. Certainly this is comfort after the fact for the dead and grieving, though it was also a central motivation for a heroic life in the first place, as we know from Achilles's famous reflections on preferring a short life with the promise of resounding glory as his epitaph. And yet, as commentators have observed, the phrase *sunt lacrimae rerum* is ambiguous in its reference:[11] the turmoil of life

10. See *Aeneid,* bk. 1, line 462. I have followed the formulation in *The Aeneid,* trans. R. Fagles (New York: Viking, 2006), 63, lines 558–59.

11. For a conspectus of the issue, see D. Wharton, "*Sunt Lacrimae Rerum*: A Linguistic Exploration," *Classical Journal* 103 (2008): 159–79.

is itself a vale of tears, but so too are those pulsing products of art that mimetically attests to it and transfer the sorrow of the artist into their chosen medium. Perhaps Virgil meant both. And so, just as the *Aeneid* is a testimony of anguish, other poems can similarly convey our mortal sorrow and elicit empathetic solace from one soul to another. Thus, do the *lacrimae rerum* ("tears of existence") bespeak the bottomless sorrow of the human heart; they are an evocative testament to the silence of the soul. Tears flow from the font of memory's dark well: words are their secondary witness—however they come or in whatever form they speak. Because they emerge from a font of raw experience, they are as close to existential truth as possible. It therefore behooves the mimetic accounts to remain close to the engendering moment, through the genius of tone, image, and suggestion. Then they, too, may similarly provide testimonies of the heart—in their own right and for all who will appropriate them.

Lyrics of Tears, Self-Reference, and Sorrow

In addition to epic, there are personal lyrics that convey identity and tears. Among the greatest poets that merit consideration on this theme is Shlomoh ibn Gabirol. He was one of the most prolific and profound individuals that produced the renaissance of Jewish literary culture in Spain during its Golden Age. His own floruit was the eleventh century, and he wandered within Majorca and Saragossa—but mostly he traversed the singular depths of his luminous mind and anguished spirit. Within his secular oeuvre, nothing quite matches the cryptic mystery and emotional force of "Ulay Dema'ot" (If Tears)—a poem replete with an exchange of diverse voices from the outside world (perhaps based on some actual critique addressed to the poet, perhaps also based on the inducements of friends) and his personal, inner turmoil.[12] Like a thick swell and swale, these voices jostle among the concatenated lines and accentuate the poet's frequent swings of mood—until light dawns in the form some sidereal specter that helps Ibn Gabirol recover his primordial connection with Divine wisdom

12. See *Shlomoh ibn Gavirol: Shirei Ḥol*, in the edition of Ḥ. Brody and Ḥ. Schirmann (Jerusalem: Schocken Institute for Jewish Research of The Jewish Theological Seminary of America, 1975), no. 52, pp. 28–29.

and transcend his earthly pain—both physical and mental.[13] Tears reveal the torrent of his fractured personality as well as the reflections that pummel his heart toward a personal truth. This poem gives testimony to both.

From the beginning, the themes of night and tears and the subjunctive voice (of possibility) intersect, setting a mood of personal sorrow and confession. Tonal echoes and end rhymes reinforce the lexical and thematic figures that recur in this lyric. Listen to the opening evocation—spoken by the poet to himself, and to those (inner voices) that populate his mind.

> If bitter tears had poured out, / my cheeks would have sprouted a beard of sorrow;
> And had they lingered ever so slightly, / my groaning would chase them in flight.
> All night my eyes teared up in torrents, / as if the hired fare for guarding its stars.
> Should you see them yourself, / they would be visible, fixed beyond the firmament.
> While crying, my heart swore to cease, / lest my eyes be wasted: but to no avail;
> Had I not walled-off my pain, / my neighbors would have washed away in my tears.

To whom is this soliloquy addressed, if not to the poet's inner self, swelled by his unceasing sorrow? The hypothetical and the actual combine in the stress on possibility (*ulay*, "if," in line 1; *lu* and *lulei*, "if" and "had I" or "if I had," in lines 3 and 6) and situation (*leil*, "night," in line 3). The uncontrollable tears are a witness to his distraught emotions—for which the stars stand testimony. Using a variety of biblical tropes,

13. The place of discourse in ibn Gabirol's poetry has been studied by T. Rosen-Moqed, "*Tekhniqah Dialogit ve-Siṭu'aṣiyah Dramatit ba-Shirim ha-Ishiyyim shel Ibn Gavirol*," in *Meḥqarim BiYṣirat Shlomoh ibn Gavirol*, ed. Tzvi Malachi (Tel Aviv: University of Tel Aviv Press, 1985), esp. 148–74. For a conspectus of the poet's life, especially his emotional and physical condition, see Ḥ. Shirmann, "*Le-Ḥeqer Ḥayyav shel Shlomoh ibn Gavirol*," in his *Le-Toledot ha-Shirah veha-Dramah ha-'Ivrit* (Jerusalem: Mosad Bialik, 1979), 1:216–33.

Ibn Gabirol, presents himself as a night "watchman," awake and alone with the evening eyes of heaven (a Spanish and Arabic trope for the stars of night)[14]—so much so that he cannot even keep his own promises of self-restraint or adjudication. There is something in the pains of life and "time" that has rankled him. Perhaps it is the provocation of friends who mock his personal depression over illness; or perhaps it is his despair over a lack of social approbation. Hints of this emerge in subsequent lines where he channels their appeal that he focus on his youth and join them in wine and its fellowship. This request is rejected, and the scene shifts to a vision of the stars above and the writing of the heavens. The poet sees them sprout like flowers (inverting his opening lament) and thereby signal a silent, eternal truth (lines 24–37). Those in drunken stupor would hardly see the multiple images (*tzurot ve-tzurot*) that are visible in the sky and can excite the eye of poetic imagination (*tzurot tedameh 'ein enosh ki niftaḥu* figures that the human eye can imagine, being opened to their wonders and flowering; l.25). In this turn inward, the poet exults in the silence and eternity of the stars—which reveal their "mystery" (*sod*) and "wonders" (*nifla'ot*) and the eternal "laws of their God." For the stars are the cosmic "guardians" of the "heavenly cycles" (the verb *yishmeru* and the noun *mishmeroteihem* in lines 30–31 anticipate the formulation *eshmerah* in l.44, which marks the poet's assertion that he will not "set" a muzzle to his voice). In his concluding assertion, Ibn Gabirol recovers his true identity and destiny. He will "not be silent" (*lo aḥrish*) but will contemplate the eternal cosmic glory of heaven and broadcast its splendor (*zohareha*). He even avers that his illumination (both philosophic wisdom and poetic vision) is conjoined with the wisdom and clarity of the sun, to which he is both virtually and verily a nearest kin (lines 47–50).

Thus the poet proclaims his cosmic destiny, but now before he traverses the jagged edges of despair—soaked in tears and seared by internalized critiques. In due course, Ibn Gabirol overcomes these emotional caesuras with a sudden resolve, and the lyric culminates in a spiritual triumph. This notwithstanding, throughout, like a leitmotif (shared with other Jewish and Muslim poets of the age), we hear

14. Cf. Y. Ratzhabi, "*Mar'ot-laylah be-shirat Ha-Nagid ve-Ibn Gevirol,*" *Tarbiz* 47 (1978): 56–90.

the term *dema'ot* ("tears") recurrently echoed in the term *dam* (the "blood-red" of wine and the "blood" of grief); and intoned in the verbal resonances of *ha-dami* (the "wages" of sorrow), *adamah* (the "earth" or mortality), *adummim* (as the "reddish flush" of inebriation, and *tidom* (marking the "silence" of reproof). This thematic complex finds further echoes in the verbs *yidmu* (the "seeming" or likeness of the metallic shine of the stars) and *tidmu / adameh*—terms that are used to mark the poet's figural "imaginary" (lines 25–26).

The dynamic of this soliloquy is a working through of doubt and despair. It is a testimony to the poet's process of coming to terms with the words of his inner world through the countervoice that flooded his mind like tears. The final result is a respite of issues that plagued the poet during his short life. The stars in heaven hold a mirror to Ibn Gabirol's soul: they are initially the focus of his vigil of tears, hidden behind the firmament, but they eventually emerge as a script of eternity. Poetry (*ha-shir*) is the true "glory" (*yaqar*; l.38); and it "recalls the glory" (*yaqar*) of the sun (the star supreme). The poem is thus marked by a transformative shift, a shift to poetic expression asserted in the first-person singular: "I shall not be silent until I inscribe my poems on the tablet of the earth—so that they shall never be erased" (*lo aḥarish 'ad eḥerosh shiray 'alei / luaḥ lev teiveil le-val yimmaḥu*). At this triumphant conclusion, the poet deems his destiny to be immortal, like the rays of the sun and its wisdom. The flowers of his poetry will be like the flowers (or stars) of heaven—fixed, eternal, and a testimony to his transcendent ardor and song. Just this polar swing from self-doubt to self-aggrandizement induced rancor among his peers. But this shift notwithstanding, no achievement could finally remove the poet's tears. The poem testifies to a momentary pause and a sense of inner glory.

Ibn Gabirol's Avatar

The modern poet Bialik not only collected and annotated the poems of Ibn Gabirol[15] but was profoundly influenced by him and his imagery. Like his poetic "master," the night sky recurrently figures as a time

15. See *Shirei Shlomoh ben Yehudah ibn Gevirol*, ed. Ḥ. N. Bialik and Y. Ḥ. Ravnitzky (Berlin: Masada, 1924–32), in 7 volumes; this poem is in vol. 1 (1924), no. 5, pp. 10–13, with notes and explications in pt. 2, pp. 10–17.

of personal sorrow and vision in Bialik's oeuvre. The exemplar I wish to highlight here is where he confesses to his own despair and turns to an abandoned star to shine light on his lonely soul. Perhaps with his mentor's work in mind, Bialik opens a soliloquy to a "Kokhav Nidaḥ"[16] (A Remote / Abandoned) and thereby discloses his own distraught sensibility. This poetic topos is signaled and developed in the opening lines. Here the poet reveals his personal crisis and longing for spiritual healing. It begins with a mixture of depiction and petition:

A remote star shone from the glomming—
O my star: illumine my sorry state!

His existence is "without hope" (he states): it is overburdened and desolate, "a life of wormwood and rot . . . drowning in pitch dark." And with this confession Bialik repeats his request for poetic inspiration with painful pathos and beseeches his star to illumine his despair and distress.

Who would know the duration of my night,
Or the wandering darkness that remains my lot?

From the black of night I lift my eye to heaven;
Whence a glimmer of your light I see—and find comfort.

I still retain (*shemurah*) a pure drop of my tears (*mi dimʿotai*)[17]—
May it flow anew, to water this last bud of hope.

There yet remains a primal spark in my roiling heart—
May it be kindled again—even now, before it is snuffed out.

My still remaining vigor returns, pulsating within:
Let it now wage a final, all-consuming battle!

16. See *Kol Kitvei Ḥ. N. Bialik*, 23 (my translation).

17. In the poem "Dimʿah Neʾemanah," he likewise confesses, "I have one faithful tear" (*li dimʿah aḥat neʾemanah*), attesting to a lost but remembered poetic perfection. The use of the verbal stem *shamar* echoes the use of it in the poem by Ibn Gabirol examined above, where it also serves to mark the poet's inner conviction of spiritual talent.

The tremor of Bialik's verse underscores the poignancy of his hope. Both he and his star are cast off and alone, each within a consuming darkness. The despair of the poet is palpable. The star, so slightly illumined above, quickens the sense of some flickering spark within the speaker. Suddenly the verbal hints marked by *'od* ("still") or *'ad* ("until") become a confirming intimation: the bright glimmer of the star hints at the poet's rekindled inwardness—still only a mere presentiment, for it is not yet a reality. This feature of emergent light (and inspiration) is also revealed through a "tear" or bud of hope in Bialik's heart, and he longs for it to nurture his spirit and (paradoxically) kindle the sundering flame. Both elements conjoin in the poet's soul: the *tzitz* (or "bud") evokes the primal *nitzotz* (or "spark") of creativity. By the end, the poet has regained his vision and verse—of this the poem is proof positive, a testimony of this achievement. Slowly there is a shift from the impersonal to the personal voice: when the poet again asks for illumined hope, he states "here I am, ready to go; here I am, borne by hope" (*hinneni ve-halakhti, hinneni va-ayaḥeilah*). This readiness is both a moral and a spiritual disposition gifted by a glance at the faraway star—though still capable of regenerating hope. With that perception there arises a renewed awareness of the speaker's true nature. He has a poet's soul; it beats within, and he is ready to fight so that it may flare up in verse. Every word attests to this process of poetic longing and recovery. Even more, the poem is itself a testimony to his yearning spirit. There is thus a profound continuity of the poetic self to which the verse attests—even as we experience it in the halting pathos of its development. In the end, this lyric is a triumph of the poet's self-disclosure through tears: a testament to the spiritual star reborn in his soul.

Bialik's voice and tears were also shed for his people. Most horrendous was the Kishinev pogrom of 1903, and most unsettling was the poet's wail and torment. It shook the soul of a nation well battered by persecution, and it sundered the poet to the core. Like a reborn Jeremiah, the poet cast his woes to the wind. His voice is a forecast of tragedies even more unspeakable to come, even as his words draw from a well of unquenchable national tragedies—the *Leidensgeschichte* (or "history of sorrows") of Jewry, multiple millennia old.

And now, O son of man, why stay here? Flee to the desert;
And bear with you, there, your cup of agonies!
And rip up there your very soul into a hundred shreds;
And let your heart feed upon an unbearable fury;
And smash your mighty tear (*dim'atekhah*) upon the rocks;
And unleash your bitter roar—to be lost in the whirlwind.

So spoke Bialik in his searing lament-rebuke, "Ba-'Ir Ha-Hareigah" (In the City of Slaughter).[18] The multiple ligatures ("And") underscore the repeated intonation of sorrow—which could continue until they are jolted to a precipitous close. In this climactic outcry, readers don't know whether the voice of the prophet (to himself) exhorts only the roar to be unleashed on the all-erasing wind or whether it also includes himself with the verb *to'vad* (to be lost [in the whirlwind]). I do not doubt this second possibility. Lament is as recurrent as timeless suffering, but it falls silent on deaf ears and is lost in the vapors of forgetfulness. As the threnody states, words die first with the dead and soon thereafter with the witnesses. What remains for us latecomers? Even the most poignant of verbal testimonies may lose their imprint in time—emptied of the tears they once shed.

Tears and a choking sorrow mark the section to come. But we must first ask, For whom and for what are these testimonies? Are they ever otherwise than a betrayal of the shattering pain that we must acknowledge so that the images of suffering might lacerate our hearts? Heeding their call, we are summoned to make these words part of our biography and fill the abyss of oblivion with awareness. Through these raw enunciations, we are initiated into a chain of inconsolable memory.

In the Fold of Impossibilities: The Tears of Testimony

We are in the fold: in "the between" of mind (with its knowledge) and body (with its feeling). Philosophers make a lot of this "and," and rightly so. We also wonder about this connection when we try to feel

18. *Kol Kitvei Ḥ. N. Bialik*, 95–98; the citation is at the end (my translation).

the pain of others with a measure of wisdom. But testimonies of degradation shatter our mind—leaving us mindless in grief—unnerved and numb. Only in this nullified state can we possibly share in the fold of impossibilities that is revealed. Only in such an altered state can we perhaps sense the surreal quality of this searing reality. Poets like Nellie Sachs bring us to this abyss and evoke the shattering horror of the Holocaust. Through the spectral tremor of their work, we experience a representation of undeniable truth—denying which there would be no truth at all. Let the glib liars not say it is unsayable. If it happened, it can (and must) be said, again and again.[19]

What fiery planet, what alien reality is this, she asks? "Agony, metronome of an alien star, / Staining each minute with an alien darkness"[20]—and the answer is precisely this world. What reality is it where we hear the voice of a child from beyond the grave, where a testament (like the following) is even possible?

> My mother held me by the hand.
> Then someone raised the knife of parting:
> So that it should not strike me,
> My mother loosed her hand from mine.
> But she lightly touched my thighs once more
> And her hand was bleeding—
>
> . . . .
>
> As I was led to death
> I still felt in the last moment
> The unsheathing of the great knife of parting.[21]

19. Cf. G. Didi-Huberman, *Images in Spite of All* (Chicago: University of Chicago Press, 2012), 24: "The very existence and the possibility of such testimony—*its enunciation in spite of all*—refute . . . the closed notion, of an *unsayable* Auschwitz." The work of G. Agamben, *Remnants of Auschwitz* (New York: Zone Books, 2002), is a sustained analytic refutation of the false claim of the "unsayable" with regard to such suffering and inhumanity.

20. See N. Sachs, *O the Chimneys* (New York: Farrar, Straus & Giroux, 1967), 7 ("Agony, metronome of an alien star"; translated by M. Hamburger).

21. Sachs, 13 ("A dead child speaks"; translated by R. and M. Mead).

Here is the testimony of a child led to slaughter bearing her mother's love and compassion in her heart. It is a fragment worthy of Scripture: with just enough words to scream in mortal protest. Who could deny that we have hit the bedrock of expression, the point where figures of the impossible testify to the real and unbelievably actual? No tears can stanch such horror. The poet's words eviscerate our heart.

We earlier observed the role of "if" clauses in the poetry of Ibn Gabirol, a poetic device that set up conditionals of experience or self-development. These clauses focus on time and transformation, but there are "if" statements that summon readers to impossible self-reflection. Just this consciousness is at issue in a poem by Primo Levi, written in January 1946, when the pain of internment had not yet molted into an artistry of recollection. The query "if" that is evoked remained so searing that it became the very title of his second book, *If This Is a Man*. In the jolting central section of the poem "Shemà," this phrase forms the central stanza. It formulates a damning rewriting of Scripture: a cry addressed to all those who dwell in safety and satiety.[22] Listen and hear!

> Consider if this is a man
> Who toils in the mud
> Who knows no peace
> Who fights for a half a loaf
> Who dies by a yes and a no.
> Consider if this is a woman,
> With no hair and no name
> With no more strength to remember
> And a womb as cold
> As a frog in winter.

22. *The Complete Works of Primo Levi*, edited by A. Goldstein (New York: Liveright, 2015), 3:1187–88 (translated by J. Galassi). This poem was originally titled "Psalm."

What are we asked to consider? Is it not a query about a shard of humanity—"who" is barely human and lives in the mire like an animal? Who is this nearly unrecognizable she-being depleted in mind and beyond reproductive capacity (the double simile is horrendous)? Is this a man—a "he," or a "she," a female—without countenance and without consciousness? The cipher of "if" begs a response, for the poet does not ask rhetorical questions. He demands that we realize that there is still something living and human in this decay. Levi doesn't wait for us to respond but insists that we "ponder that this happened" and trust the "I" (the testifier) who "consigns the words to you" (the addressee). And he then demands, "Carve them into your hearts / at home and in the streets, / Going to bed or rising: / Tell them to your children." This is the obligation of being the witness of a witness—all those who faithfully recite the language of the Shema-prayer (from Deut. 6:4–6). The poet wants his words (as memory) to be burned into one's innermost being, like the identification brand of camp inmates. And Levi doesn't wait for the reader to reflect on this imperative; for he follows it with the dire consequence of curses, also derived from Scripture: "Or may your house fall down, / May illness make you helpless, And Your children turn their eyes from you." This is a torrential outrage that blasphemes and damns all those who forget this crucible and get on with things. Auschwitz is a new and inverted Sinai. It hangs above our heads and will crush us to death, grinding our lives, like bones and marrow, if we disregard this obligation to testify and remember.

The poem lies in the fold of impossibilities. What can one internalize of this horror at the distance of years and a few stanzas? And yet there can be no evasion. To forget is to curse our culture and its generations. The speaker has identity only through his cry, and he beseeches us to "Hear" and know that Yes, this is a man and a woman—however defaced by demonic evil. Heed the summons to see in this withering depletion the image of the still-human; and heed the plea not to shut our eyes or deaden our heart. Forgetting becomes a supreme act of debasement. The poet demands an ineradicable memorialization.

This notwithstanding, a radical silence remains. This is the "mute silence beyond words" (*demamah ha'ilemet midevarim*) within which there is a bottomless abyss (*hamon rabbah*). This silence is "like the silence of God's muteness" (*ke-demamat elohim ilmim*) . . . ; and "like the muteness of the mourner" (*ke-demamat ha-avel*) whose heart breaks from within.[23] His heart is a flaming hell, as he "sits silent and mute." In this threnody, the poet Aharon Mirsky bleeds words that evoke an ultimate absence: a murmuring muteness, in which the horrendous assonance *elohim ilmim* (Divine muteness) is a vocal rebuke.[24] This poem of tears and silence was written in 1944.

In another elegy of loss, Mirsky envisions (through the stained mirror of memory) his native land: "town and cities and village"—and their Jews—blown into the whirlwind of death. He stands in prayer alone with a "silent groan" in his mouth, a "tombstone" in his heart, and "in his eye: a pool of bitter tears."[25] The poet's truth bursts forth like Primo Levi's curse, with a malediction directed at those who would somehow forget.

> Cursed be whoever restrains his eye from crying (*bekhi*)
> And cursed be whoever wipes his tear (*dim'ato*) from his cheek,
> Let it remain as a scar stamped upon his face;
> As a sign (*ot*) between his eyes: a frontlet (*ṭoṭefet*) of lamentations.

Here is a voice sunk in sorrow: it is a survivor's threnody poured out in tears from hollowed sockets of suffering. The poet does not speak for himself; for his identity is marked by the inconsolable memory of death and loss. As he does in other laments, Mirsky is a voice for the dead, unable to express syllables adequate to the void he feels.

23. The verbal stem *damam* evokes the same range of topics here as in the poem by Ibn Gabirol, presented above (and, by association, the figure of *dema'ot*, "tears" is also suggested).

24. A. Mirsky, *'Aley Siaḥ* (Jerusalem: Mosad Harav Kook, 1966), 67 ("Yeish demamah ilemet," my translation). This theological figure evokes the famous midrash on the phrase *mi kamokha ba-eilim YHWH*, "Who is like you among the gods, O YHWH?"), but radically inverts it. Instead of praise of Divine might and redemption, the exposition exemplifies God for His capacity to absorb the insults Israel bears (in history) and remain "silent" (*ilmim*)—a bold theological image of silent suffering. In Mirsky's version, it depicts a radical Divine silence and absence. The original midrashic inversion occurs in the *Mekhilta de-Rabbi Ishmael*, ed. Ḥ. Horowitz and Y. Rabin (Jerusalem: Bamberger and Wahrman, 1960), *Beshalaḥ* 8, p. 142.

25. *Mekhilta de-Rabbi Ishmael*, 74 ("Reshut le-Qinah").

Tears are the scar of memory, a memorial that bespeaks an inverted covenant. Hear now his confession:

> How can I form a dirge in my heart and pour my soul in lament;
> Or come with my sorrow and anger, and my heart-loss of woe;
> Or how can my heart not suffer the horror of what has occurred?
> It is like an anvil pounded by pain: by misfortune beyond sense.
> How could I even explain to my soul this brutal rupture and loss—
> Of a nation, once like heaven soaring oaks, now utterly uprooted?

The poet shouts *eikh* (how?) in sorrow and bewilderment, for how can he intone the Scroll of Lamentations (titled *eikhah*)? This is a pun of pain (borrowing from ancient models) that is an undoing of an "I" that must formulate words for this horror. Four times the speaker uses the first-person singular in these initial lines, so much is he aware of his inability to offer adequate voice or sufficient testimony. This rift concludes with a cry to God to arise and shatter the heavens with His dirge! The speaking "I" knows the depth of tragedy but now yearns for a Divine manifestation so that he can sit alone in silent suffering with the other mourners (*ve-anaḥnu neisheiv ve-nidom*).[26] This wasteland of sorrows must remain as a searing scar, and so he once again curses those who would dare rebuild from the smoldering ashes. The smoke of "devastation" (*ḥurban*) must remain—as an enduring "sanctuary of mourning" (*miqdash aveilim*), as a monument to *ha-shem ha-meḥullal* (the desecrated Name of God).[27]

What poet still remains, Mirsky asks, whose heart could channel the carnage? Polish Jewry is no more, and absent, too, is the faith and practice (*omanut*) of the ancestors. "Every hill of my childhood," he mourns, "seems to me like a mountain of death." Physically eviscerated, he proclaims: "I have forgotten my song, and only know how to curse (*qaleil*)" So let someone else rise to mourn; but there is no one left to say "amen."[28] Speaking from France in the midst of the war, Hannah Arendt anticipated this lament and wrote, "There is No One to Recite

26. Cf. *Mekhilta de-Rabbi Ishmael*, 83 ("Eikh evra'ha-mispeid").

27. *Mekhilta de-Rabbi Ishmael*, 86 ("Yagorti eimei tanḥumim"). This poem was composed in 1946.

28. See *Mekhilta de-Rabbi Ishmael*, 79–80. It was written in 1947.

the *Kaddish*."[29] This is the ultimate undoing. Summoned in absentia, a congregation of mourners is called upon to testify; but they are not adequate, for they did not see the events with their own eyes or hear it with their ears. How can such individuals bear witness, or recite the mourner's *Kaddish*? Scripture and its tradition cannot answer this query; the voice of the people has vanished in the rubble of death. There remains only a survivor's broken heart: a plaintive echo of lost lamentations.

29. "On ne prononcera pas le kaddish," in *Auschwitz et Jérusalem*, trans. S. Courine-Denamy (1991; Paris: Deuxtemps Tierce, 1997), 39–41. This was written in 1942.

7

Poetic Longing, Mysticism, and the Ontology of Language

Introductory Comments

For well over a century, since the watershed achievement of William James's great *Varieties of Religious Experience*,[1] the phenomena of mystical consciousness have attained a privileged position of study and appreciation. In its wake scholars have turned their attention to diverse states of mystical awareness, sensibility, and knowledge. This spectrum of spiritual states has resulted in a corresponding range of evaluative dichotomies. Of particularly broad influence is the distinction between "sacred" and "profane" mysticisms first employed by R. C. Zaehner.[2] And even if we characterize this second pole as "secular," so as to evade a tendentious binary, it remains to be determined whether such evaluations are productive or even adequate.

It is perhaps more compelling and helpful to say that the language used by adherents of normative religions to describe their mystical states derives from canonical sources with well-established or authoritative terms,[3] whereas the figures employed by individuals in-

1. Based on the Gifford Lectures on Natural Religion, 1901–1902, the book was first published by Longmans, Green and frequently reprinted. It deserves note that the subtitle is *A Study in Human Nature*.

2. See his *Mysticism: Sacred and Profane* (Oxford: Clarendon Press, 1957). His subtitle is *An Inquiry into Varieties of Praeternatural Experience*. I doubt that this allusion to James's work is altogether unintentional.

3. Cf. the formulation of G. A. Coe, in "The Sources of the Mystic Revelation," *Hibbert Journal* 6 (1908): 367.

dependent of such constraints tends to be more personal or private in nature. Considered in their varieties, these modes of expression help authenticate the experiences felt by the individual and together constitute the genre of mystical literary testimonies. For traditionalists, therefore, certain images precede mystical experience and confirm its validity after the fact, whereas individualists try to state their experiences in self-authenticating ways. The highly personalized accounts of a Symonds or a Bucke (precisely documented by James), or the literary ecstasies composed by Tennyson and Shelley, are cases in point. These private testimonies tend to stand at an autarkic point on the spectrum of spiritual authority, and this raises the question of the status of such ecstatic reports when they are confessions of psychological moods or are inflected by the posttraditional situation of the writer. Such considerations raise other issues that bear on the particular ontology of poetic language, especially when they purport to portray unique or private mystical states of linguistic inspiration.

I take up these topics through the prism of a poet whose work reveals the hazard of the contemporary spiritual enterprise[4] at the crossroads of tradition and its literary sources. Chaim Nachman Bialik, the master elegist and voice of Modern Hebrew poetry, felt the rupture of authentic language in the depths of his soul and experienced this depletion as a personal, psychic wasteland. Only a lonely longing for inspired speech remained, casting a shadow over his childhood memories of pure vision. Hope for Bialik is the poetic resurrection of his tears by an angel of light, mediating once again the ontological mystery of language. Poetry, longing, and ontology repeatedly combine—bemoaning loss and awaiting the rebirth of authenticity.

Initial Considerations of Linguistic Ontology

The notion of linguistic ontology should not be deemed conceptually fixed or formal. Numerous varieties are in evidence, and these determine the authority of language in any given culture. The status of language—be it supernatural or natural—affects how it is presumed

4. See especially the various essays in E. Heller's *The Disinherited Mind* (Harmondswoth: Penguin Books, 1962). The concluding meditation, "The Hazard of Modern Poetry," is particularly significant.

to express the felt truth of an experience or to resonate with readers. Accordingly, a Divine or Divinely derived language will condition whether some textual sense is deemed inherently finite or infinite, and what it means to be a speaker or interpreter of this language. Such considerations affect reformist and secular trends as well, including the sense of linguistic depth or vitality when creativity has cut loose from the moorings of religious tradition. Readers may then circle the received canon and try to rescue one formulation or another, importing it into new meanings and sensibilities. The phenomenon of literary "fragments" has provided a stimulating literary category since the work of Friedrich Schlegel;[5] and on this basis newer questions arise. What is creativity under these circumstances, when fragments become wholes, and wholes are comprised or diverse fragments? Eliot's *Waste Land* comes to mind.

The verbal pathos of Bialik's poetry is the focus of the present discussion.[6] Since his spiritual formation was established within the environment of traditional Jewish text study, the ontology of language in which he was nurtured may be epitomized through the theological masterwork of the founder of the rabbinic academy where he studied in his youth. R. Chaim Volozhiner (1745–1821), the founding rector of the Volozhin Yeshiva in Lithuania,[7] wrote *Nefesh Ha-Ḥayyim,* which articulates a religious worldview totally grounded in Divine language: principally, the supernal and primordial Torah of Heaven; and relatedly the revealed Torah of Moses, whose esoteric dimensions are symbolically encoded in the various commentaries found in the *Book of Zohar*. As "Gate Four" of Rabbi Chaim's work states, a

5. Of central importance are his essays in *Lucinde and the Fragments* (Minneapolis: University of Minnesota Press, 1971).

6. I shall cite from the classic anthology of his literary works, *Kol Kitvei Ḥayim Naḥman Bialik* (Tel Aviv: Devir, 1938). References to oral talks will be annotated accordingly. All translations are my own.

7. See the striking memoir by a fellow student, A. Blosher, *Ḥayim Naḥman Bialik be-Volozhin, u-Volozhin be-Bialik* (Kaunas, 1935). Bialik's immortal rendition appears in the poem *Ha-Matmid* (The Talmud-Student).

person's immersion in the language of ancient rabbinic lore (in all its legal and homiletical iterations) is the linguistic highway to Divinity. Even more: this textual immersion is nothing less than a mystic contact with God through God's will, as formulated by the sacred tradition. Accordingly, study not only extends this verbal will into worldly forms (since the religious world of Judaism is textually inflected at every level), but it is the linguistic link to the primordial Torah. As a result, perpetual study sustains the sacred fonts of existence encoded in its supernal expressions. Or, put more ontologically: all of being, and our natural universe as a concrete particular, is an infinitely formulated Divine language—from supernal top to mundane bottom. Everything is some modality of this all-comprehensive enunciation and partakes of the most primordial and infinite emanations of Divinity. Stated more concisely, there is nothing other than Divine language. Inspired perception is cognizant of this linguistic manifold, and it is the desire of the adept to experience its resonant reality. Indeed, every worldly element is a refraction of this seminal truth—a truth which, through devotion, can be perceived by the inner eye of the beholder.

Epistemological breaks with religious tradition have ruptured this sacred syntax and resulted in the demystification of the world—to employ Max Weber's famous locution. Hence persons born into this modern era, and impacted by such a modernist sensibility, must make do with their options: either to reform this cognitive situation from within, or experience themselves as tone-deaf to this resonance and move to other cultural spheres for inspiration. In the first instance, there is an ongoing attempt to revitalize the linguistic terms of one's religious canon; but this becomes increasingly difficult when the world to which the older language points seems no longer real or revelatory—or when the canonical center of the tradition no longer holds (to paraphrase Yeats). What can one do when it seems no longer possible to wholeheartedly engage in the exegetical projects of the normative culture? And what can one do when one feels compelled to build a new epistemic worldview from the canonical deposits? For these and other reasons the strong poet, in a teetering and but lonely virtuosity, has become a spiritual hero in modernity. Aching for the renewal of a personal language, certain poets have strived to reread the now demystified book of nature through the prism of their heart, and thereby renew a vision of the external world. This was the vaunted program of

Romanticism, in all its varieties. Regenerated, language could reveal the depths of nature (they believed) through sudden flashes of words that might irradiate a mystical spectrum of new perceptions. This goal was also the center point of Bialik's poetics. It was his ever-recursive longing to retrieve a lost sense of wonder—a yearning to perceive the world as an effulgence of light and render it in lyrical verse. Because of his integrity and the circumstances of his life, this profound desire marks the rhythms of despair and ecstasy in his soul.

Sources of Illumination

Toward the end of his poem, "Eḥad Eḥad uve-Ein Ro'eh" (One by One, and without Seeing), Bialik laments, "I know that only once does a person drink from the golden cup / and that the vision of splendor and radiance (*ziv ve-zohar*) will not happen to one twice"—as he feels the fading of this illumination into abject nullity (*va-yikhlu be-yagon dumam*). It would be hard to deny that a recurrent feature of Bialik's poetry is the longing to retrieve the near-mystical experiences of that time—a period of inspired and luminous wonder. Writing about these occasions in his later years, Bialik strived to recapture both the crystalline quality of its light—the veritable light of creation experienced as the illumination of consciousness—and its inspiring benefactions. Translucence is therefore a recurrent trope of the mature poet, an experience enfolded into his deepest being. It is not accidental, therefore, that the prior citation speaks of the recipient of light as both *adam* and *ish* (as an adult man), since it is just the older self that "knows" the cycles of inspiration and their tangible memory. Looking back, his poetic compositions are, repeatedly, a waiting in hope for some "sudden" bestowal of Divine "blessing" (*birkat pit'om*), when the visions of youth will once again flood his soul with their transformative power. I shall return to this trope, but for now we need only add that this moment is a return to a preverbal state of awareness: the pure ontological ground of his poetry.

Reflecting on the peregrinations of his soul as an itinerary of consciousness, the poet depicts a dialogue with his tutelary angel. At the outset of the poem "Ve-Im-Yish'al Ha-Mal'akh" (And Should the Angel Ask), the stark query is posed, "My son, where is your soul?" (*beni, nishmatekha ayeha?*) Note well that the temporality of its whereabouts is stated in the concurrent present (*ayeha*)—for the soul is both present-absent. To somehow annotate its lost immediacy the speaker recalls the childhood home of the poet overarched by a radiant sky within which there is a "single cloud" (*'av yeḥidah*)—to which, long ago, the dreaming boy was drawn in an ecstatic ascension of vision. "Drawn" upward to this luminous element, the eyes of the poet "saw" (this cloud depicted as "the single one, the refined one, the pure one")—after which "his soul departed" (*nafsho yatze'ah*), flying upward like a "dove." The overlapping soul-symbols reinforce this event of transport. (The original *neshamah*, or "soul," of the angel's query, being depicted as a *nefesh* and figured as a dove, joins the cloud, called *yeḥidah*—a word that refers to a still higher gradation of soul in the Jewish mystical lexicon). Referring to this mystic transport, the speaker says that his soul was saved by a ray of golden sunlight—riding on the "wings of splendor" for days on end. With time, this supernatural bliss mutated into a tear of loss that fell into the Talmudic folios of his ancestors, where it mingled with the letters of tradition and the candle wax of ascetic nights—each a memorial of prior vitality. Fallen from its transport, his soul writhed in moribund death throes until it was revived by the gift of poetry. The speaker now proclaims that the "dead letters" of the old rabbinic tradition were wondrously "visited (*heqeiru*) by the songs of life"—miraculously "changed" (*shanu*) into vivified verse.

On Bialik's testimony, poetry is no mere mimesis of nature but its linguistic transfiguration—the recrudescence of the silent luminosity of creation through the words of the canonical culture. Accordingly, if the ontology of traditional linguistic forms could speak anew, it had to be transmuted by a far more primordial ontology. This experience marks the revival of the poet's soul, save for a profound yearning for human love: "crying in silent inwardness" (*bokhiyah be-ḥasha'i*). It recurs as a recurrent desire to view some transcendent light. Such longing evokes a palpable (and deeply personal) metaphysical ardor.[8]

8. This latter conjunction is one of the great tasks of poetry. See the concise formulation of John Crowe Ransom, "Poetry: A Note on Ontology," in his *The World's Body* (Baton Rouge: Louisiana State University Press, 1968).

Light and Its Variants

The poetics of light dominate Bialik's sensibility, redolent in stunning visions of nature or refracting their likeness in childlike dialogues. Light is the medium of sight and insight.[9]

As with phenomenology generally, so, too, in Bialik's poetry light is sensed as a presence before it is experienced as a specific summons or verbal inspiration. Two modalities exemplify this feature. The first depicts the silent incursion of light through a window of sorts and its invasion into one's preternatural consciousness. The figure of an illumined awakening, repeatedly portrayed as the arousal of a child in bed, is certainly a trope for poetic arousal, since it provides a transition to the flooding sensibility of awareness before verbal creativity. Just this is enunciated by the mature speaker of the poem, "'Im Petiḥat Ha-Ḥalon" (At the Opening of the Window). This verse begins with the first shafts of dawn as they invade the sleeping boy's bedroom and stimulate his heart: "Arouse yourself . . . light has come, light has happened!" Slowly, the gleam of radiant splendor turns into "beams of light" (*qarnei ha-or*), and then a "billow of lights" (*naḥshol orim*) follow, manifesting a visitation of effulgence (*va-yaqeiru negohot*). Suddenly the world is illumined like a heavenly canopy of "sapphire and splendor" (*sapir ve-zohar*): radiant "fragments of the supernal throne" (*shivrei kisei ha-kavod*), dispersed into the "depths" (*tehom*) of existence.[10] In mystical ardor (evinced by these images and others) the eye and heart and soul of the subject is "engorged by the light" (*sovei't*

9. The primacy of light as a constitutive metaphor was articulated by Hans Blumenberg in his classic (1957) essay, "Light as a Metaphor for Truth," in *Modernity and the Hegemony of Vision*, ed. D. M. Levin (Berkeley: University of California Press, 1993), 30–86. A valuable conspectus of light in world religions can be found in *The Presence of Light: Divine Radiance and Religious Experience*, ed. M. Kapstein (Chicago: University of Chicago Press, 2004).

10. I shall return to the hermeneutical import of such language below. Here it suffices to note the panoply of mystical allusions that pervade the terminology, like fragments of dispersed light, so redolent in Lurianic Kabbalah, but also the reference to sapphire, to the *'arpelei tohar* (clouds of purity), and even the ivory (*shayish*) seeming splendor whose impression could bedazzle the mystical adept from Talmudic episodes on (cf. *B. Ḥagiga* 14a).

ha-or), and the speaker exudes: "O God of light, give (more) light!" Such is the saturation, filled to overflowing.

Light is the source of all awakening, whose advent is the sacred expectancy of the poetic temper. The poem "Mi-Shomerim La-Boqer" (From Those Who Await the Dawn) continues the foregoing themes but brings the speaker to another state of mind. The poem is set in four stanzas divided into two rhetorical structures (of query and answer) and a complex rhyme scheme repeated throughout. The dialogical nature of the queries invites the listener into a personal disclosure of the wonders of the morning glow and its strong impact upon the attendee (this being an imparting to the hearer of the effect of dawn's light on the speaker). The poem begins by asking, Have you attended to or awaited the morning? (*ha-shamarta la-boqer*), when the "reddish hues of the sun" (*dimdumei shemesh*) burst on the rim of earth and extend in all directions—even before the day is "ready" (*nakhon*) to receive them. This "vision" of colored light is an awesome spectacle, "and like a great retinue (*sod*) of holy beings (*qedoshim*) before the disclosure" of its mystery the envisioning heart is "filled with murmurings (*higayon*)." Dumbstruck by an ineffable splendor, the speaker wonders what mouth could "call it by its name" (*yiqra'ennu be-shemo*), "speak of it" (*yesiḥennu*), or ever know "what language (*lashon*) could configure it (*kanoto*)?"

The silence of the splendor, a mysterious hiddenness, seems beyond the capacity of verbal expression. Evoking this imponderable reality, the poet now—somewhat repeating the opening stanza in the third—asks whether one has even seen the myriads of cavorting radiance that "burst" and "scatter" roundabout at dawn. And now alluding to the "spectacle" (*mar'eh*) noted earlier, he speaks of this "supernal vision" (*maḥazeh*) and exclaims, "Happy is the eye that has hidden (*tzafenah*) a ray of light as a remembrance (*mishmeret*)"—so that when this emotional turbulence gives way to halting speech and the palpable ray is transformed into a "tear" of a lost radiance, the poem will remain as dim but "glowing (*mazheret*)" memorial.[11]

11. The word *mazheret* also connotes a thing of "caution." Cf. Psalm 19:12, where the worshipper is "warned" or "illumined" (*nizhar*) by the teachings of Torah, and all those who "keep" or "observe" its teachings will find great treasure.

Hidden Lights for the Eye and Heart

The true light of day, for the awakened soul, is more than daylight. It is a Divine effulgence that emanates from every element of the external world, beckoning like glistening "sprites" (*tzafririm*)—as in the poem of the same name ("Tzafririm")—to see everything from the inside out. To see "hair on sheaves of grain," the "rush of waves," a "sleeping child's smile," "tears," and "fractures of glass"—even, and perhaps especially, the "rhymes of song." For is this not, truly, the memory and longing of the poet, saying, "how the heart melts" (*mah namog ha-lev*) at this spectacle and exulting, "O God, light has flooded me!" (*Elohim—shiṭafatni ha-ʾorah*). Who affirms, if not the poet, that all this radiance has entered the "depths of my eyelids" (*maʿamaqei bavotai*)—to "purify me (*haziquni*), flood me, penetrate my heart, come and descend into my soul, be there and shine (*va-ʾoru*)"? Surely this is the testimony of mystic inspiration rising from the ontological depths—a prelude to creativity: "the heart floods (*shoṭef*) [its banks] . . . bursting forth like a font of streaming light (*nogah noveʿa*)." The waking boy is the aroused poet, seeing with new eyes.

The great poem *Zohar* (Splendor) brings us totally into this spiritual reality. It is a testament of "hidden mysteries and silence" (*setarim u-demamah*) to the inwardness of light beyond the "physicality of the world" (*gufo shel ʿolam*) where the youth who speaks perceived supernal realities "as if gazing into the eye (*ʿeino*) of the world" where his companion spirits "revealed . . . their secrets" (*niglu . . . razeihem*), and "received" (*qibbalti*) them in the "mute silence" (*ha-ʾilem*) of his heart. Here is a verbal token of an inner vision whose colors and secrets were absorbed as hidden mysteries—and now disclosed as verbal song.[12]

The languages of light and its invocation make up the mystic consciousness of the poet, and their many refractions constitute

12. Nearly every word of this first stanza is drawn from Jewish mystical language: the poet speaks of the "inner essence" (*ʿetzem*) of his "solitary" youthful soul (*yeḥidi*); of the disclosed "mysteries" (*setarim, razeihem*); of visionary sights (*nistalkalti, tzofeh*). Notably, too, the "eye" of the world is its "font" and "color" (recurrent puns and allusions in mystical texts) and most especially the "reception" of the mysteries (*qibbalti*). Among the most salient of the biblical allusions, are Isa. 29:11; Jer. 32:11; Dan. 12:9; and, suggestively, Song of Songs 4:12.

diverse tropes within *Zohar*. There are cascading flashes and dazzling images—giving voice to the first shining or illumination of his eyes, as the summoning sprites lighted upon him, purifying his vision (*qaloti, zakoti, kenaf*, or *tissa'eini*). Like infinite prisms, this light blinded him (*sanveirim la-'ayin*), weaving a web of golden chords around his soul. And then, suddenly, the older poet reveals not just the child's revelation but his own as well, when an "illumined youth was aroused and renewed within me" (*hitna'arah, hitḥaddeshah bi yaldut me'irah*).[13] Suddenly, "my mouth rejoiced, [and] in [my] heart a song of sun (*shemesh shirah*)." And then also: "from the touch of sun beams" (*qarnayim*) came joy and radiance—"I was sun struck, illumined, overcome and melted" (*eqranah, enharah, eivoshah, emogah*). Totally transformed, the poet attests to some mystic state of ecstatic dying, when he was "drunk with luminous splendor" (*shakhur zohar*) and "striated by a dazzling radiance" (*requmah negohot*)?

Vision within vision, the poem transports the inner eye (of the speaker and reader) to a pool of absolute purity (*ke'etzem peninim la-ṭohar*), reflecting the heavens "like a polished mirror" (*ke-re'i melutash*), even "like an inverted world" (*ke-'ein 'olam hafukh*). This pool (and its refraction in the soul) is a visionary speculum that echoes the opening stanza, when the poet spoke of attaining the very source of existence.[14] Surely it is the reflecting glass of supernal realities into which the poet gazes—"so effulgent" (*koh bahir*) and "dreaming" (*ḥolem*), like his own eye, shining and bending the lights of reality into ever-new refractions. In a stunning series of images, the visionary beholds the world in new forms and sinks into "this ocean of fiery light" (*yam di-nur zeh*), wholly "saturated with this sea of light" (*va-espog yam orim*), emerging like a priest from his sacred immersions "refined sevenfold" (*pi sheva' mezuqaq*). Once again the elder poet reveals that such light was and remains the purifying agent of his language (its ontological agency). For Bialik has left us a trace of his feelings—through words that echo Psalm 12:7, where the psalmist contrasted the false

13. The verb *hitna'arah* coveys the dual sense of "arousal" and "becoming youthful."

14. The topos of prophets "seeing" God through a visionary mirror of water is classically enunciated in *Midrash Vayiqra Rabba* 1.14, ed. M. Margulies (Jerusalem: Wahrmann Books, 1972), 1:30–32. Note the pun on Ezekiel's vision (*mar'eh*) as a mirror (*mar'ah*) at the waters of Chebar (Ezek. 43:3).

speech of dissemblers with the "pure words of God . . . refined seventyfold (*mezuqaq shiv'atayim*)." And if this verbal hint does not suffice, we also have the youth summoned by a "supernal splendor" (*zohar 'elyon*), the veritable "radiance of the Shekhinah" (*ziv ha-shekhinah*), proclaiming that the wish to "immerse you [him!] (*nitbolekha*) in the splendor . . . (and) bring you into the treasury of the hidden light (*or ganuz*) in the depths of the abyss (*be-ma'amaqei tehom*)."[15] Here now is a summons to an ultimate experience, an invocation to pass beyond the holy radiance of Divine immanence to a mystical light hidden (according to rabbinic tradition) at the creation of the world. And it refers (according to other traditions) to a primordial light emanating from God's robe, an effulgence made manifest when God said "Let there be light."[16] But there is more: the speaker was summoned still farther, into the depths of the *tehom*—this being a truth beyond being, beyond the sensibility of light or of any natural perception. As we shall indicate later, the *tehom* is the most radically primordial of all ontological dimensions.

Returning to the theme of immersing in this light, Bialik concludes the poem by saying that even though the primary *shirat zohar* (song of splendor) has long since been stifled and stilled, "its echo is nevertheless hidden deep within his heart" (*akh 'amoq be-lev kamus 'immi heid qolah*)—and, he confesses, "I have guarded (*shamarti*) the radiance of its light under my eyelids (*bavot 'einai*)"—a light from whose well (*'einah*) came his dreams and visions "pure . . . and blessed from its source" (*ṭehorim . . . u-berukhim mi-meqorah*). This is a double hiddenness: the revealed luminescence of the primordial light (*or ganuz*), which is an interior vision of true existence, sequestered within his

15. There are many examples of mystical visions of light and the symbolism of water and sinking. A classic instance occurs in R. Isaac de-min Akko's *Otzar Ḥayim*, MS. Moscow-Günzberg 775, folio 161b.

16. The light of God's garment is first mentioned in Psalm 104:2; the theme is taken up in *Midrash Bereshit Rabba*, ed. J. Theodor and Ch. Albeck (Jerusalem: Wahrmann Books, 1965), 3.7 (I, pp. 19–20); the light "separated" for the righteous at the creation is specified ibid., 3.6 (I, p. 22). This same light is first deemed "hidden" (*ganuz*) in *Babylonian Talmud*, *Ḥagiga* 12a, and subsequently in numerous mystical sources. For a notable exploration of this theme, see in A. Altmann, "A Note on the Rabbinic Doctrine of Creation," *Journal of Jewish Studies* 7 (1956): 195–206. The mystic illumination is wholly other than any natural light.

mortal eyes as the source of his poetry of a pure presence, his apperception of a Divinely irradiated world. Accordingly, the poet says that his verbal creativity reveals, when purified by light, the transcendent radiance "preserved" (*meshumar*) since the creation. By this testimony, the poet expresses a primordial inwardness still shining in his memory.

Silence and Spiritual Inception

There are still other soundings from the depths, primary evocations at the cusp of language. These, too, are the ontological sources of Bialik's poetic speech. Among the most salient are silence and sorrow. Reverberating throughout the poet's work are expressions of profound solitariness and loneliness. They evoke language at the brink of the inchoate, in the silence of longing and profound interiority.

The confession "Yam Ha-Demamah Poleṭ Sodot" (The Sea of Silence That Emits Secrets) is revelatory. From the pervasive stillness of night—from this "silent" (*shoteq*) blackness, composed of layers of shadow—a "silent" (*domam*) star fell into a "sea of darkness" (*yam ha-maḥashakim*), foreboding the onset of song. Amid this quietude (*be-hishtateq*) of existence, an emergence was sensed: "I trembled (*argish*): my heart aroused and speaking (*er u-middaber*); / I felt (*argish*) a pure fountain welling up, / slowly surging (*homeh*) in greater strength."[17] And then the speaker realized, "silently" (*be-ḥasha'i*), that his dreams were fulfilled and that this astral event was not his true muse, for he perceived his own star's light in the heavens above, shining with compassionate care.[18] In his contemplative gaze, he knew that the "only" true world, hidden within all the silences, was "the world in his heart" (*ha-'olam she-bilvavi*), the font of inwardness and poetic vision. Within this dark space, the poet senses his ultimate truth: the vision of his heart. The language of poetry now reveals this reality.

17. The verbal stem *r-g-sh* conveys both a shuddering tremor and an inward sensibility, and *h-m-h* conveys both the swelling of sea waves and the vibrations of the heart and mind—as innumerable biblical references attest.

18. The image of a star conveying compassion to the poet, grieving over memories and dreams and ever longing for redemptive inspiration (the star being a heavenly semblance of childhood radiance), also occurs in *Kokhav Nidaḥ*.

The fullness of inspired silence, before poetic speech, and the culmination of a lamented longing for the illuminations of childhood, is momentously conveyed in the extensive closing stanza of "Eḥad, Eḥad." The trope of *'ayin* (eye) is its leitmotif, borne by the knowledge (*yada'ti*) that "there" the world is bathed in a radiant "splendor" (*zohar*), and that a "hidden light" illumines the blue of sky and the "color" (*'ein*) of greenish grass, and that the "eye" (*'ein*) of the child may merit this vision only once; but the poet also believes that "God has a blessing of suddenness" (*birkat pit'om*), reserved for those "faithful in His eyes" (*'einav*). Alas, "no visionary can predict" its advent, and "no eye (*'ayin*) can behold its channels (*tzinoreyha*)" of inspiration.[19] But Bialik nevertheless avers, "I shall prepare (*e'erokh*) for it silently (*dumam*)." With his heart "strung taught" (*'arukh meitarim*) like a lyre, he will await its coming, assured that it will break on him "suddenly" (*pit'om*) and illumine his soul with a glorious splendor. Though this glory will last a moment, "flooding me" (*sheṭafani*) with the wave of its sweetness, the poet knows he will "stand tremulously" (*e'emod nif'am*) again before the primordial world of riddles and marvels—on which "no hand ever rested (*ḥalah*),[20] or any speech occurred." Overwhelmed, "my heart will be filled with an overwhelming sound [*hamon*], and the tremor (*timahon*) of God upon my face; / in my eyes (*'einai*) a tear will glisten, and in my soul a silent blast (*teru'ah ne'elamah*)." Beyond language, the silent splendor of being is evoked. The poet is transfused by an expectant readiness—the pulse of the ineffable resounding in his heart.

In tremulous terms, poetic revelation says one thing and does another: it reveals the moment before language, when the poet experiences the mystery of a pregnant silence. Among other attestations, the poem "Besorah" (Message) conveys such an ultimate inwardness—each stanza a portent of the mystical transport of selfhood. When light breaks forth anew, sending its sacred shafts to earth, each like a "golden arrow" that "speaks . . . its splendor" (*millel . . . zoharo*). The poet's eye is transported on high, transfused like a prophet by this

19. These channels (*tzinorot*) import mystical revelations. A similar sequence of language is at the end of *Tzafririm*.

20. Deftly, the poet conveys this primordial moment of pure happening (the verb *ḥalah* also conveys, by suggestion, the absence of desecration).

luminous glow. "Face to face I shall speak / with the beauteous heavens; / mouth to mouth I shall open the channel (*tzinor*) of my heart: / the sky will pour forth its bounty . . . the radiance of its light." His heart will then be filled with a heavenly azure, and his heartstrings will be strummed by the play of light (*pizzuz . . . orot*) radiating into his soul. Totally transformed, the poet's "entire being will resound with new song (*kol qerovai / shirah ḥadashah yehemayu*)"—a murmuring song born of a profound interior illumination.

For Bialik, vision has other, contemplative dimensions—equally fundamental for the poet and his inspiration. We have a personal accounting of this toward the end of the lyric "Ha-Bereikhah" (The Pool). In the penultimate stanza, the poet returns to the imaginal dimensions of this reflecting surface (first taken up in *Zohar*).[21] Bent in meditative pose, and caught between the world without and its features on the waters, the speaker is suddenly "aroused . . . by a silent streaming" (*margish . . . nevoʿa ḥeresh*), filling his heart and plunging it into this reality—attentive to the onset of a revelation. And then his heart "in its holy desires . . . trembled, was extinguished, [and] expired (*yaḥil, yikhleh, yigvaʿ*)" in ecstasy—as if eviscerated in his very being, to such a degree that a heavenly voice asked, from within the surrounding "silence" (*demamah*), "where are you?" as the natural world looked on in astonishment.

Coming to his senses in the final stanza, we are given a veritable poetics of this experience. For hereby we are told that there is a primary language that precedes human speech. It is a "silent, divine language" (*sefat elim ḥarishit*), a "language of silences (*lashon ḥashaʾim*) / without any voice or sound (*lo qol ve-lo havarah*)" a primordial medley of colors and shapes and spectacles. This is the language by which "God makes Himself known" to his favored ones and from which the artist shapes "the stirring of his heart (*hagig levavo*)" and seeks solutions to an "unvoiced dream (*ḥalom lo hagui*)." Even more, we are told that this is "the language of visions (*lashon ha-marʾot*)"—revealed in the colors

21. *Zohar* is dated to 1901; *Ha-Bereikhah*, to 1908.

of the firmament, the wings of birds, the sparkle of an eye, the shapes of human form, and the host of phenomena on sea and land. Reaching a pitch of disclosure, Bialik adds that it is just in this "language, the language of languages" (*be-lashon zo, lashon ha-leshonot*) that the pool conveyed its truths to the speaker—through a vision whereby everything may be envisioned in all its mysterious and ever-changing diversity. The "eye" of the pool is thus a font of perception and projection—a veritable "visionary" (*tzofeh*) in its own right, "envisioning" (*tzofiyah*) the multiplicity of worldly sights and their "previsioned" (*tzafui*) occasions in all their great "variability" (*mishtaneh*) and variety. Through this prism, the dreamer may now imagine all manner of likeness and comparison, each "as if" of the imaginal life (*li nidmetah ke'ilu*), each speculation of awareness.[22] Arising through such visual associations, human words construe the inmost figurations of its imaginal consciousness.[23]

A Hermeneutical Interlude

We have repeatedly noted that a fundamental source of Bialik's creativity derives from the memory of ecstatic visions perceived in his childhood and later reprocessed through the canonical tradition. The first type is preverbal and sensate; the second constitutes the argot of language preserved in ancient folios but needing to be revived through the prism of poetic speech. It is this process that changes their ontological character. The visions of the outer world—be they of its sacred, interior light or its external images—are evocations of the creation: God's

22. The poet himself is thus included in this "seeing," as he says at the onset of *Zohar*, that in his youth he was "like a *tzofeh* at the *'ein* of the world," where primal mysteries were revealed (*niglu*). This verb has recurrent iterations. Bialik's use of *ke'ilu* marks his acute consciousness of the role of similes to convey imaginal effects. He also uses *kemo* in the second stanza of *Mi-Shomerim La-Boqer* to indicate the near ineffability of mystical experience. His use of this form is a remarkable stylistic enjambment. For this and other reasons, I believe that Hillel Zeitlin misspeaks and greatly misprizes Bialik's use of similes. See his "*'Al Bialik*," *Ha-Tequfah* 17 (1918): 430–42.

23. The imagery of mirrored worlds, with diverse refractions, is a fundamental feature of Kabbalistic hermeneutics and is a topos employed by E. Wolfson to articulate mystical *poesis* in his illuminating essay, "Showing the Saying: Laying Interpretative Ground," in *Language, Eros, Being: Kabbalistic Hermeneutics and Poetic Imagination* (New York: Fordham University Press, 2005), 1–45.

language made manifest to the human eye. The words of tradition had become, for young Bialik, mere shells that no longer retained the aura of sacred speech despite their revelatory origins and reinterpretation over the generations.[24] What, then, is the status of a poetic argot (Bialik's oeuvre) that culls from this canon and produces a new melody of sound and significance? How can we understand such literary refractions—creatively educed from nonverbal channels of the spirit?

Bialik's emphasis on personal and immediate experience is essential: it is the inner fire that refines older terms and melds them (or "hammers" them, as he says in his "Winter Songs") on the anvil of his heart. Three examples may illustrate this vortex of creativity. The first is the reference to spiritual yearning at the beginning of the poem *Zohar* where the speaker says, "I pined to go from the physical body of the world to its light" (*mi-gufo shel ʿolam el oro ʿaragti*). This use of the verb *ʿaragti* evokes spiritual longing as well as Psalm 42:2, wherein the adept's soul yearns to be sated with God, like a hart seeking streams of water, since he likewise thirsts for the living God like a pilgrim who, upon traversing sacred sites, is aroused by memory and loss (vv. 3–7). Surely, in the foregoing quote, Bialik has reminted the verb *ʿaragti* to express his lifelong yearning for the mystery of light. But what else drew him to this passage? Might we not also hear the poet's mourning for his spiritual loss of the tradition and its capacity to inspire? For the psalm depicts the seeker's longing with the figure of waters breaking over him: "Deep calls to deep (*tehom el tehom*) at the sound of Your channels (*tzinoreykha*)," (v. 8) in terminology redolent with Bialik's own language of inspiration, noted earlier. Even more striking, the psalmist says that during the night God's "song (*shiro*) is with me" (v. 9)! This is, quite evidently, another indication that the language of the psalmist resonates with the longing of the poet's soul. And finally, might we not also hear in Bialik's figure of longing an echo of the great medieval "Song of Unity," wherein the liturgist states, "I will compose (*eʿerog*) songs to God, because my soul pines (*taʿarog*)" for His Glory?[25] A bold fusion of linguistic ontologies (sacred Scripture and the author's soul)

24. See the poignant lines in "Lifnei Aron Ha-Sefarim" (Before the Bookcase).

25. A stimulating linguistic discussion of the verb *ʿarag* in Bialik's oeuvre appears in D. Sadan, *Ḥayim Naḥman Bialik ve-Darko bi-Leshono ve-Leshonoteyha* (Tel Aviv: Ha-Kibbutz Ha-Meʾuḥad, 1989), 15–34. The "Song of Unity" (Shir Ha-Yiḥud) is recited each Sabbath according to the Ashkenazi rite.

marks these allusions and constitutes their intertextual significance. Bialik's composition is manifestly resonant with all these features.

Of a quite different type is his use of the figure *genuvti yom* to convey the phenomenon of poetic revelation.[26] Literally, the phrase means "taken by stealth," and it occurs in Genesis 31:39 when Jacob protests to Laban of his honesty and that he made good any losses of the flock, be they "snatched by day" or otherwise. At first glance this image is odd, and its form requires some explanation. In fact, the "*i*-suffix" here is an old linguistic (gentilic) feature (see Rashi and Ibn Ezra), not a personal pronoun, and the verb is also used to indicate a Divine revelation in Job 4:12 to refer to some form of unintended overhearing (a kind of spiritual stealth) of a heavenly word.[27] What does Bialik do? He uses the verb *gunavti* as an innuendo of inspiration but also appropriates the suffix as a marker for his own, personal experience. The upshot is that the formulation *genuvti* now conveys "*my* purloined inspiration"! Sensitive to his own reuses of traditional language, he characterizes his poetic inspiration as a kind of "reappropriated treasure."[28] The complex layering of his poetics and the Scriptural originals is a hermeneutical tour de force and strikingly exemplifies the convergent literary strata in Bialik's poetry. The ironic mixture of the patriarch Jacob's protest with his personal confession demonstrates that the older, canonical authority (its Divine ontology) is not obscured but strategically elided in order to give the poet's innovations their new ontological resonance. Such is the spiritual cauldron of Bialik's soul. In his view reappropriation and transformation is the singular way to sanctify an ancient language (Hebrew) that has lost its traditional resonance and been depleted by secular usage (among the pioneers of post–World War I Palestine).[29]

26. See near the end of "Razei Laylah" (Mysteries of the Night), where it is paired with a *bat qol* (Divine voice).

27. The literary figure is *davar yegunnav* and has a positive sense. The verb was also employed to give an ironic echo to the words of Laban, Rachel, and Jacob himself in Genesis 31:19–20, 26–27. The term conveys plagiaristic or false prophecy; see below.

28. In Jeremiah 23:30 the prophet lambastes those who have "stolen" or plagiarized his prophetic words (*megannevei devaray*); but this usage may be an ironic outlier here for the poet. By constrast, see his striking usage below.

29. Bialik addressed these matters in his celebrated lecture, "'Al Qodesh ve-Ḥol be-Lashon," in Ḥ. *N. Bialik, Devarim She-Be'al Peh* (Tel Aviv: Devir, 1935), 2:128–30 (delivered in 1927).

As a final example, I turn to the lyric poem "Lo Zakhiti Ha-Or Min Ha-Hefqer" (I Didn't Merit Light by Accident). In it Bialik adapts verbal elements from the legal and prophetic traditions of Scripture to express personal sources of his creativity. At the outset, the poet avers that the "light" of his inspiration was neither the product of happenstance nor patrimony (*me-avi*) but something he "hewed" from the "rock" (*sela'*) of his "heart"—employing several allusions to Isaiah 51:1 that refer to the ancestral rock of the "patriarch" Abraham as the source from which the nation was "hewn." Bialik then adds that his creative "spark"[30] was neither "borrowed" nor "stolen" (the verb *genavtiv* here cleverly denies the theft or misappropriation of inspiration) but was rather the product of the "hammer of my sorrows" (*paṭish tzorotai*). Under the weight of its blows, "my heart burst (*yitpotzetz*)" and a flame entered his eye and inspired his "verse." Such imagery personalizes the language of Jeremiah 23:29–30, wherein the Divine Word is compared both to "fire" and to a "hammer shattering a rock" (*kepaṭish yefotzetz sela'*)—a figure set in contrast to the speech of those who misappropriate or "steal" God's Word (*meganvei devari*). At the end, the poet adds a melancholy note. He reports that his verse also ignited the cultural "fire" (*'ur*) of his listeners, although it disappeared from sight (snuffed out by the indolence of his audience). Thus, in conclusion, the poet laments, "And I paid for the conflagration / with my flesh and blood" (*ve-anokhi be-ḥelbi uve-dami / et ha-be'eirah ashalem*). In this passage, the reader can hear an allusion to the forensic situation in Exodus 22:4–5, which adjudicates that if a person ignites a fire on their own property but the flame burns another's fields, the one who causes the "fire" (*ha-be'eirah*) must "pay" (*yishalem*) the requisite damages. Bialik uses the language of sacrificial offerings to indicate the personal cost and does so with another double entendre (*dam* indicates "blood" in biblical Hebrew, but "money" in rabbinic parlance). It is a further testimony to the poet's adaptation of canonical terms and figures to convey a personal truth—and exemplify at the same time the power of linguistic renewal. The convergence of diverse linguistic ontologies (sacred and profane) is a subject in itself.

30. The mystic innuendo of *nitzotz* (soul spark) here is freighted with significance.

The Ontology of Language as Such

For Bialik, personal immediacy and primary experiences are at the core of language. He articulates this linguistic anthropology in his essay "Gillui ve-Khisui ba-Lashon" (Revealment and Concealment in Language).[31] Adam is paradigmatic, being the first speaker and first artist. Responding to the unknown terrors of existence—both its sounds and sights—the primal creature emits tones that mimic the phenomena of nature. Such enunciations are reactive, often onomatopoetic, and only subsequently reformulated into communicative meanings (the sound "r-r" that precedes the word *roar* is emblematic). These articulations arise from the primary terror of existence and the emergence of a self-aware "I." The result is the emergence of verbal remedies to displace the unnerving *tehom* ("depths"—or the primordial deep of Genesis) of nameless being. Social language reinforces this remedy and further tempers the fears of raw experience. But, Bialik avers, it nevertheless happens that this protective veneer is repeatedly ripped away, and the chaotic foundation of existence is exposed by death, grief, or sudden joy—and then the reality of ineffable mystery overwhelms the now shuddering self—until some new image assuages the unhinged soul to allow one to return to the tasks of life. Poetry is distinctive among the verbal forms of culture. It hovers close to the hylic abyss in its capacity to express raw emotions that require new terms to respond to the issues at hand. Poetry is thus the counterpoint to chatter and common speech, and its dense syntax and word choice attest to this reality. Poetry stands close to the abyss because its language is a prism of the unsayable. For Bialik, the query *mah* (what?) symbolizes this truth, and the mythic word *tehom* names the primal upsurge of terrors from the abyssal depths. It is from this font that we feel sorrow or emit a cry; that we feel the surge of happiness and laugh; or sense the play of

31. See *Kol Kitvei Ḥayim Naḥman Bialik*, 207–9 (for a translation, see the Introduction to this volume). The essay was first published in 1917. There have been some attempts to correlate Bialik's linguistic theories with Russian symbolists, German Romantics, and others. See, Ḥ. Bar-Yosef, *'Al Andrei Biely, Ha-Simbolizm ha-Rusi ve-Bialik*, discussed and translated in *Miqarov* 10 (2003): 44–57; and also R. Cartun-Blum, *Diesendruck ve-Bialik, Moznayim* 41, no. 2 (1965): 90–97. See Tzvi Diesendruk *Ḥiyuv ve-Shlilah ba-Vitui, Revivim* 3/4 (1913): 5–18. Both he and Bialik were influenced by G. Herder's *Abhandlungen über den Ursprung der Sprache* (1770; Stuttgart: Reclam, 1966).

melody and sing. These are the preverbal modalities that Bialik deems "languages without words" (*leshonot be-lo millim*) but that a human speaker (*medabber*) can reformulate in ever-new ways. They are ultimately the echoless and unanswerable words of God arising from the *tehom* that can drive a person mad—but that also elicit responses that testify to the primordial Word of God, to the extent we can bear it.

Surely Bialik speaks from experience. Every word he uttered needed to be shaped by these primary experiences—be they the mirth expressed by the cavorting sprites and youth in the sunlight or the dance of imps in the dark, or the primal breath of existence that glistens from icy roofs in winter, or the simplicity of being figured by butterflies alighting on a young girl's locks in springtime. Such images are due to the poet's primordial sensitivities. In like measure are images of sorrow that mourn personal loss, that remember the poet's childhood poverty (and the dough soaked by his mother's weeping), or that evoke the whirlwind of wounds due to brutality and the ravages of war. In this sense his poetry is a long "scroll of fire" (*megillat esh*) whose flames curl up as figures of inconsolable mourning for his world-weary and suffering people. But most of all, Bialik's language arises from his profound sense of the ultimate abyss. It is this dimension that brings him to a heart-shattering groan at the climax of this realization. The poem "Hetzitz ve-Nifga'" (He Gazed and Died) is a formulation of his lifelong attempts to see ultimate realities. Absent here is any light but the torch he bears to guide a pilgrimage into the abyss of the "nihil," of which nothing can be said—not even a perplexed or anxious "what?" (*mah*). This abyss is the incomprehensible "no-thing" that mystic tradition dared call *beli-mah* (an ultimate dimension without a *mah*). As the pilgrim-poet proceeds past every cognitive limit, he sinks to the borderland that is marked by this term and roars a primal scream—having just glimpsed at a state beyond being. No one can return whole from this perception, and there is no similitude or verbal likeness for it. The *tehom* is the end of imagination—its dark hole.[32] At the closure of this poem, we are left to ponder, Is this the end of poetry or its true source?

32. It would surely not have been lost on Bialik that the image of the world suspended over *beli-mah* in Job 26:7 is preceded by the figure of the north (*tzafon*) stretched out over *tohu*! Might *tzafun* (the hidden) also be intoned here?

Whether linked to a psychic event or not, Bialik wrote another poem that same year (1915) wherein he speaks of the snapped chords of his voice and depicted this rupture as a punishing silence. In acutest language, he portrays the impurity of his words. Repeatedly, in "Ḥalefah 'Al Panai" (There Passed over Me), the poet laments his stained words, seemingly beyond refinement,[33] and determines to "go out" to hear the pure speech of children and the chirping of birds in the morning. To catch these tones we can best turn to his childhood jingles, modulating babbles of rhyme and echoing joy.[34] Perhaps none of these "songs of innocence" so purely evokes these tonalities as the poem "Nadnedah" (The Seesaw). Within the compass of a seemingly simple chant, the poet conveys a profound insight. Tongue in cheek, he has the children sing, as they cavort up and down, "What is above? What is below?—Only me (I), me and you" (*mah le-ma'alah? / mah le-matah— / raq ani, / ani ve-attah*).[35] With a barely disguised irony, the word *mah* marks both a query and an assertion! Above and below, there is only *mah*—only wonder and the certitude of "I and thou" in simple dialogue. Metaphysical angst is replaced by the joy of shared life. The mystery of childhood has returned again.

My end is my beginning, where I spoke of how the ontological language of older religious tradition was challenged by modernity and how contemporary poetry has tried to recover the loss of wonder and meaning. After the fracture of a Divine language that unites heaven and earth, the modern seeker is left with verbal fragments that try to evoke a new spirit and sensibility from their linguistic husk. Such attempts at hermeneutical transfusion are the hazard of modern poetry. During the past century, the achievements of Rilke and others are emblematic of the struggle to recover a lost immediacy of experience, and thereby the renewal of vision. We initially portrayed Bialik in this

33. The poem marks this desecration through numerous inversions of old sacrificial terminology.

34. See his *Shirim u-Fizmonim LiYladim* (1933; reprint, Tel Aviv: Devir, 2008).

35. Cf. *Shirim u-Fizmonim LiYladim*, 19. For an extensive study, see D. Marom, "Bialik 'al ha-Nadnedah," *Dor le-Dor* 53 (2017): 33–72.

light, and this alignment cannot be denied. But is there more? Can we integrate such a portrayal with the "silent language" of God that is, he says, the external world of appearances? And more, can we even relate this to the Divine "language without words" that pulsates within the abyssal depth of being? If so, are we not perhaps compelled to regard everything as Divine language—as a Divine evocation in some palpable mode or respect? May we even say that the true poet is an inspired witness to all this—trembling before emptiness and fullness and perceiving the beckoning of the transcendent mystery in his heart before it coalesces in the imagination as figures of a sudden sensation? So understood, all poetic speaking emerges at the border of sound, where God's word may be heard anew. And thus to think with poetry is to sense the nascent creativity of speech and the ineffable Divine Voice at its base. This is a near-mystic cognizance of revelatory significance: a spiritual awareness at the silent verge of language.

8

"The Between"

SPACES OF MEETING, LANGUAGE, AND THE ABYSS

When we open our eyes to the day, the world is already there as a presence, and I and you participate in what comes to sight and mind. A mysterious bond joins us to the physical world and to its creatures; it is a conjunction of relatedness and difference. Just what is between one thing and another, when we experience such connection and separation? We certainly sense the significance of these correlations as they increase or diminish in emotional quality, or as the quantities of physical space affect our perception and memory. Is this "in-between" zone merely some artificial construct, or does my lived relationship to this particular "other" (person or thing) have some ontological reality? As I shift locations, and move across the street to greet you, what is happening "between" us through our mutual regard or anticipation of the encounter?

Beyond these interpersonal events, we may also wonder, What is between me and some book or art object, as I enter into a lived relationship with it—at a specific moment, or intermittently over time? And further: if, in a manner of speaking, a person uses a simile or metaphor, or imagines that "this" is *like* "that" in some particular way, what is "between" these presumed correlations? Do such acts of conjunction have ethical implications or are they mere acts of the imagination—literary constructs that have no actual bearing on the world or our lives within it? Surely we balk to think that nothing "more" is involved. But what is "between" these differences-in-unity? What kind of world do we inhabit when we think across these distinctions?

There is no simple answer to the mystery of "the between" or its occasions. Even thinkers like Martin Buber, who pondered these matters over a lifetime, struggled between perplexity and certainty about the meaning of the term and the conditions necessary for it to be a human reality. At an early stage of his work, he considered "the between" the terrifying abyss of being that must be overcome through resolute, creative acts. At later points, he perceived this in terms of interpersonal communication and dialogue. His formulations take us to the heart of the matter, and we shall follow the lifelong track of his thought. But this notwithstanding, I must demur with respect to the linear progression of his work. Its positivity is not fully satisfying, for the recurrent ruptures in relations are not simply the great difficulty in sustaining mutuality (whenever some "mismeeting" or "objectification" dislodges a true encounter between persons). In many cases, distrust and disconnection (or other disruptive elements) have a decidedly more negative root that can implode our sense of meaning or undermine the very possibility of human relations. Certainly Buber was not naive. After the abyss of the Holocaust, he, too, stood silent in its horrendous aftermath, altogether bereft—though he remained resolute in his belief (or hope) that earlier attestations of dialogue might condition the renewal of social trust. His repeatedly revoiced determination was therefore to hold firm in the palpable void.[1] But the question remains how one might reaffirm trust in others after such radical evil. This remains the challenge in times of crisis. Renewal of "the between" between persons then requires a patient and diligent reconstruction of our best cultural resources. Standing in this void, we too must wonder, Is there a voice in the whirlwind?

First Formulations

In the midst of the third of five "Dialogues on Realization," titled *Daniel: Gespräche von der Verwirklichung* (published in 1913),[2] Buber diagnosed a crisis of the contemporary European spirit (when the older verities were emptied of their former significance) and offered a

1. See *At the Turning: Three Addresses on Judaism* (New York: Farrar, Straus and Young, 1952), 61–62; and in the original, *An der Wende: Reden über das Judentum* (Cologne: Jakob Hegner, 1952), 105–7.

2. It was published in Leipzig by Insel. The English version was translated as *Daniel: Dialogues on Realization*, trans. M. Friedman (New York: McGraw-Hill, 1965). In the references below, the German text is cited first.

solution rooted in the notion of authentic self-realization. He was not unique in this quest, and repeatedly shows the influence of Nietzsche, whose brooding meditations in *Thus Spoke Zarathustra* had a youthful impact. A similar temperament of spiritual dislocation recurs in Rilke's writing at this time and many years later.[3] No wonder that when their joint publisher, Insel, sent Rilke a copy of Buber's *Daniel*, Rilke responded with enthusiasm.[4]

How did Buber diagnose this crisis? He speaks of a shattering upheaval of consciousness wherein every semblance of the coherence of things was ruptured: "I felt [says 'Daniel'] no connection (*Zusammenhang*): but rather shriek, shriek, and in between (*dazwischen*) the abyss (*Abgrund*)." And again, in a more intense specification, he also stated, "The abyss was between piece and piece of the world, between thing and thing (*zwischen Ding und Ding*), between image and being, between the world and me."[5] Certainly this devastating rupture (induced, in part, by the social collapse of the "Old Europe" and onset of the First World War) was also experienced in the depths of the self—splitting the person "not into spirit and body . . . but into the thousandfold Protean doubleness of the bright One and the dark Other, with the eternal abyss in between (*mit dem ewigen Abgrund dazwischen*)." This sense of a radical fracture signals the end of "security" and the onset of a "discordant, disjointed life."[6]

In conjunction with this confession of a primal alienation, the speaker refers to a ruptured *Zusammenhang des Seelenlebens* (the interconnection of the spiritual life). Significantly, Buber's philosophical mentor, Wilhelm Dilthey, had promoted the term *Zusammenhang* to specify the primary "interconnection" that individuals experience between themselves and the world.[7] Buber's *Daniel* upends this crucial harmony. With striking pathos, the speaker feels caught on the horns

3. See E. Heller, *The Disinherited Mind* (Harmondsworth: Penguin Books, 1961), 109–55 ("Rilke and Nietzsche, with a Discourse of Thought, Belief, and Poetry").

4. Cf. R. M. Rilke, *Briefe auf seine Verleger* (Leipzig: Insel, 1934), 180, 182.

5. *Daniel*, 64–65 (English, 86).

6. *Daniel*, 65 (English, 86).

7. See W. Dilthey, *Gesammelte Schriften VI, Die Geistige Welt: Einleitung in die Philosophie des Lebens*, ed. G. Misch, 3rd ed. (Stuttgart: B. Tuebner, 1958), 144; and the discussion in R. Makkreel, *Dilthey: Philosopher of the Human Studies* (Princeton, NJ: Princeton University Press, 1975), 98–100.

of multiple antinomies without hope of resolution and bereft of any metaphysical ground. Here and everywhere is the primal *Abgrund,* the abyss that surges up and sunders any semblance of relations among the elements. It roils between "thing and thing"—the term *between* marking the gaps and emptiness of all disconnection. In this protean abyss, what promethean acts might counter total despair or nihilism and create something out of chaos? Buber's dire answer: there is nothing that can eradicate this primal *Abgrund;* hence, one must resolve to repeatedly transform the elements through creative acts, since only in this way can one achieve any personal integration and self-realization (*Verwirklichung*). With courage and determination, one must descend into the "nameless polarity of all being, between piece and piece of the world, between thing and thing (*zwischen Ding und Ding*)"—a cleavage that even splits one's "inmost self." The supreme task is "to create unity out of your and all duality," a "fulfilled unity out of tension and stream, such as will serve the polar earth—the realized countenance of God illuminated out of tension and stream." In an even more poignant challenge, one must acknowledge the terrifying *Abgrund*[8] and resolve to live with "holy insecurity" (*den heiligen Unsicherheit*).[9]

A variety of factors challenged Buber's commitment to this personal position, avowedly disconnected from the stream of ongoing social life. Among his companions it was Gustav Landauer who had the greatest impact in urging Buber to turn from acts of self-creativity and its enthusiasms toward social communities and issues of political justice—a veritable transvaluation of values.[10] This revision of orientation came to full expression in 1918 in Buber's essay "Der Heilige Weg"

8. Remarkable to say, this notion first appears in Buber's early (1908) work on the Baal Shem, where he similarly says that "all things" were "in the Abyss," and that "the Abyss (*Abgrund*) was between one thing and another (*zwischen jedem Ding und dem andern*)," and that only by virtue of the holy helper (the Baal Shem) were things joined and healed. See *Die Legende des Baalschem* (Frankfurt am Main: Rütten und Loening, 1920), 67–68.

9. See *Daniel,* 83–84 (English, 98–99).

10. For a nuanced examination of both Landauer's early intimacy with Buber's *Daniel* and his later repulsion at the moral blindness that mystic enthusiasms (like

(The Holy Way), a work dedicated to his slain friend's memory.[11] Herein, Buber came out decisively against the spiritual path of private intuition and intensity and on behalf of the interpersonal social realm as the sphere of truest realization. He stresses that although the Divine may come to life in an individual person, "it attains its earthly fullness only where individual beings open themselves to one another, . . . help one another; where immediacy is established between one human being and another (*zwischen den Wesen*) . . . where this takes place, where the eternal rises in the Between (*Dazwischen*), . . . that true place of realization (*Verwirklichung*) is community (*Gemeinschaft*), and true community is that relationship in which the Divine comes to its realization between man and man (*zwischen den Menschen verwirklicht*)." Or, as he had just stated, God "must be realized between [all] the things (*zwischen den Dingen zu verwirklischen*)" of existence.[12] The striking conceptual and verbal counterpoints to *Daniel* cannot be missed. It is now *between* the multiple things or realities of existence where true realization occurs, and it is effectuated in the depth of life, with all its antinomies and contradictions. These elements are not to be overcome through some creative individuation or integration but "lived through" in all their complexity. For it is precisely in the thickness of life, Buber stresses, that Judaism builds its home on earth; just here, in the world, does it strive for "the realization of true community" and the "realization of the [religious] spirit."

Five years later, in 1923, following continuous thought and revision, Buber published his momentous *Ich und Du* (I and Thou), in which the notion of a "lived actuality" (*Wirklischem Leben*) becomes a repeated theme to specify the realization of personal relations.[13] Significantly, these latter do not have their interconnection (*Zusammenhang*) in the realm of things or objects but in the center (*Mitte*) where the lines of

---

Buber's) could lead to, see P. Mendes-Flohr, *Martin Buber: A Life of Faith and Dissent* (New Haven, CT: Yale University Press, 20019), 73–74, 100–108.

11. See *Der Heilige Weg* (Frankfurt am Main: Rütten und Loening, 1920). Landauer was murdered at a political event.

12. *Der Heilige Weg*, 15–16.

13. *Ich und Du* (Leipzig: Insel), 1923). English renditions are adapted from the R. G. Smith (London: Keegan Paul, 1937) and W. Kaufman (New York: Scribner's, 1970) translations.

all true relations intersect: in the eternal Thou of God.[14] Buber returns to this locution at the conclusion of the book, when he refers to this sphere as one "between beings" (*zwischen den Wesen*) and "hidden in our midst (*Mitte*)—there between us" (*im Dazwischen*).[15] What is conveyed by this realm, and what is its nature? A lifetime of reformulations and explications followed. Before considering these ruminations, two phrases found in Buber's lectures on "Presence" (which preceded *I and Thou* by two years and was delivered at the Freie Jüdisches Lehrhaus in Frankfurt at the request of Franz Rosenzweig) deserve consideration,[16] for they bear on his emergent understanding of the "Between" in a striking manner.

Premonitions of a Conceptual Shift

In the course of his reflections on "the mystery of presence," Buber asserts that the latter is a primary experience of a pure or absolute relation. It confronts the individual as an undifferentiated immediacy—not cognizable as such, and thus not known through the particulars of worldly awareness. Something happens—something is given—and the self may receive it in a total, undifferentiated way. This something cannot be named but is revealed to awareness as a total presence. Suddenly, reality addresses the self in the most immediate way. To characterize this presence, Buber now speaks of an "Absolute Thou." This term points to the absolute actuality of existence that confronts the individual and lifts one beyond the facticity of subject-object differences. What surges from eternity, and sustains these moments, is a feature of this Thou "between" them. Reaching for a teaching from Jewish tradition that might mark this Absolute, Buber suggests that "this is no doubt what is meant by the saying that the *Shekhinah* is

14. *Ich und Du*, 116.

15. *Ich und Du*, 137–38.

16. These lectures were preserved in stenograph form and only subsequently published. See R. Horowitz, *Buber's Way to "I and thou": the Development of Martin Buber's Thought and His "Religion as Presence" Lectures* (Philadelphia: The Jewish Publication Society, 1988). Her book was originally published as *Religion als Gegenwart* (Heidelberg: Lambert Schneider, 1978). German citations are from the latter publication.

between the beings (*zwischen den Wesen*)."[17] Quoting from an ancient rabbinic source, Buber glosses this experience by stating that when we face one another and sense that something is held in common, we are gifted with the eternal all-present revelation of God in the here and now. Based on the Hebrew formulation of this traditional adage, he averred that this is the reality of the "Divine presence *beineihem*"[18]—"between" these conjoined realities. One may feel that Buber's use of this figure goes too far, and that by invoking a *theologoumenon* that names the phenomenon of presence he veers toward an objectification of the mystery. And yet, remarkable to say, in his draft of the lectures from 1918, Buber recognized this point and nominated "The Between as an Hypostatization of the *Relation*."[19]

A second passage offers another consideration of the mystery of Thou that may surge into consciousness. Each such moment is a revelatory breakthrough in human terms, and each one varies by what it helps bring to expression in art and religion. No formulation is fixed, and each breakthrough is distinct in terms of its shapes or appearance—not to mention the human experience itself. What abides or sustains the multiple moments of presence? Trying to give expression to this issue, while avoiding any hint of some substantive reality, Buber remarks that each gap between moments of manifestation is like a "holding of breath: [like] the silence between (*zwischen*) word and word . . . between forceful revelation and forceful revelation." In this context the "between" is the eternal mystery, an ineffable manifestation of the eternal Thou. "We stand and remain in the mystery. . . . We stand to it in community. We stand to it in its reciprocity (*Gegenseitigkeit*). We stand in its presence (*Gegenwart*)."[20] This *Zwischen* is therefore not the *Abgrund* but rather something like

17. See *Ich und Du*, 144.

18. The classic enunciation is in *Mishnah Avot* 3.2.

19. Horowitz, *Buber's Way*, 135. In the German original of her book (*Religion als Gegenwart*, n. 16), the terminology is *Das Dazwischen als Hypostasierung der Beziehung* (in facsimile). In a different formulation in "I and Thou," that still echoes the lectures on presence, Buber evokes the imagery of Isaiah 6:1 when he says, "In every sphere, through everything that becomes present to us, we gaze at the train (*Saum*) of the eternal You." See *I and Thou* (in the W. Kaufmann translation, n. 13), 57 (German term inserted).

20. Cf. *Das Dazwischen als Hypostasierung der Beziehung*, 152.

the pulse of presence—binding the moments of manifestation like a covenant between the parts in which the ultimate mystery (*Geheimnis*) hides in plain sight. The eternal Thou (in these lectures) is thus deemed both manifest and concealed: one simultaneous truth. The seeker strives to live this reality—to be a participant in its ever-new actuality. By contrast, the philosopher seeks words of specification so that the lived event can be thought and (somehow) held in mind.

Speaking of "I and Thou"

Buber's transformation of consciousness is thus a shift from a conception of the world "as idea and representation" (a being engaged by the super creative ego for its self-centered individuation) to the interpersonal realm of lived reality. How can we understand this move? It is, I suggest, not so much marked by the hyphen that conjoins "I-Thou," or the conjunction (*and*) that bridges "I and Thou," as by the interactive preposition "with" (*mit*). The "between" is the interactive dynamism of "with" (as in "being with," "living with," or "speaking with") that reaches across the difference of persons. Language is such an expressive medium, and so is an engaged silence or the meeting of eyes. These moments are the activation of presence: a dialogical confirmation of shared sociality. Persons evoke this ontic realm. It only exists, as such, amid the concrete particularities of human relations, when one person turns to another, with the requisite focus or intention of the soul. "Only the being whose otherness, accepted by my being, lives and faces me in the whole compression of existence, brings the radiance of eternity to me. Only when two say to one another with all that they are, "It is *Thou*" (*Du bist es!*), is the indwelling of the Present Being between (*zwischen*) them."[21] The phrases used here are evocative, for in this influential 1929 essay called "Zweisprache" (Dialogue), Buber underscores his discussion with a near-literal reference to his earlier, pivotal work *Der Heilige Weg*—composed a decade earlier in memory of Gustav Landauer. Not for nothing does this paragraph precede the section titled "Gemeinschaft" and its discussion of a true community—where

21. See the rendition in Buber's *Between Man and Man,* trans. R. Gregor Smith (London: Routledge & Keegan Paul, 1947), 30.

people are "no longer side by side but *with* one another of a multitude of persons." Significantly, the key terms in this confusing formulation are *Beieinandersein* and *mitsammen sich*—both of which express the relationality of being "with" another one in community. The stylistic redundancy has a striking rhetorical effect on the reader.

It would take another decade for Buber to return to the phenomenon of "the between" and the meaning of dialogue in interhuman relations. Many topics only adumbrated earlier, and others needing philosophical clarity, were explicated and sit on a firmer foundation. If the melodic language of *I and Thou* was replaced with a more prosaic (and sometimes ponderous) syntax, the urgency and directness of Buber's voice remains. The leitmotif of authentic personhood and the centrality of communication reverberate and address the reader to attend and respond.

Pondering the nature of the person through a series of possibilities discussed by thinkers over the millennia, Buber turns directly, near the end of the book *Das Problem des Menschen* (*Was is der Mensch?* published in 1948 and based on his Jerusalem lectures from 1938) to his major concern: not to the essence of man but "to the reality of the relation *between* man and man."[22] Making his key point even more decisively, Buber stresses that the individual is "a fact of existence" insofar as he steps into a "living relation" with others, just there where "something takes place between one being and another (*zwischen Wesen und Wesen*)," which never occurs in nature. It is something established through the existence of individuals, this being "the sphere of the between (*die Sphäre des Zwischen*)," and he goes on to assert that this sphere is a "primary category (*Urkategorie*) of human reality (*Wirklichkeit*)." This bold formulation is a *novum* for Buber. Now we are clearly told that "the between" is something unique: a distinct category whose grounding is repeatedly constituted as a "fact between" (*faktisch zwischen*) people. Hence, it is a "real place" between them, and not to be found either in one person or in another. This reality is ontological and not reducible to the ontic facticity of any one partner in a

22. *Das Problem des Menschen* (Heidelberg: Lambert Schneider, 1948), was translated as the unit "What Is Man?" a year earlier in *Between Man and Man*, 118–205. The quotation appears in the English language Foreword. The concluding *Ausblick* (Prospect) appears in the German edition on pp. 164–69.

relationship—precisely because this reality is "between" the partners joined in dialogue (accordingly, the various modes of interpersonal communication, whether this be language or a silent gesture, are only signs of this happening). The between is therefore a realm that comes to pass as its own dimension, "on the far side of the subjective, on this side of the objective, on the narrow ridge, where *I* and *Thou* meet."

Or do they? How can we comprehend this formulation? If the "dialogical situation can only be grasped in an ontological way"—and not on the basis of the "ontic of personal existence"—in what sense do the partners meet and cognize one another? If the truth is between persons, isn't its authenticity somehow in the lived differences or mutuality of communication? Indeed, if the Thou (as Buber himself stresses) is only a noumenal presence (and not a reality in the phenomenal world), does authentic dialogue falter as an unbridgeable aporia? Or must we nevertheless admit that we do experience such connections as a "real presence"? Indeed, serious philosophers have argued that such a sensed, interactive presence among persons gives good reason to say that "the between" is something more than a hypothetical construct one must posit in order to ground authentic communication.[23] Somehow, "the between" is a reality that constitutes our lifeworld.[24] Considering this complexity led Buber to assert that the "eternal Thou" is the ever-present, ungraspable foundation of presence and that the upsurge of the "between" becomes an ontic human experience of the reality of God. Or, perhaps, such moments are but a fleeting "glimpse" (a *Durchblick*) of God.[25]

Expanding the Philosophical Scope

Admittedly, Buber does not directly tackle these problems, but his ongoing writing reveals his great desire to expand his formulations and so move into new philosophical territory. The essay "Elements of the

23. See J. Habermas, *A Philosophy of Dialogue* (Jerusalem: The Israel Academy of Sciences and the Humanities, 2013), Proceedings, vol. 8, no. 6, p. 114.

24. Cf. M. Theunissen, *The Other: Studies in the Social Ontology of Husserl, Heidegger, Sartre, and Buber* (Cambridge, MA: MIT Press, 1984), 291.

25. See J. Bloch, *Die Apriori des Du: Probleme der Dialogik Martin Bubers* (Heidelberg: Lambert Schneider, 1977), 80–86.

Interhuman" (Elemente des Zwischenmenschlichen), published in 1954,[26] exemplifies a new phenomenology of the dialogical situation and the topic of "the between." The first term (*Elemente*) marks some distinctive features that characterize the ontological dimension of the second (*Zwischenmenschlichen*). This raises a complexity similar to the one noted earlier, namely, that the concrete actualities (or persons) of an authentic dialogue can neither be thought nor objectified—for if I do so, and somehow concretize or conceptualize my dialogical intention, the other would not be a "Thou" but an "It," and there would also be no pure event or presence. What, then, is the actuality of the "Between"? It would be paradoxically (and ontologically) absurd to say that "it" was "something" and that it joins two distinct "thous," neither of whom could be even abstractly substantivized. Such considerations presumably galvanized Buber to some notable reformulations.

The first expression to be noted is that the interhuman realm is now called a "special dimension" (*Sonderdimension*) of human existence, an actual "happening" (*Ereignisse*) whose "mystery of contact" (*Geheimnis des Kontakts*) is the true core of interpersonal relations (*Wirklichkeit des Zwischenmenschlichen*)—and that what unfolds in the "living interplay" of the participants in a dialogue is the "between (*zwischen*) which they live together." All modalities of objectification sunder the potential bond between persons. For Buber, it is only in "partnership" that one can become an "existing whole"; it is only in a nonobjectifying relationship (whereby one can paradoxically intend to engage in a specific relationship without thinking the other as an "other") that an authentic interpersonal reality may be activated and unfold. True dialogue is where one person enters into an "elementary connection with" another. This mode of turning toward other creatures is what Buber calls a "personal making present" (*Vergegenwärtigung*)—which he means as the intention to help realize the other person in all their creaturely uniqueness. I would further suggest that such a "turning toward" the other is a modality of the dative. The lived syntax of the dative is thus a wholehearted intention "toward" a relationship. For

26. Originally in *Merkur* 7, no. 2 (1954): 112–27, and in *Neue Schweizer Rundshau* 21, no. 10 (1954): 593–608, then in *Das dialogische Prinzip* (Heidelberg: Lambert Schneider, 1962), 269–98, and *The Knowledge of Man*, trans. M. Friedman and R. Gregor Smith (London: George Allen & Unwin, 1965), chap. 3, pp. 72–88.

Buber, this is a primary feature of human nature. It also suggests that this "turning toward" another (the dative element) is also primary for an authentic meeting with others. Indeed, this intentional movement is the onset of the ontological sphere that is unique to human beings. In Buber's terms, this is called an *Einschwingen ins Andere*—a "bold swinging" into the life of the "other"; an "imagining" the particular "real" of the other person, a bold readiness to "expose" oneself fully to the "common situation" between them. If and when "mutuality" (*Gegenseitigkeit*) stirs, genuine dialogue may also blossom.

Making oneself wholly present to another person through the requisite traits or attitudes constitutes a fundamental spiritual disposition of the soul so necessary for authentic dialogue. Buber calls these traits *Seelungverfassungen,* and they are similar to Kant's ethical prescription that one must never treat another person as a means but as an "independent end" (*selbständiger Zweck*) only. This includes the requirement that one "intends" or "means (*meine*) and makes present" the other in their personal being—precisely in the way that is peculiar and possible for them. Herewith we return to the basic intentionality of the other's possibility, mentioned earlier—an intentionality bent on a confirmation of the other's independent being and not on any particular content. By his use of the term *Meinung* (intention), Buber differs appreciably from the more conceptual notion of intention as used by Husserl.[27] Here, it seems, the verb *to mean* has the strong sense of "intending" the concrete reality of a person and their situation. This is neither the perception nor representation of some object in consciousness but the making another person an "actual real"—to themselves and to oneself. It is "to exercise that degree of making [oneself] present" to another person at a shared "moment." The result is deemed an "elemental togetherness" (*elementaren Mitsammenseins*)—and, insofar as the other person is confirmed in their being, this mode of relationship has an ethical accent if not character. It must be stressed that this confirmation of another person does not mean any "approval" of the other person or the particular event. Rather, integrity requires that nothing be held back between the partners. In this context, intention changes into the positivity of the particular. One must "be intent"

27. Cf. K. Shurtz, "Husserl and Meaning," *Aporia* 1, no. 1 (1991): 43–51.

(*bedacht sein*) to "raise into an inner word" that which will only later be spoken. Such an intention is a true bending of one's mind toward the other person in the specificity and demands of an authentic dialogue. It is therefore an expression of "the ontology of the interpersonal" (*die Ontologie des Zwischenmenschichen*) in all its mystery.

It must be emphasized that the sphere of Dialogue (*Gespräch*) is not the factual occurrence of this word or another drawn from the historical thesaurus that may be available to a historical speaker at a given time and place. It is rather the more elementary reality of *Gesprochenheit* or "spokenness." *Gesprochenheit* is that which occurs in the lived "between," where one person turns toward another from a primary "will to communicate." This new point is made in Buber's late but significant 1960 essay "The Word That Is Spoken" (*Das Wort, was gesprochen wird*).[28] The German formulation makes the primary point: there are many words that occur in language, but it is only that particular word that expresses the will toward relationship that is of ontological import. When such a vital word emerges, "communalizing" our verbal formulations, that human being becomes a person. Indeed, it is the very "striving toward language" (*Sprachstrebigkeit*) whereby one may reach beyond monologue and one's private inwardness toward the world and confirm the shared reality of their lived creaturely being. For Buber, it is the will to communicate that generates the ontological sphere of the "Between," and points to a concern to build a common lifeworld and resolve the ambiguities and multiple meanings (*Mehrdeutigkeit*) that complicate relationships. Deeper than the specific meanings of words, then, is the address *to* (the dative again)

28. This essay was first printed in *Worte und Wirklichkeit: Sechste des Jahrbuch Gestalt und Gedanke*, ed. Bayerischen Akademie der Schōnen Künste (Munich: R. Oldenberg, 1960), 15–31, and later in *Logos: Zwei Reden* (Heidelberg: Lambert Schneider, 1962), 7–29, and in Buber, *The Knowledge of Man*, 109–120. It was suggested by a close associate of Buber that this essay was written in response to Heidegger's lecture "Der Weg zur Sprache" and its central motif that: *die Sprache zur Sprache bringen*. For Buber, it is not language itself that speaks but human beings. On this point, see W. Kraft, "Martin Buber über Sprache und deutsche Sprache," *Hochland. Zeitschrift für alle Gebiete des Wissens und den Schōnen Künste* 60, no. 6 (1968): 525.

another person "whom the speaker *means* as such." "To mean a man (*einen Menschen meinen*) means nothing less than to stand by him and his insight with the element of the soul (*Seelenelement*) that can be sent forth." When this occurs, we may stand in the "between" of genuine interrelations. To repeat: whatever individuals are in their private inwardness, it is precisely here, in the profundity of their mutual *Gesprochenheit,* that they can be fundamentally confirmed as persons. Let it then be said that the narrow ridge stirs toward actuality when one person swings *toward* another, *intending* their lived reality to the extent possible. The two are no longer separated as subject here and object there but are rather connected by the Divine dwelling in their midst. When a person intends another as a "thou," the "eternal Thou" dwells between them.

This is a hard hope and unremitting task. Is it a voice from the whirlwind?

A Ḥasidic Postscript

Over his long lifetime, Buber narrated the *Tales of the Hasidim,* seeking to exemplify modes of sacramental existence in both word and deed. Indeed, Buber's interest was sustained for over thirty years, beginning with narratives and teachings of individual figures, such as the *Tales of Rabbi Nachman* (*Die Geschichten des Rabbi Nachman*) in 1906,[29] and culminating in the massive collection of narratives of holy teachers from throughout the eighteenth and nineteenth centuries based on earlier but also subsequently added sources during the war years of 1938 and 1946. There is no reason to suppose that Buber's modern temperament identified with all this material, but there is ample evidence to assert that his editing and stylization of the texts was often in accord with his aesthetic taste and dialogical philosophy. A striking instance of the latter serves as final postscript to the preceding discussion.

29. See the revised German edition of *Die Geschichten des Rabbi Nachman* (Heidelberg: Lambert Schneider, 1988).

In 1922 Buber published a book on the great disciple of the Ba'al Shem Tov known as the Maggid of Mezeritch—a charismatic preacher whose teachings cover a range of theosophical topics set within a radical spiritualized panentheism.[30] The original edition of this work offered only selected teachings from this master along with several of his followers.[31] This selection was later considerably expanded by Buber in the magnum opus of the legends of Ḥasidic masters, early and late. It is in this anthology that a particular term stands out. That term is *Dazwischen*. What does it mean in this context? In an oral account of one of the Maggid's sermons,[32] we are informed (of the theosophical teaching) that "nothing (*kein Ding*) in the world can change from one reality (*Wirklichkeit*) to another unless it first comes to the absolute state of Nothing (*Nichts*)"—this being the transcendental reality that preceded the creation, and it is utterly beyond all human comprehension.[33] Thus this reality has an ontological character, one that is often designated (as in this Hebrew original) by the term *ayin* (or Nothing). To further characterize this transitional state, the Ḥasidic report also utilizes the Talmudic term *beinei beinei* to designate an intermediate stage "betwixt" or "between" one thing and another.[34] But Buber diverges from this meaning and imports his own philosophic conception here and significantly translates this intervening sphere as *Dazwischen*—clearly suggesting something far more ontologically recognizable and, if it is not entirely beyond human grasp, can at least be referred to as something "there" (*Da*)—this prefix being a marker that only makes sense for a reality in the human (not theosophical) realm. With one stroke the supernal domain referred to in the original teaching has been domesticated and brought down to earth.

30. The Maggid (or Preacher) of Mezeritch was the cognomen of R. Dov Ber Friedman (1704–1771), a Ḥasidic master of great influence. We have noted his teachings and influence in earlier chapters of this book.

31. It was titled *Der grosse Maggid und seine Nachfolge* (Frankfurt am Main: Rütten & Loening, 1922).

32. See the tract *Yosher Divrei Emet* in the collection *Liqqutim Yeqarim* (Jerusalem: Ma'arekhet Divrei Emunah, 2004), 116b–117a (no. 13).

33. See *Der Erzählung der Chassidim*, in *Martin Buber Werkausgabe*, Chassidismus III, 18.1 (Gütersloh: Gütersloher, 2015), 254–55. The original edition appeared in 1949.

34. This is also the terminology found in the earlier Hebrew edition. Cf. *Or Ha-Ganuz: Sippurei Ḥasidim* (Tel Aviv: Schocken Books, 1946), 110–11.

To be sure, in Buber's reformulation, we are not dealing with an interpersonal or relational reality but rather with something that marks an organic shift in existence (the purported change between a seed and its fruit being one of the Maggid's several examples). All this notwithstanding, the choice of terminology is significant. The long path from the abysmal *Dazwischen* in *Daniel* to its more positive usage in the *Tales of the Hasidim* (the English title) reverberates to the attentive ear. It is a further indication of Buber's monumental change of consciousness and orientation.

9

Alone-Together

CONTEMPLATION AND COMMUNITY AS INTERSECTING VALUES

Introductory Consideration

The conjunction of "self" and "other" evokes a primary precondition for social ethics—all their situational and historical differences notwithstanding. Its roots are the most radical of all: as mammals, we emerge from a maternal womb dependent on others for nurture and protection. Parental care or its substitutes are necessary for survival. Long before the self develops a sense of separation, entwinement with caretakers takes precedence for ego identity. This includes dependence at the sensory, affective, and visceral levels; and shapes our nature long before social-moral values are enunciated or modeled in a family setting (or its surrogates). Who would deny it? And it is in this setting, moreover, that we first learn to set limits through raw experience or instruction; only later do we learn this virtue culturally through tradition and its norms. This difference notwithstanding, these two factors are thickly intertwined: patterns of life and culture seem, from the first, part of the "nature of things"—and this helps constitute their fundamental, transcendent authority.

Developmental and social psychologists have proposed various reasons for personal preferences for one's psychic or social segregation from normative community practices, and the history of religions gives bountiful evidence for personal withdrawal—even when individuals are committed to the beliefs and structures of a given faith community. In these cases the factors inducing separation vary and are often marked by an intensification of an inner demand to purify one's mind or senses. Similarly, along this spectrum of segregation there is a corresponding social desire to be among likeminded persons who share a certain ascetic discipline. Nevertheless, even in these elective communal settings, the practitioner feels charged by a hyper-demand for a radical "aloneness": the ascetic condition of being alone with oneself, at all times and in all circumstances.

Søren Kierkegaard was certainly not the first to think of the "solitary" as more than a state of existential being, chosen by will or supported by proclivity; nor was he the first to elevate the ideal of the "purity of the heart" as a decisive priority. He was long preceded by religious seekers of many sorts, and modernity has served up its own variations. Characteristic of this spiritual type is the intensified ordering of value and consciousness around the "solitary self"—an ideal demanding the overcoming (or suppression) of one's natural endowments (or animal nature) and the yearning to be constantly in the presence of Divinity (through verbal prayer or silent contemplation). This achievement requires total commitment and diligent devotion, and there is no lack of cultural evidence for the inevitable tensions such a lifestyle elicits for established religions and their concern for public regulations or norms. At the sharpest point of distinction, "the solitary" puts maximum emphasis on inwardness and self-monitoring, whereas the communal ideal highlights a shared public ethos and its regulative authority. For the latter, certain ascetic values are also frequently noted in spiritual handbooks, but their implementation was geared (or intended) for public execution within a normative framework. Judaism is no different: it, too, exhibits a multiplicity of virtues that require excessive self-monitoring, although the normative obligation to fulfill most religious duties within a communal quorum put considerable constraints on the pure ascetic ideal of social withdrawal. How this tension was resolved varied over the centuries.

Except for extreme cases of exclusion, a person lives with different degrees of paradox whenever they are bent on self-development but nevertheless respect the traditions of the social order. As noted, the tension (particularly with respect to public prayer or marital duties) can lead to resolvable or merely endured situations and contradictions. Maimonides may serve as a paradigmatic case, not solely for how these matters expressed themselves in his life and writings but for how they were received and modulated by those who fell under the spell of his ideals—even when they extended to quite different social and spiritual modalities (as we shall soon). The "Great Eagle," as this religious philosopher was called, flourished within the twelfth century culture of Islamic civilization, especially as it affected Spain and North Africa, with pinnacle points in the cities of Fez and Cairo. This was an intellectual and spiritual universe that had fully absorbed Aristotle's *Nicomachean Ethics* in Arabic translation, and on that basis it was led to consider the ideal and actual relationships between the political (the societal writ large) and the ethical (personal virtues), and this heritage had long since inspired Maimonides's intellectual forebears. Among the most notable was Ibn Bajja, who wrote a treatise called *Governance of the Solitary* that pondered the position one should take if they should find themselves within an imperfect societal environment—one that was harmful to their physical or psychological well-being, and he went so far as to advocate both a physical and mental isolation from these negative conditions or ill effects.[1]

Maimonides followed this suggestion and even noted the alternatives of changing one's domain or retreating to the desert if need be.[2] Commenting on the final chapters of Maimonides's *Guide of the Perplexed*,[3] the philosopher Shem Tov actually referred to the private meditative practices depicted there as the master's own "governance of the solitary." We may ponder the paradoxes involved, given this sage's renowned stature as the foremost legal codifier of his age whose massive achievement helped determine the law and practice that should regulate all Jewish religious and societal behavior—an ideal that was applied to the entire community of believers, whether intellectual adepts or mere followers of tradition (or what was referred

1. For the parallels between Ibn Bajja and Maimonides, see L. Berman, "Ibn Bajjah and Maimonides: A Chapter in the History of Political Philosophy" (PhD thesis, Hebrew University of Jerusalem, 1959 (Hebrew with English summary); and H. Blumberg, "Al-Farabi, Ibn Bajja, and Maimonides on the Governance of the Solitary," *Sinai* 78 (1976): 135–45 (in Hebrew).

2. See his comments in *Mishneh Torah, Hilkhot De'ot* VI, 1, to be dealt with more extensively below.

3. Translated by S. Pines (Chicago: University of Chicago Press, 1963).

to as "received opinion," as Plato had determined it). This ideal notwithstanding, private, personal practices (even tinged by Sufi-like practices and terminology) are evident in this sage's great philosophical treatise.

In brief, at the conclusion of the *Guide* (3.51 and 54) Maimonides presents his own contemplative practices and his ideal of an individual perfection limited to an elite few—those capable of the discipline and intellectual training required in contrast to the social ideals of the normative religious tradition. In particular, he stresses that what is required is a "total devotion" to God through intellectual love, and he adds that this is "mostly . . . achieved in solitude and isolation" (3.51). This ideal of perfection is all the more striking given Maimonides's high exaltation of the Law and its forms, which make monastic seclusion an unnecessary practice (2.39), and also his emphasis on the way the Law can cultivate the spiritual ideal of a holy community for the masses (3.32). In these and related cases, we can readily note the gap between these two ideals (philosophy for the few and tradition for the many). We can conceivably only bridge this distinction if we assume that he wrote his Code (the *Mishneh Torah*) as a beneficent "outflowing" for the spiritual benefit of the larger community—an act of graciousness he deemed to be the highest level of *imitatio dei* (3.54).[4] If so, we can suggest that Maimonides regarded his work as the gift of a philosopher to those dependent on the Law and Tradition as the true end of religious practice. If the Law establishes the public ideal of the community, the ultimate ideal is philosophical perfection and contemplative conjunction with Divinity. Thus, despite his efforts for the masses, the Great Eagle yearned to stay "frequently in solitude and . . . not meet anyone unless it is necessary" (3.51).

Other religious teachers gave a different expression to the tension between a perfected selfhood and social-legal practices. Among the most famous of these is Nachmanides (a slightly later contemporary

4. Cf. the judicious analysis and reasons of R. Lerner, "Maimonides' Governance of the Solitary," in *Perspectives on Maimonides: Philosophical and Historical Studies*, ed. J. Kraemer (New York: Oxford University Press, 1991), 42–46.

of Maimonides), who voiced his view in his comment to Deuteronomy 11:22. There, Moses admonishes the people "to faithfully observe all this Torah [Instruction] that I command you, to love the Lord your God, to walk in His ways, and to cleave (*le-davqah*) to Him (*bo*)." This text and its ideal of a total commitment to the Lord and His teachings was examined by earlier sages, both with respect to the admonition and to the stages of spiritual development involved. In his exposition,[5] Nachmanides clearly notes that Moses's statement to the people is a great mystery (*sod*), and he deems it to be a "warning" to follow a spiritual regimen whose end is an unswerving "adherence" to God. In his own treatment, he stresses that "cleaving to God" is a mental-spiritual ideal: a focusing of the mind (he speaks of "thought" or *maḥshavah*) on God alone) at all moments and in all places. In his view, the admonition at the outset exhorts the individual to cleave totally to the Lord and not grant a reality to anything other than God: "only the Lord alone should one serve in his heart and deeds." But then the sage remarkably adds the following clarification and caveat: "It is possible [to interpret the word] *deveiqah* (cleaving)" as subsuming [the ideal] that you should 'remember' (*tizkor*) the Name [of God] and His love always and never allow your thoughts to cease from [connection to] Him—*even* when you go on the way, when you lie down or rise up; [a consummate ideal to be practiced even to the degree that] one's outer speech is with people whereas their heart [or inner attachment] is not with them but [only] before God." Nachmanides goes on to suggest that some practitioners of this ideal (of being alone with God even when one is engaged in mundane matters with other persons) might achieve a measure of immortal life in this world—since they have become persons whom the Divine *Shekhinah* inhabits—as other philosophers, like Judah Halevi, hinted.[6] Without a doubt, this double consciousness long preceded Nachmanides, albeit in different forms, and one must note that his emphasis on remembering God also exceeds the stated biblical ideal. Indeed, it evokes the Islamic practice of *zikr* ("remembering" or "mentioning" God at all times), which other Jewish thinkers in Spain (like Ibn Gabirol) had deemed

5. See *Peirush Ha-Ramban 'al ha-Torah*, ed. and with a commentary by Ch. Chavel (Jerusalem: Mossad Harav Kook, 1960), 2:385.

6. This point is made by Nachmanides himself in this passage.

a cherished ideal. It is also notable that Nachmanides's ideal of having God in one's mind or thought (*maḥshavah*) may be an oblique reference to the supernal realm of "Thought"; for this is a heavenly reality mentioned by the Kabbalists of Provence,[7] and it would have had a special resonance in Gerona[8]—where Nachmanides was a renowned mystical adept. Thus, in a remarkable way, Moses's admonition to the common person is transformed into an elite ideal of a singular and constant God consciousness, namely, that one should strive to be alone with God in every single life circumstance.

With this background, we turn to a striking expression of these matters in an early Ḥasidic homily, initially delivered to a select circle of disciples but later revised and published so that contemporary masses and subsequent generations might have some access to the master's teachings. The homily depicts a tension between two social groups: those who practiced a rigorous spiritual piety but were repelled by acts of impiety in their social domain (and wanted to distance themselves from its invidious aspects), and those ordinary worshippers who wished to remain within the communal fold and follow the social regulations of the Law. The teacher engages these differences and tries to formulate several resolutions to the issue. It is likely that several of these proposals were delivered over several years, but they have been melded together in the redaction that has been preserved. We shall therefore read the topics and solutions sequentially in the form

7. For a discussion of these early usages, see G. Scholem, *The Origins of the Kabbala* (Philadelphia: Jewish Publication Society of America, 1987), 270–77.

8. Of particular note in this context is the commentary of R. Azriel of Gerona on Babylonian Talmud, *Ta'anit* 16a, where he states that in focused prayer one's *maḥshavah* spreads out and ascends to its source; and how the earlier pietists would "mention" or "recite" (*mazkirin*) their words, and because of their *hazkarah u-maḥashavah deveiqah* (recitation and cleaving thought), their words would ascend until they opened heavenly channels of blessing that flowed down into the world. The parallel with Nachmanides's comment is obvious. For R. Azriel's remark, see *Peirush ha-Aggadot le-Rabbi 'Azriel*, ed. I. Tishbi (Jerusalem: Magnes Press, 1983), 39–40. Tishbi also adduces the observation by G. Scholem in "Der Begriff der Kawwana in der alten Kabbala," *Monatschrift für die Geschichte und Wissenschaft des Judentums* 78 (1934): 501n1.

that they have been edited—for it was in this collated form that they were disseminated among the wider public. This notwithstanding, a thematic development and harmonization of positions is discernible (and it will guide the ensuing presentation).

Spiritual Instructions and Social Ideals

The collection of homilies to be considered are by the Ḥasidic master Rabbi Kalonymos Kalman Epstein of Krakow (1754–1823) and preserved in his collected teachings called *Ma'or va-Shemesh* (first published in Breslau in 1842 and frequently thereafter).[9] His teachings are especially influenced by his major teacher, Rabbi Elimelekh of Lizhensk (1717–1786/87), who was sent by his master, R. Dov Ber of Mezeritch, to spread Ḥasidism throughout Poland. R. Epstein also considered himself to be a disciple of other Polish and Galician masters, and his teachings reflect several strands of second and early third generation Ḥasidism in eastern Galicia.[10] The entire homily is a series of comments on verses from Leviticus 19, recited on the Sabbath Torah lection of *Qedoshim*. As remarked, this series of teachings probably reflects distinct or independent homilies, but these are now collated into a coherent sequence and present a distinctive Ḥasidic "take" on a number of key religious topics. The range of sources cited or alluded to is quite broad and includes the work of Maimonides and R. Isaac Luria as well as the oral teachings of Rabbis Elimelekh and Dov Ber. This content suggests an initial presentation to an elite coterie of disciples even though the teachings are now formulated in a popular style with a minimum of esoteric allusions. In this way the content would have been instructive beyond the immediate circle of original listeners—particularly by a laity that came in contact with the emergent world of Ḥasidic doctrine via popular preachers and the printed book.[11] But despite these secondary transformations, one

9. I shall be citing from *Sefer Ma'or va-Shemesh, Ha-Shalem Ha-Mefo'ar* (Jerusalem: Machon Even Yisrael, 1992), 2:363a–67b.

10. For a concise overview, see A. Aescoly, *Ha-Ḥasidut be-Folin* (1954; reprint, Jerusalem: Magnes Press, 1999).

11. On the phenomenon of publication and distribution of these oral teachings, see Z. Gries, *Ha-Sefer ke-Sokhen Tarbut ba-Shanim 1700–1900* (Tel Aviv: Ha-Kibbutz Ha-Me'uḥad, 2002).

can still perceive traces of the oral style and intonation of the original presentation—both via the pedagogical emphases of the preacher and the modes of thematic repetition.

For presentation purposes, I shall cite the opening portion verbatim, since it provides the fulcrum of the entire teaching, and thereafter I will present the structure of the various other teachings through partial paraphrases and a selected translation. The overall structure is subdivided into four parts: Part 1, the Prologue, introduces the discussions of Leviticus 19:2; Part 2 is composed or three units dealing with the meaning of this verse; Part 3 has two units that deal with two laws found in Leviticus 19:3; and the concluding unit, Part 4, is made up of a single section dealing with laws found in Leviticus 19:23–25.

Prologue

> And the Lord spoke to Moses, saying [Lev. 19:1], "Speak to all the congregation of Israel, and say to them: Be holy (*qedoshim tiheyu*), for I the Lord your God am holy (*qadosh*), etc." [v. 2]. [Regarding this verse,] Rashi of blessed memory commented: This teaches that this [lectionary] portion was recited in a public gathering (*be-haqheil*), since it contains most of the core Torah regulations (*gufei Torah*); hence [the injunction] "Be holy" means: "be *perushim,* etc." Now [adds the Ḥasidic master] the words of Rashi require explication. What do they teach us by this formulation, since this portion was recited in a public gathering? And it is moreover a reasonable implication that all the commandments that are practiced by the entirety of Israel were [similarly] said in a public gathering (*be-haqheil*).

The homily opens with this prologue. Rashi's comment, which is actually a direct citation from *Midrash Torat Kohanim* 1.1, is triggered by the key Scriptural reference to a public gathering for "all the congregation of Israel"—one that serves to emphasize that Leviticus 19 includes a number of central laws for communal practice.[12] In actual

12. Two classical medieval commentators, R. Shimshon (the Ra"sh) of Sens and R. Avraham b. David (the Ra'avid), both stress that the pericope was enunciated *be-haqheil*, "for it is not like other units," wherein Aaron learned it first from Moses,

fact, Rashi's comment goes beyond the terse comment adduced here and specifies that to "be *perushim*" means to be separated from "illicit sexual acts and sins" (and just this is the way this passage, cited in the halakhic midrash *Torat Kohanim*, is explained by Rabbeinu Hillel ben R. Eliakim of Greece, who was a student of Rashi).[13] By not adducing this additional clarification, Rashi's comment is intentionally truncated; and instead of being a normative admonishment of restraint, R. Kalonymos initiates a broader consideration of the religious asceticism (unqualified, the word *parush* refers to a person who has "withdrawn" from the community for various reasons). By stating that "the words of Rashi require explication," the preacher prepares to consider the complex interrelationships between asceticism and communal practice. The condensed citation of Rashi is therefore both rhetorically intentional and tendentious.

Part 1

The first interpretation by R. Kalonymous takes up a structure that the other units will follow.[14] It includes (1) a citation and discussion from an authoritative thinker or teacher, (2) a citation and discussion of a passage from classical Midrash (*Leviticus Rabba*), (3) a specific interpretation of a passage from Leviticus 19, and (4) an application of the teaching to the spiritual act of *devequt*,[15] or "attachment" to God.

---

then taught it to his sons, then to the elders, and finally to the people—the chain of instruction noted in the *Babylonian Talmud*, tractate *'Eruvin* 54b. See in *Sifra de-Vai Rav hu Torah Kohanim 'im Peirushei Rabboteinu Ha-Rishonim Ha-Ra'av"d ve R"Sh. Mi-Sens* (Jerusalem: Sifra, 1959), 86a.

13. See the edition of *Sifra de-Vai Rav hu Torat Kohanim . . . 'im Peirush . . . Rabbeinu Hillel b"R Eliakim*, edited by S. Koletditzky (Jerusalem, 1961), pt. 2, 39a. In his comment R. Hillel actually refers to illicit acts and "all forbidden things (*issurin*) in the Torah"; whereas Rashi speaks of "transgressions (*'aveirot*)."

14. See *Sefer Ma'or va-Shemesh*, 363a–64a.

15. The topic of *devequt* is repeated in various ways and referring to various techniques in this collection of homilies. For the religious theme overall with a focus on Ḥasidic themes, see G. Scholem, "Devekuth, or Communion with God," in his *The Messianic Idea in Judaism and Other Essays on Jewish Spirituality* (New York: Schocken Books, 1971), 203–27. For a conspectus on this topic in early Ḥasidism and its place in the teachings of a contemporary of R. Kalonymus Epstein in eastern Galicia, see M. Krassen, *Uniter of Heaven and Earth: Rabbi Meshullam Feibush Heller of Zbarazh and the*

In this case, the master first turns to a passage adduced from Maimonides's *Mishneh Torah, Sefer Ha-Mada'* (*Hilkhot De'ot* 6.6).[16] The discussion in question deals with the importance of living within a civilized province, and stresses that "a person must (*tzarikh*) always conjoin with righteous persons and live near scholars in order to learn from their ways." This means moving to such locales when the people in one's environs are bad or don't follow "an upright path" of life. And if this proves unfeasible or impossible, "one should dwell by himself alone (*yeḥidi*)"—even to the extent of leaving habitable places and living in the desert."

This explicit allowance for ascetic withdrawal in extreme circumstances is transformed by R. Kalonymos. He begins with a paraphrase of the source and key terms (even stressing that "one must flee" bad environments and "separate (*lifrosh*) oneself" from the rabble. By alluding to the term of withdrawal, the preacher hints at the problematic issue of being *perushim* (engaged in ascetic withdrawal) from the community. The preacher adds that such acts of separation are only advisable in those cases where such behaviors would not "prevent" (or "impede"; *me'aqvim*) the proper communal "worship" (*'avodah*) of God, since (he stresses) one can only achieve the "higher holiness" (*ha-qedushah ha-'elyonah*) when "one cleaves" (*yidbaq 'atzmo*) to true worshippers and joins "together (*yaḥad*)" with them in communal prayer. The ensuing citation from the Talmud (*b. Berakhot* 49b), that one should bless God among a "multitude (*rov*) of the congregation (*qahal*)" reinforces his point. In context, the Mishnah cited means that the Name of God that one uses in the "Blessing after Meals" varies relative to the number of the participants. R. Kalonymos adduces it to emphasize that one should (ideally) bless God in a public quorum, since the degree of holiness one attains is related to whether one prays alone of with a congregation. The implication of the Scriptural lemma (Lev. 19:2) is thus: to "be holy" by praying in a communal setting. Accordingly, the preacher concludes by warning that "if one isolates himself (*yevodded 'atzmo*)," as a solitary, "he will [thereby] be separate

---

Rise of Hasidism in Eastern Galicia (Albany: State University of New York Press, 1998), chaps. 2–3.

16. See the critical edition of *The Mishneh Torah,* bk. 1, ed. M. Hyamson (New York, 1937).; and also *Mishneh Torah,* ed. S. Fraenkel (Bnei Brak, 1995), 1, ad loc.

(*yifrosh*) from the community (*tzibbur*)."[17] The issue condemned is thus not ascetic withdrawal (in principle) so much as self-isolation from the required ideal of communal worship (and the special holiness that it accrues).

Given this point, it is notable that the master stresses that one should "cleave" (*dabbeq*) to those who serve God, since one cannot "merit *qedushah*" in isolation. No doubt this riposte is directed against certain ascetic trends in his day that considered ascetic withdrawal a way to attain the highest level of holiness. To counter that conclusion, R. Kalonymos adduces a passage from *Midrash Leviticus Rabba* (24.9).[18] In context, that source proposes and rejects the following interpretation of Leviticus 19:2 (the command to "be holy"): "One might suppose [that this exhortation means] 'be holy—like Me'; therefore, Scripture (adds) 'for I am holy' to teach you that 'My holiness is higher (*le-ma'alah*) than your holiness.'"

Originally, this teaching was preached to delimit any sense of *imitatio dei* with regard to this ideal. But the Ḥasidic master explains it differently. One might think that if one were commanded "to isolate oneself alone" (*le-hitbodded le-hiyot be-yaḥid*) it would be possible to attain the "higher holiness"; therefore, Scripture adds "for *I* am holy," which is to teach that "My holiness" is superior to yours—for God alone is "one and unique" (*yaḥid u-meyuḥad*). And to reinforce this critique, R. Kalonymos adds, that a worshipper can only "draw down" (*le-hamshikh*) the "holiness of God" on himself within a "collective congregation (*be-haqheil yaḥad*)"—where one is "in social solidarity." Presumably the teacher evokes this "higher holiness" on the basis of the phrase *qedushah ila'ah* found in the *Book of Zohar* (on this Torah portion)—but in adducing it he ignores its original context (regarding Divine unity) and emphasizes the liturgical ideal of accessing

17. This refers to *Mishnah Avot* 2.4 (in the name of Hillel): *al tifrosh min ha-tzibbur* (do not separate yourself from the community). In his commentary on this passage (2.5 in his text), Maimonides again avers that "it is not proper to separate oneself from the community except because of *sheḥitutam*, their destructive ways." See in *Mishnah 'im Peirush Rabbeinu Moshe ben Maimon*, ed. Y. Kafiḥ (Jerusalem: Mosad Harav Kook, 1965), *Seder Niziqin, Avot*, p. 276.

18. See *Midrash Vayiqra Rabba*, ed. M. Margulies (Jerusalem: Wahrmann Books, 1972), 2:565.

the holiness of God through theurgical prayer (the drawing down of Divine energy into the community).[19] So doing, R. Kalonymos interprets the old Midrash passage in a mystic manner; for now God's holiness is not simply something "superior" but is an entity in the "supernal heights" (*le-ma'alah*)" and ontologically superior to any earthly holiness. To achieve this spiritual level, he avers, one must be in a worshipping community. Thus, the ritual act of "cleaving" to fellow worshippers in communal prayer is elevated above all else and is deemed the sole means of "drawing down" Divine blessings "on" oneself. In this polemic, individual and social spirituality are integrated. All the cited sources are reformulated to enforce this theological point. Indeed, even the ideal of "drawing down" Divine sanctity is conjoined to this communal value.

The second interpretation of the biblical verse deepens the spiritual issues involved[20] and addresses the concern that individual contemplation has no place in this new communal ideal. The new exegetical point begins with the recitation of Leviticus 19:2, and invokes another passage from *Midrash Leviticus Rabba* 24.4 that explained the Scriptural citation as if it had God exhort Moses, "Go to the Israelites and say to them: My children just as I am *parush* so should you be *perushim*; [and] just as I am *qadosh* so should you be *qedoshim* [as Scripture says]: *qedoshim tiheyu* (become holy)!" One must "be astonished" (*tamoah me'od*), by this teaching, says the Ḥasidic master, since it flies in the face of the preceding polemic. R. Kalonymos wonders whether this can be meant seriously, for how can an individual or community "be holy" like God, or even *parush* like Him? Stymied, he has no recourse other than to interpret the midrashic teaching in a straightforward manner (*'al pi peshuṭo*), and in so doing he produces a novel and paradoxical conclusion.

The teacher begins with the observation that though there are many ways to worship God, the central way is to worship God out of

19. See *Zohar* 3.81a.

20. See *Sefer Ma'or va-Shemesh*, 344a–b.

love in order to arrive at "*devequt* with God." Now many people (he adds) naturally think that the assured path to spiritual "attachment" is by way of ritual isolation (*hitboddedut*), alone in one's room—neither speaking nor looking at any person. But this is not the "true" way, he says, since it is possible to follow this practice for years and not attain the spiritual goal. He bolsters his assertion by referring to an exegesis of Jeremiah 23:24 that he heard from his own master, Rabbi Elimelekh. The verse is ironic: it refers to a query by God that even were a person to hide in isolation, wouldn't He still see him? And the polemical explication is derisive. For if a person were to engage in ascetic isolation, God would certainly not pay attention to him (the language of the question is inverted into a rhetorical joust)! "True . . . worship," R. Kalonymos stresses, is to join a community of righteous persons; for although "the ideal way" (*ha-'iqar*) is one of "contemplative isolation" (*hitboddedut ha-maḥshavah*), whereby one "thinks" or "continuously" attaches their thought "upon God's exalted Divinity," it is nevertheless possible for one to "cleave (*yidbaq*) to God in one's mind" while in a group setting—by imagining (*yidmeh*) that one is alone with God and devoid of human contact![21] Indeed, performing such a private meditation during communal prayer will lead to the highest isolation (not of one's body but of one's mind) with God alone. The supreme ideal is thus to be *parush*, or "separated" in one's mind or "thought" (*maḥshavto*)—in a state of contemplative isolation.[22] Just as R. Kalonymos used Maimonides in his earlier teaching, so he now adduces Rabbeinu Baḥye ibn Paquda to support this ascetic ideal of mental asceticism within the community.[23] (And certainly one can also hear the influence of Nachmanides's ideal of attachment to "Thought" cited earlier, together with the vaunted ability to simultaneously engage in worldly matters.)

21. Recall Maimonides's person ideal in *Guide* 3.51, cited above, regarding the ideal of solitude and limited social contact.

22. For the notion of *hitboddedut* as mental concentration in earlier sources (and not only as physical isolation), see the discussion of M. Idel, "*Hitboddedut* as Concentration in Ecstatic Kabbalah," in *Jewish Spirituality from the Bible Through the Middle Ages*, ed. A. Green (New York: Crossroads, 1986), 1:405–38; an earlier, more extensive Hebrew version, appeared in *Da'at* 14 (1985): 35–82.

23. See his *Sefer Ḥovot ha-Levavot*, translated from the Arabic by Y. Kafiḥ (Jerusalem: Feldheim, 1984), Gate 9, .chap 5 (esp. the end).

It is thus evident that R. Kalonymos has rhetorically flipped the midrashic passage he cited; for now the "plain-sense" is its "inner-spiritual sense." And if one were also to wonder how one can be *parush* "like God," the answer is a theological tour de force. The Ḥasidic preacher states that although God "fills all the worlds . . . and there is no place devoid of Him," God is totally "separated" (*muvdal*) from all "materiality" (*geshem*). Similarly, every person should strive to "be" (*tiheyu*) spiritually separated from material matters. The ideal is "to be *parush*" even within the community by being *davuq* ("attached") to the Divine name and by not mingling with their "physical" or "corporeal" nature (*be-gashmiyutam*). It is an ideal of spiritual interiority requiring a maximum of mental focus while praying in the midst of society. One may thus perceive a progression from the first interpretation to the second and note its assertion of a radical duality been corporality and spirituality. One comes to "be like" God through a purified mind and spirit—an inner separation from worldliness and a refined attachment to God Alone.

The third interpretation expands the ideal of mental attachment to God[24] and provides a technique for its enactment in all circumstances. This exegetical development opens with an explication of the Midrash adduced earlier from *Leviticus Rabba* 24.9, in which God asserted that "My holiness is higher (*le-ma'alah*) than your holiness (*mi-qedushatkhem*)." We noted earlier that the reference there to Divine superiority was transformed and given a mystical valence (referring to the supernal heights), and that the emphasis was on a theurgical access to Divine holiness through communal prayer. This mystical aspect is further developed by an interpretation that R. Kalonymos says he heard from Rabbi Dov Ber in his youth. His report requires explication. It states that God's holiness is the higher one precisely "because Israel's *qedushah* on high is through their good deeds" here on earth; that is, "because you [Israel] sanctify yourselves[on earth] below." Nothing more is stated, but the mystic implication is that God's

24. *Sefer Ma'or va-Shemesh,* 364b–65b.

holiness on high is *affected* by Israel's acts of sanctity in the world below. This mystical assertion is made by reinterpreting the comparative adverb *mi-* (than)—in the expression *mi-qedushatkhem*—as agential (in the sense of "through" or "by means of"). The new point is that God's sanctity is influenced by means of Israel's deeds of sanctity on earth. The causative effect is vertical, from below to above (and the ritual inducement of Divine power is effectuated by collective ritual actions—not individual meditation).

The preacher does not elaborate on this radical reinterpretation but merely says that it is "possible to give a bit of support" to this reading from another direction. He then launches into a mystical rereading of Psalm 104:24, which says, regarding the creation, that God "made all [things] with wisdom (*be-ḥokhmah*); the [entire] earth is filled with Your creation." Understanding the phrase "with" wisdom to mean "by means of" (supernal Divine) Wisdom, R. Kalonymos presents a teaching of the sixteenth-century theosophist known as the "Ari" (R. Isaac Luria), who said that *Ḥokhmah* ("wisdom") is the most superior of all gradations emanating from God and is also the most primary element in the creation, since all things were created from its transcendent spiritual vitality. Accordingly, if a person were to "contemplate" (*yistakel*)[25] on the "Divine Wisdom" inherent in all things—by which "they live and are sustained"—they could "arrive at this most supernal Wisdom" (*ḥokhmah ila'ah*), and then, "being connected (*davuq*)" to it, "draw down" (*limshokh*) from this Source all manner of worldly benefits. Based on this reading of the Scriptural verse from Psalms, an adept is taught that one could conjoin with God above through attachment to the (inherent and omnipresent) sphere of Divine Wisdom in the creation. Indeed, it is from this supernal dimension (of *Ḥokhmah*) that the Divine soul-force joins human worshippers to God, to "inflame the hearts" (*le-hitlahev ha-levavot*) of these worshippers and induce spiritual ecstasy. Thus, becoming holy "like" God now means being attached to the Divine dimension of Wisdom in all things—it being their true supernal vitality. This ideal of the spiritual elite is now extended as a mode of contemplative access for all

25. This usage is akin to the use of Aramaic *istakkel* in the *Zohar*, though *histakkel* does mean "contemplate" in early rabbinic sources (cf. *Mishnah Avot* 3.1).

worshippers. Hereby, R. Kalonymos not only wishes to incorporate the mystical elite into the community through contemplative ideals during communal prayer but also to encourage the common worshipper to attain spiritual heights during their public worship.

But one may still ask how, apart from its teaching of an expanded notion of spiritual conjunction with God, the master's words find support in the teaching of R. Dov Ber. Precisely this is the focus of the final rhetorical turn of this section. The homilist states that it is "known" (among mystical adepts) that the word *qadosh* is a synonym of *ḥokhmah* (*Zohar* 2.121a). Hence the meaning of the exhortation to "be holy" in the Scriptural citation means to "be" attached to the Divine sphere of Wisdom (which is also God, who is also called *Qadosh*), and thereby (through one's attachment to the principle of Wisdom in all existence) to "draw down" "vitalities and benefits" into this world. In this way, the puzzling passage in the Midrash takes on a new meaning: namely, that God's *qedushah* (holiness) can be drawn down to earth through the ritual acts of *qedushah* performed by the people Israel. The emphasis is not merely on ritually activating the Divine level from below but on drawing it down (by theurgical meditation) from on high. This contemplative act is special, for it goes beyond attaching one's mind to the vital principle of God in all things. Indeed (as we are now informed) it is a practice that also "effectuates (*tif'alu*) great and sacred mystical unifications (*yiḥudim*) in all the worlds; and even brings pleasure to God, Who spoke and the world came into existence"![26]

In this way, R. Kalonymos has it both ways: a meditative attachment to "Divine Wisdom" by all persons (the entire community of Israel addressed by the biblical command) *and* by those initiated into the most recondite acts of mystical theurgy. It is thus evident that this contemplative ideal remained a fundamental substratum for R. Kalonymos and his disciples. The esoteric import is that human attachment to God may not only induce worldly beneficence but a Divine benefit as well. We are thus left with a further resonance of the Midrash taught by R. Dov Ber; namely, that God's holiness is influenced

26. On the beginning of a shift away from Kabbalistic unifications in early Ḥasidism, see J. Weiss, "The Kavvanoth of Prayer in Early Hasidism," in his *Studies in Eastern European Hasidism* (Oxford: Littman Library, 1985), 95–125.

by the meditative acts of Israel and that human deeds can actually elicit Divine bliss (*naḥat ruaḥ*) on High.

Part 2

The first interpretation of the next part of this homiletic ensemble turns to an example of the "fundamental laws of Torah" (*gufei Torah*), found in the liturgical portion of *Qedoshim*.[27] It seems originally to have been an independent unit, since it is concerned to clarify the relationship between the initial commandment to "*be holy*" (v. 2) and the ensuing exhortation that "a person shall fear his mother and father" (v. 3)—but does so in a distinctly esoteric manner. What is the import of this conjunction of verses? The preacher offers a transitional link with the phrase, "on the basis of the preceding [discussion about 'being holy']," one can understand the verse "a person shall fear his mother, etc." This phrase would seem to invite some form of pious explication as often occurs in classical rabbinic sources. But R. Kalonymos, remaining true to his interest in mystical-meditative modes of relating to God, takes the discussion to an arcane level. He begins by summarizing key points of the earlier unit—that a person attached to the Wisdom of God will be enflamed with the love of God—and adds that "it is known that *Ḥokhmah* [Wisdom] and *Binah* [Understanding] are two [supernal] companions who are never separated."[28] With this phrase, the preacher invokes an exceptionally esoteric teaching and exalts the parental references of father and mother in Scripture to a cosmic-heavenly domain; namely, that the two gradations (*Ḥokhmah*, a "masculine modality" of Divinity; and *Binah*, a "feminine modality") are understood as the "supernal parents" of all being. They are known in classic mystic sources as "father and mother" (*Zohar* 2.281a) insofar as they conjointly symbolize (as primordial archetypes) a mythical-mystical way of alluding to the engendering and propagating dimensions of all Reality. On this basis, R. Kalonymos teaches that a person who wishes to ascend to the Divine source of

27. *Sefer Ma'or va-Shemesh*, 365b–66a.

28. The original wording of "two companions that are never separated" is *trein re'in dela mitparshin*. On the related motif, cf. Y. Liebes, "*Trein urzilin de-ayalta'. Derashato ha-Sodit shel Ha-Ari Lifnei Moto*," *Jerusalem Studies in Jewish Thought* 10 (1994): 113–69.

all being can only do so through acts of "repentant-return [to God] in love"—which involves turning to God with reverential "fear" (or *yir'ah*), since it is from the supernal gradation of *Binah* (which symbolizes the reparative integration of all being within Divinity) that Divine "judgments" (or *dinim*) come. Speaking thus, the master signals that the "loving gifts" of God's laws are entwined with "legal punishments" for their malpractice. Hence, one must come to God with the spiritual consciousness of the mystic conjunction of Love and Fear in the Godhead. Speaking this way about the love and fear of one's parents (father and mother), the Ḥasidic master suggestively evokes in his listeners the famous rabbinic explication of the difference between the formulation of parental obedience in Leviticus 19:3 (which speaks of the "fear" of parents and mentions the mother before the father) and that found in Exodus 20:12 (which commands one to "honor" their parents, and puts the father before the mother). According to the explanation found in the Babylonian Talmud (*B. Qedushin* 30b), the difference between the two is pedagogical, since (it is presumed) that one would naturally fear one's father and honor or love one's mother. By inverting this "natural" order, Scripture (we are told) wishes to stress the duty to love and fear both parents. On this basis, R. Kalonymos teaches that this double disposition should also condition one's theological disposition and that the love and fear of God should be realized as entwined or integral duties.[29] One is to love God through reverential fear and obedience and fear God through loving devotion and obedience. The spiritual emotions are deemed one and inseparable. Filial piety thus has profound supernal effects and implications.

Having dealt with this spiritual matter, the commandment to love and fear one's parents is linked to the exhortation to "be holy" and is mystically explicated on this basis. The teacher begins by stating that this exhortation enjoins one to be *davuq* (spiritually attached) to supernal Divine "Wisdom" and "Understanding." This is explained to mean that the worshipper should seek (mystically) to conjoin the Divine levels of "Father" and "Mother," which (as just noted) symbolize the holy and supernal dimensions of "Love" and "Fear." And

29. This correlation between attitudes to parents and to God also appears in an old rabbinic explication of Exodus 20: 12. See *Mekhilta de-Rabbi Yishmael*, edited by H. Horovitz and I. Rabin (Jerusalem: Bamberger & Wahrman, 1960), 231.

furthermore, immediately following the commandment of parental devotion (in v. 3a), there occurs the injunction that the worshipper should "observe My Sabbaths" (v. 3b). Rather than regarding this conjunction as a non sequitur, this commandment is interpreted to make the same mystical point as the prior one about two parents—since "it is known" that on the Sabbath one can attain the spiritual gradations of both Father and Mother. This elusive statement is based on the fact that the word *Sabbaths* appears here in the plural and thus (states the master) does not indicate all the Sabbaths of the year but rather specifies that on this one day a devotee may ascend to the levels of both Wisdom (*Ḥokhmah*) and Understanding (*Binah*), the first being the gradation of Love, and the second the gradation of Fear (alluded to by the verb *observe*). Thus the second phrase in verse 3 contains the same double mystical reference as the first (regarding parental obedience), and both actions are enjoined by the initial exhortation to "be holy" (v. 2). Given these valences, there can be no doubt that R. Kalonymos is speaking to those disciples for whom the esoteric (contemplative) meaning of Scripture and its observance was of major significance. It also indicates that a worshipper could be engaged in public piety (with one's parents) and worship (on the Sabbath) and retain a solitary focus on God. Through these distinct acts of religious obedience and their integral contemplative conjunctions, the multiplicities of existence could be reintegrated and restored to their primordial Divine source.

The second interpretation of Part 2 also takes up the conjunction between the commandment to "be holy" and to "fear his father and mother," and between the latter and the commandment to "observe My Sabbaths."[30] As before, this homily concerns the mystical valences of "Love and Fear" and "Father and Mother" noted earlier but adds a theological twist. To properly arrive at the gradations of Love and Wisdom, an individual must first pass through Fear and Understanding (symbolized by *Binah* or Repentance—lower on the hierarchical

30. *Sefer Ma'or va-Shemesh*, 366a–b.

scale of Divine gradations). According to R. Kalonymos, an individual's penitent return to God requires the spiritual disposition of reverence (before love) as its precondition. This sequence is linked to the commandment about the Sabbath in Exodus 20:5, since its use of the verb *zakhor* (remember) was taken to allude to the masculine term *zakhar* (male), which points to the Divine gradation of Male-Father, whereas the later Sabbath commandment in Deuteronomy 5:12 uses the verb *shamor* (observe; guard), and its formulation was taken to refer to the Divine gradation of Female-Mother. Hence, the Sabbath has two mystical dimensions (Female and Male), and, accordingly, one must come to the higher of the two (Father-Love) through its lower counterpart (Female-Fear) by being diligently on "guard" and "examining one's deeds" during the week. The commandment to fear and love one's parents thus parallels the two dimensions of the Sabbath in both their dual structure (sequence) and form (content). The spiritual upshot is that a worshipper lives on two levels: the earthly and the supernal, which are mystically integral to each other.

R. Kalonymos makes this esoteric truth explicit throughout his sermon. By conjoining the most exoteric or public aspect of worship with a more esoteric dimension, the master addresses two religious constituencies simultaneously: the average worshipper, concerned with the public performance of the Law, and the contemplative elite, correspondingly concerned with supernal acts of personal consciousness. In a remarkable act of exegetical pedagogy, the master conjoins the two and establishes the new ideal for his mystical fellowship: a new integrated "governance of the solitary."

Part 3

The final unit of the homiletic series focuses on laws in Leviticus 19:23–25, specifically those dealing with planting trees in the land of Israel and the absolute prohibition of eating any of their fruit during the first four years after planting (in the fourth year the fruit must be a sacred donation) or from deriving any benefit or personal pleasure from it. Only in the fifth year may the produce be consumed and used. The preacher opens by citing this rule and raising questions about its import. As elsewhere, R. Kalonymos's concern is not to expound on the law as such but to use the topic to give an instruction bearing on one's spiritual life.[31] In the process, he returns to the theme of the interrelationship between individual and community.

The preacher begins his exposition by narrowing his rhetorical strategy on a selective presentation of the sermonic composite on this passage found in *Midrash Leviticus Rabba* 25.1.[32] The format there follows the ancient form of old rabbinic (homiletic) proems: it first cites the Scriptural citation (here: "And when you come into the land you shall plant"; Lev. 25:23), and then juxtaposes it to a passage from the Writings (here: "It is a tree of life to those who hold fast to it" [*maḥaziqim bah*]; Prov. 3:18). The hermeneutic strategy is to arouse curiosity about the correlation and then develop a new instruction through various analogies or parables. In the present case, the cotext was chosen to counterpoint a law about tree planting with a metaphor about a tree, and this choice was exploited for full rhetorical effect. R. Kalonymos hits his rhetoric stride directly. After stating that the conjunction of these two passages is "very puzzling," he cites a portion of the old rabbinic homily to highlight the issues involved: first, by stating that the verb *hold fast* is problematic, since one would have expected a reference to an act of "labor";[33] and second, by remarking that the midrash is verbose and never explains the linkage between its elements. Now the teacher is certainly correct in strictly formal terms; but he is also disingenuous, because every rabbinic audience would know that the tree of life mentioned in the cotext from Proverbs refers (symbolically) to the Torah.[34] This aside, the queries serves the preacher's rhetorical purpose, and he goes on to say that he will resolve the various problems *'al pi peshuṭo*, by interpreting the passage "according to its straightforward sense." What this means remains to be seen.

31. *Sefer Ma'or va-Shemesh*, 366b–67b.

32. See *Sefer Ma'or va-Shemesh*, 566–69.

33. The verb used is *'ameilim bah*.

34. Among the celebrated passages is *Mishnah Avot* 6.7. Another key instance is in *Midrash Genesis Rabba* 89.13—a passage that R. Kalonymos was certainly familiar with. It discusses the Torah as the Tree of Life and refers to the relations between Issachar (who studies Torah) and Zevulun (who supports him). Precisely this correlation is specified later in the homily (see below). For this passage and commentary, see the edition of J. Theodor and H. Albeck (Jerusalem: Wahrmann Books, 1965), 3:1281, and the extensive notes of *Minḥat Yehuda* (J. Theodor).

The link of this homily to the preceding teachings becomes apparent at the outset. R. Kalonymos begins with the fact that the law about the planting and use of produce from a tree comes into effect upon entrance into the "holy land," where it is possible to "worship God in truth" (this point is stated three times at the outset). He then goes on to say that this beneficial "plus" includes a corresponding "minus," since the bounty of the land and its pleasures can induce a person to forget the true spiritual service of God and "be drawn (*limshokh*) after materiality." This being so, the laws in Leviticus 19:23–25 provide necessary spiritual "counsel" that these beneficences are not for one's personal boon (*bishvil 'atzmo*) but rather serve "to effectuate" (*mashpi'a*) their good for all—most especially the indigent. Serving as a channel for the distribution of the goods of the earth is a spiritual challenge for the worshipper. Hence, says R. Kalonymos, the law comes to advise or "warn" the worshipper that intentions of future social care should be one's spiritual concern at the moment of planting. Accordingly, he states, the sacred goal is to "effectuate" (*le-hashpi'a*) material benefits to others—the physically poor and the "students of Torah." He makes his point with reference to the famous midrashic analogy of Issachar and Zebulun (sons of Jacob-Israel) who supported one another: Zevulun engaged in physical commerce in order to provide material welfare for Issachar so that he might devote himself to study; and reciprocally, the latter's scholarly merits benefited Zevulun's financial welfare (*Midrash Genesis Rabba* 88.9). To support his point, R. Kalonymos sneaks in an allusion to an adage of Ecclesiastes, stating that the "the shelter of wisdom is to be also in the shelter of money" (7:12), and he then proceeds to remark that to work (*'avodah*) for others is difficult, "but through this one may come to the true worship (*'avodah*) of God." One may presume that this popular analogy was not lost on the recipients of the teaching, and similarly, we can presume that the verbs *limshokh* and *mashpi'a* echoed well-known terms for spiritual beneficences. As noted, the issue of effectuating Divine blessings through ritual practice is a theme throughout the various sections of this homiletic ensemble. It would undoubtedly have had a strong resonance here as well.

R. Kalonymos concludes that this counsel to benefit others through one's daily labors is the straightforward meaning of the Midrash, which juxtaposed the law of planting trees to the proverb that "it is a tree of life to those who hold fast (*maḥaziqim*) to it" ("it" refers to this teaching), whose primary intention is to help and support (*maḥaziqim*) others, particularly Torah scholars; and that this spiritual beneficence ("it") will redound to their individual bounty. But inasmuch as it is difficult "to train a person (*le-hargil adam*)" to labor "in support (*le-haḥaziq*) of others, and not to be self-focused (*le-haḥaziq ṭovah le-ʿatzmo*)," Scripture has forbidden all use of and benefit from fruit trees for a set period of time (the first three years as a means of inculcating restraint, and the ritual devotion of the fruit to the Temple on the fourth year to inculcate the virtues of thankfulness). Such acts of selflessness are thus a mode of spiritual service for all, especially the unlettered laborers who were part of the Ḥasidic fellowship. More than this teaching being the "service of God through worldly or physical acts" (*ʿavodah be-gashmiyut*), we have here the spiritual ideal of training persons to divest themselves of material self-interest and elevate this divestment to an act of "true worship." Like the other teachings in this cluster of homilies, this practice emphasizes both personal interiority *and* community. And one will also observe that here, too (as in the first teaching), an allusion to Maimonides slips in—in this instance via the reference to the ideal of self-training through ritual practices and use of the verb *le-hargil.*

Precisely this verb is highlighted by the great sage in a paragraph that concludes a series of exhortations directing a true worshipper to be scrupulous with their habits and traits. "And how should a person train himself (*yargil adam ʿatzmo*) through (acquisition of) these character dispositions (*deʿot*) until they are firmly rooted in him? He should repeatedly exercise all the practices incumbent on him to perform [them] according to the dispositions of the middle way and should return to them continuously until these practices become easy for him and not burdensome—so that these *deʿot* [dispositions] become firmly rooted in his soul" (*Mishneh Torah, Sefer Ha-Madaʿ, Hilkhot Deʿot* 1.7).[35]

35. For a fundamental treatment of the terms *madaʿ* and *deʿah*, and the understanding of the latter as an ethical disposition (with a psychological character), see B. Septimus, "What did Maimonides Mean by Madaʿ?," in *Meʾah Sheʿarim. Studies in Medieval Jewish Studies in Memory of Isadore Twersky*, edited by E. Fleischer, G. Blidstein, C. Horowitz, and B. Septimus (Jerusalem: Magnes Press, 2001), 83–110, esp. 98 (English sec.).

Conclusion

In this notable collection of homilies, the dominant theme is worshipping God and the proper means of doing so. The relationship between an individual and the community is taken up again and again in different variations, and the spiritual challenge for finding the balance between these two poles is repeatedly negotiated. Nevertheless, an overall pedagogy is evident in the final collection. It opens with the problematic of serving God in a spiritually dangerous or negative environment and goes on to give different solutions as to how an individual can be connected to God even within a community of proper worship. The interior life is thus central, but the communal one is fundamental. The competing primacies of one's inner-state of worship (the desire for personal perfection) and communal obligations (as a primary setting for covenantal life) are in constant interplay as the preacher tries to address their integration from a spiritual perspective. The relationship between these values is also evident in the final unit, where the topic focuses on inculcating both interior (personal) values of self-discipline alongside social (group) values of communal care. Throughout, R. Kalonymos reinterprets his Scriptural and rabbinic sources to effect new motivations, new mentalities, and new ideals. For all those addressed (in the event or over time), tradition and normativity are hermeneutically revised. The revaluation and integration of primary religious issues amounts to a veritable reconstitution of Scripture. Spiritual hermeneutics is at the center of this manifold development, where the mediating (even revelatory) voice of the teacher is primary.

10

Spiritual Hermeneutics and Appropriation

THE ḤASIDIC SERMON

Preliminary Considerations

We are born into the manifolds of our family, language, and cultural forms. They compose the intermeshed primacies of our existence, conjoined to circles of belonging and interdependence. The personal "I" is a social "we" from birth, taught to echo sounds and tonalities that expand into a language of social communication whose meanings and structures are imitated and internalized long before they are perceived as communal or conventional forms.[1] It is, initially, only some error and its repair that makes us aware of the language or the behaviors that are culturally fit and acceptable. Thus, one learns the place of certain features within some scheme of values and practice—an ongoing heuristic and exegetical process. This begins within a closed frame of social significations—the sacred canopy of convention and cognition[2]—and we repeatedly strive to resolve the emergent matters of dissonance or rupture that put established matters into question.

1. We begin neither in a social vacuum nor some presumptive notion of "being." A major early formulation of these issues appears in E. Husserl's classic *The Crisis of the European Sciences and Transcendental Philosophy* (1936; Evanston, IL: Northwestern University Press, 1970), 108: "In whatever way we become conscious of the world as universal horizon, as coherent universe of existing objects, we, each 'I-the-man' and all of us together, belong to the world as living with one another in the world; and the world is our world, valid for our consciousness as existing precisely through the 'living together.'"

2. I allude here to the seminal work of P. Berger, *The Sacred Canopy: Elements of a Sociological Theory of Religion* (Garden City, NY: Doubleday, 1967). This study is

These disturbances can range from the sense of linguistic terms handed down by tradition or their value because of some exposure to elements beyond one's pregiven epistemological or axiological framework. When this occurs, strategies of repair require deliberate and socially acceptable methods of reinterpretation. This is especially momentous with regard to canonical norms and texts, especially when the interpretations lay claim to the true or fundamental meaning of a sacred source. The issue is further exacerbated when individuals claim that their explications derive from a spiritual disclosure or personal revelation. In such cases, exegesis may prove to be a radical, culture-amending act—laying claim to a sacred Scripture and its appropriation. Such matters will occupy our attention in the ensuing essay.

Setting the Conceptual Frame

Hermeneutics refers to a pivotal process in the human appropriation of sense and significance.[3] It is primary and formative. Meaning is received through acts of interpretative discernment at both individual and cultural levels. Hermeneutics also refers to the coming to critical self-awareness of the objective and subjective ways that feelings, events, and traditions are assimilated as types of knowledge and understanding. This is particularly the case when the literary or expressive content derives from the past or another culture and one is engaged in attempts to interpret it.

The challenge is to respect the unique autonomy of the datum (as one achieves competence in its lexical or historical components) while also trying to translate its content into a different mindset. Positivistic methods seek to factor out the interpreter as a mediating agent, whereas more subjectively engaged practices often idealize a

built on his earlier conceptual work, *The Social Construction of Reality: A Treatise in the Sociology of Knowledge* (Garden City, NY: Doubleday, 1966).

3. Of particular significance are the works of H-G. Gadamer, *Truth and Method* (New York: Continuum, 1975); and P. Ricoeur, *From Text to Action: Essays in Hermeneutics, II* (Evanston, IL: Northwestern University Press, 2007). Their intellectual importance notwithstanding, both their assumptions and achievements must be reconsidered and reapplied to new contexts—like Jewish religious hermeneutics. This is one of the tasks of the present discussion.

sympathetic connection with the material. Each approach pulls in opposite directions: the one lauding an objective and scientific attitude, the other creative intuition and empathy.[4] Both positions are fraught with difficulties. An analytically negotiated middle ground may provide the best dialectical practice, whereby the interpreter tries to attend to the objective and distinctive nature of the external phenomenon while grappling with its interpretation as a latter-day act of personal engagement and intellectual appropriation.[5] This process must be further accompanied by one of inner translation, which tries to render every interpretative act understandable and meaningful in contemporary terms. Cultural translation is thus an epistemic necessity, engaging the interpreter in the very act of their textual understanding.

To reformulate these considerations in more formal terms, we may state that the hermeneutical act seeks to cross from one's private (and conditioned) epistemic horizon of sense and meaning to a public datum (in nature, culture, and history) distinct from oneself. This requires one to engage the given content by entering a circle of hermeneutical understanding through a process of critical and reflective self-understanding. The interpreter begins by responding to a verbal or thematic element of apparent appeal or significance, and then, in the interpretative process, strives to assess and evaluate the emergent meanings in critical loops of reconstruction (i.e., acts of critique, self-correction, and revision). Gradually, some dominant meaning emerges (to oneself) from the factually "given." But it is vital to bear in mind that this content is never given as such but only makes sense

4. This position is exemplified by the work of W. Dilthey, most notably his *Poetry and Experience*, volume 5 of his selected works, edited by R. Makkreel and F. Rodi (Princeton, NJ: Princeton University Press, 1985). For critiques of the formalist and phenomenological counterthrust, see Ricoeur, *From Text to Action: Essays in Hermeneutics*.

5. The creative oscillation between the intellectual constitution of a text (by an interpreter) and its personal self-constitution is central to W. Iser, *The Act of Reading: A Theory of Aesthetic Response* (London: Johns Hopkins University Press, 1978). Regarding historical construction, cf. M. Thompson, "Reception Theory and the Interpretation of History," *History and Theory* 32 (1992): 248–72.

through the hermeneutical process of "making sense"[6]—through its acts of evaluation and judgment. It is in this way that the content that presents itself for understanding is reformulated as something meaningful; and it is in this way that the interpreter is transformed by the material. Reading texts is a particularly heightened mode of such acts of appropriation and transmission. As a cultural ideal in the humanities, notably in Western culture since the nineteenth century, this is the vaunted process (both personal and cultural) of self-formation (or *Bildung*) through both reading and study. Religious cultures regard such a transformation as a spiritual necessity.

Religious hermeneutics begins with the core presumption of a transcendent spiritual instruction—manifest and latent in a text—to which the self must become attuned. This instruction is deemed life bearing and transformative as such and is believed to be meaningful for every time. The primary task of a reader, therefore, is to appropriate the instruction and its inherent truths. Hermeneutics is a sacred act and process, and textual competence requires instruction in its many layers of tradition and modes of pedagogy beginning with the Divine voice and continuing with the authoritative teachers of its ongoing revelation. The keys of interpretation are themselves deemed latent in the text and are part of its overall spiritual character—be these the technical rules that give coherence and relevance to the content or the spiritual content that allows the Divine words to speak to the soul. Accordingly, in religious contexts, the individual comes to the text as a receptive disciple—not as one who has inherent regency over the material. In this sense, proper interpretation partakes of the revelation of the text for new times, and the religious reader wants to be reformed in its image to become a living expression of the text and to embody its spiritual ideals or ritual practices. Moreover, the spiritual reader comes to texts with the anticipation and expectation of significant

6. For a consideration of some philosophical issues in contemporary hermeneutical phenomenology, see J. Greisch, *Le cogito herméneutique: L'herméneutique philosophique et l'héritage Cartésien* (Paris: Librairie Philosophique J. Vrin, 2000).

instruction as well as the desire to join a chain of teachers who were similarly instructed and transformed.

Thus, to become a receptive religious reader requires one to suspend personal presumptions and privilege and to be initiated into its content. This means that, as a point of departure, one must accept the (sacred) sovereignty of the religious text as a voice of constitutive instruction. But all this is a critical challenge for the modern reader, who asserts an inherent human right to declaim the meaning of all texts from one's native point of view, often without any prior linguistic or spiritual training. Such an assertion starts with the dogmatic presupposition that hermeneutics is a private procedure and that reading generates an endless play of open signifiers. For the religious reader, by contrast, the process of reading and interpretation takes place within a community of belief, memory, and spiritual practice. Indeed, a religious reader engages the text as a spiritual practice and a traditional way to enter such a community. Not the self but a "scripture" and its "sacred order" are primary.[7]

The Ḥasidic Homily (*Derashah*)

The Ḥasidic *derashah* constitutes a distinctive hermeneutic universe with particular challenges of description and explication because of its formative and performative aspects. The very term *derashah* encapsulates these issues. Like the genre *Midrash* and the public rabbinic homilies related to it (whereby explications of Scripture were presented in the synagogue on Sabbaths and festivals), the term in a Ḥasidic religious context also indicates an exposition of Sacred Scripture and its public enactment. And just as rabbinic homilies present and integrate numerous citations from the entire biblical canon, through verbal or thematic associations, in order to produce new meanings of Scripture through the mouth of a rabbinic sage, so also does the Ḥasidic homily build on a vast matrix of sources and reconstitutes them in a living act of interpretation by a holy man—the tzaddik, or saintly teacher of the community. The onset of a homily commonly begins

7. Cf. the considered reflections of P. J. Griffiths, *Religious Reading: The Place of Reading in the Practice of Religion* (New York: Oxford University Press, 1999).

with the citation of the beginning (or other selected phrase) from biblical texts recited on a given Sabbath or festival day. There follows a panoply of sources from the entire rabbinic corpus (both Midrash and Talmud), references to medieval biblical commentaries, or passages from the *Book of Zohar* and the mystical teachings of Rabbi Isaac Luria. The strategy of explication often follows the ways the Ḥasidic masters studied the Talmud and its commentaries by first presenting the textual citations as a series of critical problems to be resolved.

Within a Ḥasidic homily these elements are frequently adduced as rhetorical props to set up a series of spiritual topics of concern to the homilist. In this way a teacher shifts interpretative planes by moving from the exoteric meaning of Scripture to an esoteric reading that induces a cluster of spiritual values that the master wishes to inculcate. Not merely a hermeneutical expert, this *darshan*, or preacher, is the acknowledged spiritual master of a sacred fellowship, and in that role he reveals the inner sense of the passage as a new word of God. Many adepts regarded their teacher's explications as ecstatic speech and often characterize them as *divrei Elohim ḥayyim* (the living words of God). In the Yiddish vernacular, this mode of "teaching Torah" was often referred to as *zogn Toyreh* (speaking Torah), for it was through the mouth of their holy master that the words of Scripture were deemed to be revealed anew.[8] This charismatic aura remained even after the original oral presentation was published as a written text. Thus, it was not merely the canonical status of the homily or its later appearance in the sacred language of Hebrew that made these literary anthologies into a *sefer*, or "holy book." It was distinctively their origin as exegetical revelations of God. As a conduit of living Divine revelation, the mouth of the tzaddik was perceived as a holy font, a shofar (or ritual instrument) that conveyed the "unceasing" Divine "voice" of Sinai (Deut. 5:19) to the covenant people in the here and now.[9]

8. The oral aspect of the Ḥasidic homily has been emphasized by M. Idel, "Hermeneutics in Hasidism," *Journal for the Study of Religion and Ideologies* 9 (2010): 3–16.

9. Aspects of the preceding formulation of revelatory speech converge with those of A. Green, in "The Ḥasidic Homily: Mystical Performance and Hermeneutical Process," in *As a Perennial Spring: A Festschrift Honoring Rabbi Dr. Norman Lamm*, ed. Bentsi Cohen (New York: Downhill, 2013), 241–42.

Let us think hermeneutically about this event, starting with the performance itself. Before and during the preacher's enactment of the words of tradition to his disciples, a multitude of voices (literary and spiritual) from the past coalesce in the cultural soul. The tzaddik creatively reaccesses them, and they become the chords of his voice, vibrating in ever-new combinations to attune the listeners to God's ineffable presence. It is this revelatory feature that makes the attentive tremble and feel the numinous reality of a heavenly voice spoken in their own *mamaloshn*—the colloquial Yiddish vernacular (or "mother tongue") of the home. It was moreover believed that God's feminine presence, denominated as the *Shekhinah*, was present with this instructing word, speaking (veritably) through the "throat" of the holy teacher.[10] Leaving the table or first place of hearing, the disciples spread this word orally to both neighbor and kin—and to further help broadcast the teachings, those who memorized these holy words, or the tzaddik himself, based on both memory and notes, reformulated the originally rendered Yiddish content into Hebrew[11] and then (often a disciple in a later generation) sent it to a printer. With this, the "living word" becomes a "text," no longer resonant with the timbre of the master's Divine voice and reduced to its literary summary—often with references to the lacunae of memory interspersed. Only a revoiced study of these transcriptions—individually or in groups—kept them vibrant and alive. Kissing the holy book at the conclusion of one's study session now replaces the holy hands of the tzaddik and his personal blessing. As a sacred text, the holy "words" of the master have renewed life—and new spiritual potential.

In their new textual settings, the transcribed words of the master are palpably gapped or elliptical, the rhetorical expansions abridged, and the original pauses and sounds erased. Not only has the homily crossed languages and life settings, but it is now present only through

10. For the phenomenon and examples, see R. Shatz-Uffenheimer, *Ha-Ḥasidut Ke-Mystiqah* (Jerusalem: Magnes, 1986), 108, 118–120; for the technical expression of this ecstatic vocalization, see below.

11. An appreciation of the differences between the Yiddish originals and the Hebrew translations can be seen through the evidence assembled by A. Mayse and D. Rieser, "The *Sefer Sefat Emet*, Yiddish Manuscripts and Oral Homilies of R. Yehudah Arieh Leib of Gur," *Kabbalah: Journal for the Study of Jewish Mystical Texts* 33 (2015): 9–43.

these absences that are hermeneutically filled in by the readers' comments, queries, and suppositions. Thus, a living engagement with the voice of the teacher is replaced by a struggle to interpret its condensed relic. The reader is caught in a double bind. One must try to explicate the received layers of sequence of the content by putting oneself at the helm of the hermeneutical flow of meaning. Thus, the voice of study replaces that of the master, which is present only through the act of recitation and interpretation. One is pulled forward by the textual content and backward by puzzlement and the search for its meaning. The prophet Ezekiel (1:14) famously depicted the alternating movement of the fiery angels in heaven as moving *ratzo va-shov*, "back and forth" in both reverent awe and spiritual yearning. Just this phrase was used by latter adepts of a master to denote the dynamics of religious reading—a repeated process of "approach and distance."[12] The sacred aura of the formulation is the spiritual force that draws the listener to the text in hopes of understanding and simultaneously distances them because of the difficulties in its appropriation. The hermeneutical constitution of the reader is directly related to this spiritual process.

The Divine Origins of Speech

What is the source of the teachings proclaimed by the tzaddik? How are the Words of God linked to those of the preacher, and what is the mystical sequence of their emergence? We may consider this in terms of the arcane hermeneutical lore taught by Rabbi Dov Ber of Mezeritch, the foundational force and master of second generation Ḥasidism (in the late eighteenth century). In his homilies, he repeatedly specifies the threefold structure of Divine language from its primal origination to its successive manifestations or expressions. Divine language begins (so to speak) in the supernal worlds and undergoes multiple transformations until it reaches the human world and its articulation through the mouth of Moses. At the primal apex, at the ineffable onset of Divine emanation, an effulgent ray of light emerged from the Absolute font of Infinite Reality—called *Ein Sof* (the "Infinity" beyond

12. For this spiritual phenomenon, see R. Levi Yitzḥaq of Berditchev's comments in his *Qedushat Levi*, edited by M. Derbaremdiger (Brooklyn, NY: Makhon Qedushat Levi, 1996), 1, pp. 9a, 215b.

being). As pure Spirit-Light, this monolithic ray of Divinity expanded and also underwent various modulations or configurations, known as "gradations," or *sefirot*. A Pure Unity thus unfolded through a process of differentiations and/or "contractions" (*tzimtzum*). In the process, the consummate Divine energy was manifested through a series of (ten) balances or realizations of creative power. This transformative sequence ultimately provided the God-given ground of language—indeed all these emergent gradations were themselves transcendent manifestations of Divine self-expression.

The highest gradation is referred to as the World of Thought (or *Maḥshavah*). It is the most transcendental mode of intelligence or mind and thus distinct from its modality of evocation, which only emerges at a subsequent stage of emanation, referred to as the Sphere of Voice (or *Qol*). This Divine modality specifies a prevocalic formulation of thought before its actual articulation or expression. This latter becomes manifest in the lowest gradation, referred to as the World of Speech (or *Dibbur*).[13] This sphere expresses the "event of enunciation," whereby the letters and sounds of language emerge from their inchoate nonverbal dimension and combine in primal vocalic units that contain all the transformative energies later revealed as the Divine word of creation specified in Scripture. This word is therefore a worldly "testament" of all these primal processes—in the image of its Divine model, the Primordial Torah in the Supernal Realms. Accordingly, the sacred instructions of the Torah of Moses are rooted in a series of inner-Divine gradations and are given oral expression through the speech of Moses at Sinai.

In his own worldly acts of interpretation, the tzaddik (like a new Moses) ascends in contemplation through all these heavenly worlds (from *Dibbur* to *Qol*, if not higher) in order to mediate new teachings through contact with the heavenly Torah. By virtue of this mystic inspiration, the tzaddik gives a renewed voice to this transcendental Divine reality and "speaks Torah." The axial interface between the Divine gradations and our world is the sphere of *Dibbur*—and through it God gives expression and instruction to the creation. This realm had

13. For texts on this triad, see his *Maggid Devarav Le-Ya'aqov*, ed. R. Shatz-Uffenheimer (Jerusalem: Magnes Press, 1976), index (pp. 350–51, letters, *otiyot*; 376–77; *'olam ha-maḥshavah, 'olam ha-dibbur*, 381; voice, *qol*).

long been referred to by the more personified cognomen of *Shekhinah*—a feminine expression of God's earthly immanence or presence. In Ḥasidic theology, and that of the Maggid of Mezeritch we have just summarized, special holy men could attain access to this dimension and through their conjunction with it speak new words of God. In this process, we are told, the *Shekhinah* "speaks through [the] throat" of the mystic (*midabberet mi-tokh gerono*). By this means, a supernal hermeneutical emanation is socially embodied and revealed to a community. The tzaddik is a charismatic agent of this exegetical enterprise.[14]

The human receivers of the tzaddik's ecstatic interpretations are doubly constrained. Those who have directly experienced the Ḥasidic master's teachings and exegetical revelations would have often strained to understand their allusive formulations and leaps of imagination, whereas those who received them in their transcribed, written form would have repeatedly struggled with the density of their idiom as remembered and recorded in stenographic shorthand. This being so, it was the task of a spiritual fellowship to devote themselves to the sparks and fragments of their master's *dibbur* and to give them coherence as a type of spiritual pedagogy. Their devotional act of study and interpretation is one of ritual service (or *'avodah*). It begins when a latter-day interpreter engages the *derashah* as a species of Divine revelation and concludes when its content speaks anew to them as devotees of these holy words.[15] These processes of reception, transmission, and interpretation are spiritually constitutive in every sense.

14. An explicit statement on this occurs toward the end of the "Second Introduction" to the teachings of the Maggid by R. Shlomo Lutzker, who brought his master's teachings to publication. See *Maggid Devarav Le-Ya'aqov*, p. 6.

15. Belief that a teacher's words remain effective in all their forms (as living a word and as a residual, textual "trace" or *reshimu*) is based on the creative principle of *koaḥ ha-po'el be-nif'al* (the power [or potential] of [the Divinely creative] action remains [effective] in that [entity] which is acted upon). For a striking teaching by the Maggid on these matters, see *Or Torah* (Brooklyn, NY: Kehot Publishing Society, 1972), 9a. Green, "The Ḥasidic Homily," 239, rightly notes that the publication of the oral teachings is part of the reverence for the written word in Judaism, wherein the study of "holy books" is a religious practice.

Hermeneutical Readings of Ḥasidic *Derashot*

We turn now from a phenomenological description of the Ḥasidic homily to a study of several examples. The purpose of this inquiry is not only to instantiate the dynamic modes of Scriptural interpretation in these expositions but to further exemplify the singular phenomenon of exegetical revelation. Three features will be highlighted: the role of the spiritual teacher as a "new Moses," giving new voice to the words of Torah; the significance of allegory as a means of accommodating the Divine message of Scripture to the spiritual seeker; and the symbolic dimension of the topics and depictions of Torah, which are ultimately archetypes of supernal Divine processes.

The Hermeneutics of Revelation: The Status of the Teacher

As noted, the supernal revelation of Torah was believed to have descended through the gradations of *qol* (voice) and *dibbur* (speech) before it was revealed to Moses at Sinai (Exodus 20:1 states that God "spoke," *ve-yedabber*, His words to Moses), and that this was similarly the gradation through which the inspired tzaddik taught his new words of Torah. This theological process is taken up by a student in the circle of the Maggid, R. Ze'ev Wolf of Zhitomir, in a *derashah* on the Song of Songs (5:13), recorded in his book *Or Ha-Me'ir*. After citing this passage—which states that "his cheeks are like beds of spices, producing thick perfume (*megaddelot merḥaqim*) . . . [and] his lips are like lilies dripping flowing myrrh"[16]—the homily shifts abruptly to another Scriptural citation, this time from Exodus 19:19. This verse forms the (ostensive) basis of the teacher's commentary.[17]

16. As typical in homilies and their transcription, the full verse is not cited; in this case, the second part is most significant, as we shall see.

17. *Or Ha-Me'ir* (originally Korsec, 1798; reprinted, Jerusalem: Even Israel, 1999), 1.272a. This text was adduced by A. Green in "Hasidism and its Response to Change," *Jewish History* 26 (2013): 13 (of online, nonpaginated version) as an example of new claims of spiritual authority. My translation diverges slightly at several points.

"Moses spoke (*yedabber*) and God answered him (*ya'anennu*) in a voice (*qol*)"; [and our sages] were inspired [to explain this, as meaning that God answered Moses "in Moses' own voice."][18] And we must [properly] understand their words, whose [inner sense] is that Moses drew Torah down from the gradation (*beḥinat*) of *Qol* to that of *Dibbur*. And those were the Ten Commandments. Now a Jew [Israelite] might say that it is impossible to comprehend God's supreme Divinity, or His awesome and marvelous secrets, except by the means of their renewal (*beḥinah meḥudeshet*), by means of the reinterpretation of Torah (*'al yedei mah she-meḥadshim ba-Torah*)—whose inner light is revealed (*nitgaleh*) by means of the souls of the *tzaddikim*, who creatively interpret (*meḥadshin*) the Torah's secrets in every generation, according to their needs and those who follow them . . . doing so . . . by means of the permutation [of letters] they employ to create new meanings of Torah.

Now it might seem that once Moses drew Torah down from the gradation of *Qol* to that of *Dibbur* "the word (*devar*) of the king could not be retracted" [Esther 8:8]—that is, once [the word of God] was said, it could not be said again. This is what the sages alluded to when they said, "in Moses' own voice." That is to say, just as [at Sinai], so now, whoever attains spiritual knowledge of his creator (*da'at qono*) is called "Moses"'—as we learn from the expression "Moses, you have spoken well" [b. *Shabbat* 101b].[19] That is to say, through God's great grace the voice that once spoken through Moses may again be heard through the *tzaddiqim* of [each] generation—giving them the power to restore the gradation of *Dibbur* to that of *Qol*—each one according to the needs of their generation and the [spiritual] service appropriate to that time. From that "voice" such a *tzaddik* might activate new permutations (*tzeirufim meḥudashim*) of Torah and thereby give God renewed joys (*ta'anugim meḥudashim*).

In this bold exposition, the hermeneutic authority of the Ḥasidic *derashah* is articulated, for the preacher states that the Torah is renewed in each generation by teachers who attain the degree of

18. This interpretation is based on the Babylonian Talmud, *Berakhot* 45a.

19. When one sage discoursed or taught well, he was given the sobriquet "Moses."

revelatory insight as Moses. Indeed, he remarks that the name Moses is an epithet for any person who could attain such a level of religious consciousness. Just as God (the King) spoke to his prophet Moses, and the assembled nation heard God through this human voice, so again, a teacher might recombine the letters of the original revelation and revivify its message (without changing the primordial "words of the King") for new hearts and souls. In this instance, the homily even provides a Scriptural justification for the revelatory import of the teachings of the tzaddik. As a new Moses, he similarly channels the Divine "voice" that "speaks" through him, his teaching being a renewed and even "renovated" revelation of the Divine letters (that are *meḥuddashim*).

But there is more. It will be observed that although the initial citation was adduced from the Song of Songs (5:13), it was not explicated in the homily, which was based on the citation from Exodus. This matter requires understanding. Normally, in classical midrashic expositions, a Pentateuchal verse from the Scriptural lection is cited first and then followed by a passage from the Writings that provides a striking intertextual corollary that in turn generates a succession of exegetical possibilities. Since the present homily was given by R. Ze'ev Wolf on the festival of Passover, when the Song of Songs was ritually recited, the verse from the Writings takes homiletical precedence. But we are still left to understand the hermeneutical correlation (between the passages). A clue lies in the fact that the Songs verse is part of a larger unit (5:9–16) that depicts the appearance of the "beloved male" (called a *dod*) by the maiden. And ever since rabbinic antiquity, the Song was interpreted as an allegory of the love between God and His bride, Israel (the female in the Song); hence, the *dod* and his ensuing depiction refers to God and His qualities. This noted, we may suppose that this *derashah* invoked Songs 5:13 as its lead verse precisely because of its depiction of the aromatic quality or effulgence that emanated from the *dod*'s lips. And if so, the connection between this passage from the Song of Songs and the verse in Exodus 19:19, is now evident: the Word of God revealed at Sinai was deemed (similar to the allegory portrayed in the Song) a continuously flowing effulgence dripping from God's mouth. So understood, the citation from the Song provides a bold theological complement to the Torah's depiction of Moses's Divinely inspired revelation at Sinai—and thereby, also, warrant for the tzaddik's statement that God speaks anew through every new Moses (himself included).[20] Put otherwise, the preacher linked the two verses (in the context of the holiday recitation of the Song) in order to enunciate a teaching about God's continuous revelation, new and renewed in each generation.

A further indication that the citation in the Song, comparing the beloved's cheeks to a "bed of spices . . . producing perfume (*megaddelot merḥaqim*)" with lips of "flowing myrrh," has hermeneutical resonance, is suggested by its citation in an older exposition found in the *Book of Zohar* (2.254a). Indeed, this medieval source illumines the deeper esoteric valence of our Ḥasidic homily—for we are informed in that account that Moses, whose "lips" were like "flowing myrrh," was granted knowledge of supernal mysteries that included the primordial souls of the greatest (future) teachers of Torah (like R. Akiva). Accordingly, Moses served as a Divine "spirit" (*ruḥa*) of interpretation that would descend through the succeeding generations and become embodied in its holy sages.

Given this precise hermeneutical tally, it is evident that R. Ze'ev Wolf considered himself a new Moses who could attain supernal gradations and effect new permutations of the letters of the Torah. Another verbal tally is also redolent with esoteric import. This one connects the initial part of the citation from Songs 5:13 (that refers the "perfume" (*merḥaqim*) emitted by the Beloved's cheeks) to Isaiah 25:1. The plain sense of this passage speaks in praise of God who "performed wonders, counsels (*'etzot*) from ancient times (*me-raḥoq*)," but the verse had long since been interpreted as an esoteric allusion to the supernal spheres (cf. *Zohar* 1.73a and 3.183b). In the present instance, the six Hebrew words of the citation were applied to the middle six Divine "gradations" of the primordial emanation (often

20. In the same work, R. Ze'ev Wolf comments on Moses levels of access to the Divine *Dibbur* and even *Maḥshavah*, in remarks that reveal more that theoretical knowledge; see *parshat Tzav*, 2.212b–213a. Immediately following this, he recalls seeing the ecstatic preaching of the Maggid, his teacher, and how the "World of *Dibbur*" would "speak through him" (*middaber bo*), and he would even "appear . . . as if he were not at all in this world, and the *Shekhinah* was speaking (*medabberet*)] through his throat" (2.231b). Another student of the Maggid, R. Levi Yitzḥak of Berditchev, gives a detailed account of a contemplative ascent to the Divine worlds, the permutations of letters, and automatic speech (*dibbur*); cf. *Shemu'ah Ṭovah* (Warsaw: M. Lifshitz, 1938), 71b.

designated as the *'etzot* of the supernal hierarchy)[21] through whose channels hermeneutical interpretations are mediated (i.e., these renewed meanings are manifest *me-raḥoq*, from the most "distant" or "primordial" spheres).[22]

We may thus suppose that R. Ze'ev Wolf also understood the passage from the Song of Songs to denote the spiritual qualities that could be imparted to a tzaddik who might thereby "produce" new Divine teachings "from the" (most transcendental) "distant" (*merḥaqim*) gradations. In this way, Songs 5:13 would lend strong esoteric support to the Torah verse reinterpreted in the homily—with the implied caveat that the Moses redivivus of each age drew inspiration from the Divine "counsels" in the supernal heights.[23] In keeping with esoteric propriety, the homilist does not directly refer to these mystical meanings of Songs 5:13 but restricts himself to proclaiming the heavenly attainments of Moses and those (like himself) who bear his mantel. The hidden import of Exodus 19:19 is similarly left for the informed student to discern—a hermeneutical hint to the wise by the tzaddik himself. Properly attuned, the addressees might draw the concealed implication: at Sinai, the earthly Moses "speaks" (*yedabber*) the Divine *dibbur* (revelatory word), and God correspondingly "responds" (or confirms it) with His heavenly "voice" (*ye'anennu be-qol*); but in due time, the avatar of Moses (the tzaddik) "will [again] speak" (*yedabber*) (from the eternal sphere of *Dibbur* through the *Shekhinah*), and God "will [again] respond to him" (*ye'anennu*) from the supernal heights (Divine gradation) of *Qol*.[24]

21. In the Kabbalistic schema alluded to here, the six gradations comprise the spheres from *Ḥesed* to *Yesod* (or "Graciousness" and "Foundation"), from top to bottom. These are part of the middle channels of Divinity, also denominated in Lurianic kabbalah as the configuration of *Ze'ir Anpin*. More symbolically, the number "six" connotes the Hebrew letter *vav*, which is the third letter of the Divine name (the Tetragram).

22. It is also possible, here and in the *Book of Zohar*, that *me-raḥoq* refers to the descent of the "counsels" from the most "distant" point in the hierarchy; namely, from the supreme point of their emergence from *Ein Sof*.

23. The word *'etzot* (or in the Aramaic argot *'itin*) was routinely used to indicate mystical "counsels" or "guidance."

24. This transformation from the Scriptural plain sense to the implied mystic sense trades on the ambiguity of the imperfect verb, which can have the sense of a continuous recurrent present as well as mark a future occurrence. For the former, see *Gesenius'*

The Hermeneutics of Accommodation: The Status of Allegory

In the process of declaiming his "Torah," the tzaddik reveals new spiritual meanings of Scripture to his disciples as well as to the public at large. Since the formulations of Torah are a Divine language, their teachings are capable of being interpreted on multiple levels simultaneously. On the exoteric plane of contextual sense (known as the *Peshaṭ*), one can construe the meanings of Scripture as if it were an ordinary discourse—in the belief that God accommodated His infinite wisdom to a linguistic form that had a popular or public resonance and intelligibility. Thus, even where these formulations appear elliptical or seem dense, it was programmatic (in the words of Rabbi Ishmael) that "Scripture speaks in the language of ordinary human discourse."

Other levels of textual sense sought the more elusive homiletical or allegorical meanings of Scripture. Special significance was thus attributed to these more esoteric layers of the text (the *Remez,* or its allusive hints; and the *Sod,* or its mystical "mystery"). In certain exegetical circles both of these latter levels were deemed a concealed dimension, with access to the former linked to some philosophical or esoteric code and access to the latter restricted to adepts and conveyed by word of mouth to prevent misunderstanding or misuse by outsiders.[25] But what was one to do if a central pedagogical goal was to inculcate larger groups in the spiritual senses of Scripture? The masters of Ḥasidism faced this issue and sought various ways of teaching their mystic theology and religious practices to a broad public. This meant finding exegetical ways of accommodating the esoteric meanings they wished to convey to a well-intentioned but spiritually undeveloped (or uninformed) public. For present purposes, a contracted excerpt from a homily by the Maggid of Mezeritch will convey the hermeneutical task. It presupposes that the language of Scripture is suffused with allegorical figures that accommodated the Divine (esoteric)

Hebrew Grammar, ed. E. Kautzsch and trans. A. E. Cowley (Oxford: Clarendon Press, 1910), 107e–f, p. 315.

25. In classical Judaism, the legal expositions of the exegetical level of *Derash* were not deemed to have an esoteric valence, though this was the case in medieval mystical traditions and their offshoots.

communication to the (exoteric) exigencies of human cognition. In the process of his pedagogical explications, the master further delimits the Divine (figural) formulations for human comprehension.[26]

> "And the heavens and the earth were completed, *va-yekhulu*" [Gen. 2:1]. Now, indeed, the *Zohar* [3.47b] asked, "Why was the darkness—which is surely not the most primordial element—created first, and the light afterwards?" This conundrum is resolved on the basis of the principle that "light is superior to darkness" [Eccles. 2:13]; and this is also in accord with what [King Solomon] said [regarding the need] "to [properly] understand a parable [*mashal*] and a literary figure" [Prov. 1:9]. Whereas a *mashal* is a means to help one understand that which is beyond their comprehension, [a speaker] reformulates what he wants to impart through the figures of a *mashal*. But the words of Torah are [different and totally] unlike [earthly] parables.... Thus, since the Torah is perfect... and no human could bear the illumination [Supernal Wisdom] of the Torah in its full essence, it was necessary [for God] to conceal [its transcendent meanings] in the letters of our Torah. Accordingly, these letters ... are in reality merely their external, material concealment within which its Divine splendor has been contracted (*metzumtzemet*). For truly, without such [linguistic] garments its [meaning] could not be comprehended at all.... This being so, these verbal garments [are not mere earthly figures] but cleave eternally to the [supernal Divine] light and ... have no separate reality whatsoever....
>
> Thus the parabolic character of Torah is not like [mundane] parables, whose primary purpose is to convey a modicum of understanding and instruction, after which ... its letters [the literary figures themselves] have no further purpose.... This difference explains the phrase [from the book of Ecclesiastes, cited earlier]: "the [value of] light is greater than the darkness." For since ... [Supernal] Wisdom [the Divine light of Torah] must [because of its transcendent effulgence] be encased in limited and functional forms ... this demonstrates the greatness of Solomon—for he was

26. I shall cite the central parts of the teaching found in *Maggid Devarav Le-Ya'aqov*, 217–19 (no. 126).

> able to take all the [transcendent Divine Wisdom] and encase it in these [seemingly] mundane parabolic figures so that it could benefit [human] devotion to God [in both knowledge and religious practice]. . . . Accordingly, one cannot separate the lower forms of wisdom [the parabolic expressions] from their higher supernal sense . . . for it is all [both the content and the form] one: [expressions of] the Infinite One [God]. . . . Precisely this is the [import] of the word *va-yekhullu* [cited at the outset, at the conclusion of the creative process that mentions darkness before light] . . . for it is only by means of a container (*keli*)—[in this case, the allegorical figures of the Torah]—that [the transcendent light of Divine wisdom may be preserved]. Consider this well!

This hermeneutical meditation conveys an essential truth of Jewish mystical language: that the words of Torah themselves, and the various parables that serve to explicate them, are merely an external vessel that accommodates God's esoteric truths to human cognition. This notwithstanding, both the linguistic formulations of Scripture (the inherent allegories of the cosmic mysteries) and the various ones constructed by sages such as Solomon constitute one seamless parabolic whole and are inseparable from their supernal Divine source. Accordingly, it is the primary task of the tzaddik (a sage in the mold of Solomon) to mediate these Divine truths to his followers by means of still other figures (where necessary) so that these adepts might ascend in spiritual wisdom and conjoin their souls to God. In the present instance (in an exceedingly obscure allusion not cited above), this task is achieved by conveying the cosmogonic mystery of creation through an allegorical figure adapted for this purpose from the rabbinic Midrash.[27] Part of that mystery is the fact that darkness preceded light—and this puzzling fact becomes the basis of teaching that the most supernal Divine light could only enter worldly existence through

27. The preacher is concerned to teach matters related to a primordial rupture of cosmogonic origins by means of an allegory about primordial *tzurot* (figures or forms) that symbolically represent the discs or *disqusin* defined as *partzufin* (the Lurianic term for configurations of the Divine hierarchy). The editor is the one who clarifies (parenthetically) that the "repair" of these figures was a cosmic *tiqqun*. The core parable is cited from *Midrash Genesis Rabba*, 10.2; there are several minor variants.

concealments of various kinds. The Torah is just such a concealment of Divine reality, and the worshipper is hereby informed that the words of Torah studied, and the world formed by the language of God, are contracted modalities of Divinity. To explicate the actual words of Scripture, and thus to properly discern the forms of the created world, is to engage the mystery of God's light in and through its infinite refractions.

World-being, we are told at the end, is itself a vessel (*keli*) that has contracted Divinity into myriads of forms. Accordingly, the task of a spiritual teacher is to reveal the holy concealments of Divine light embedded in all being—nay, it is more: to teach that this Infinite Light is refracted through the forms of worldliness as a most supreme act of Divine accommodation. Thus everything in worldly existence is subject to interpretation, for everything is a contracted embodiment or configuration of Supernal Divinity in the world. The great chain of being is one unified, intricate whole, from supernal top to earthly bottom. An illumined mind may therefore ascend toward this Source of Light and Supernal Wisdom through the external features of existence. Allegory is thus a primary (and necessary) vessel in which God's light is concealed. Guided by the tzaddik, mystical hermeneutics is an initiation (through homilies like this one) into the infinite mystery of Divine presence: that the primacy of the world is (in actuality) the primacy of God (for those in the know). The ensuing section develops this point.

Spiritual Archetypes: The Status of Scriptural Images

A fundamental component of Kabbalistic and Ḥasidic hermeneutics is the homology (or structural correlation) between the human being as a microcosm, the created universe as a macrocosm, and the supernal realm as the transcendental or hyperdimension of all being. This means that the forms of the Divine emanation (utterly esoteric and spiritual patterns of energy) are mirrored (or replicated) in the material cosmos as a whole and each person in particular. Everything participates in everything else, and the spiritual forces of creative energy pervade every aspect of being. Among these forms is the supernal or heavenly Torah. It is a blueprint or archetype of the creation in all its parts: what is described in the Torah of Moses (in its totality and variety) is in the image of God. Earthly elements like trees and rivers are not merely material realities but symbolic composites of Divine cosmic creativity. Thus, trees are symbols of the complex structure of being—its roots and branches—and rivers symbolize the interconnected flow of existence. In a similar manner, the multiple personalities of Scripture are symbolic archetypes as well: modalities of will and spiritual behavior. And finally, the Law is more than a collection of cases and norms and symbolizes the impact of positive and negative behaviors on the totality of existence. To read Scripture with a spiritual mind is to understand that everything is in the Image of God.

The following excerpt from a teaching by R. Menaḥem Naḥum of Chernobyl (another disciple of the Maggid of Mezeritch), recorded in his work *Me'or Einayim*, exemplifies the prior comments. In particular, it illustrates how the old patriarchal narratives are spiritually instructive in every detail (and are veritable archetypes of modes of religious behavior and consciousness). The homily is linked to a specific weekly (Sabbath) lection and opens with the Scriptural citation "Isaac returned (*va-yashov*) and dug the wells (*be'erot*) of water that were dug in the days of his father Abraham and stopped up (*va-yistemum*) by the Philistines. . . . [However, at a later time,] when the servants of Isaac were digging in the wadi (*naḥal*), they found a well of living water" (Gen. 26:18–19).[28] What is the spiritual teaching of this passage?

> In order to understand this verse, we must first turn to another, "They forsook Me, the Source of living water, to hew out cisterns (*bo'rot*), broken cisterns (*bo'rot nishbarim*)" (Jer. 2:13). Surely the Lord is the Source from which the bounty of life flows in all ways. There is none beside Him, and all who cleave to Him are conjoined to the Root of Life, "whose waters never fail" (Isa. 58:11)—as long as there is no separation (of this flow) from our side. But if one sins

28. See in *Sefer Me'or Einayim* (Jerusalem: Machon Me'or Ha-Torah, 2006), 1.84b–85b.

and separates himself from the Source, God's vitality will be absent to him; this notwithstanding, there is never an interruption [of this vitality] from God's side. . . . [Thus know that] anyone whose life [force] is drawn from the "Other Side"'—called *bo'rot nishbarim,* which contains . . . the remains of the sparks of vitality that were shattered (*nishbarim*) during [the primordial cosmogonic] rupture (*shevirah*)—will be separated from his Divine Source. Such a person is called "separator of [the Divine] Unity" (Prov. 16:28); meaning, figuratively, one who is separated from "the *Aleph*" [or primal principle of all being].

For this reason [to repair this primordial rupture], the patriarchs opened the channels of [spiritual] knowledge and awareness, teaching each individual how to hew himself (*et'atzmo*) into a veritable "well (*be'er*) of living water" so as to cleave to the Source, the Root of their life. Their disciples are thus called "servants," as in the phrase "My servant Isaac," since their Divine service came about through the [deeds of the] patriarchs.

However, after the death of Abraham, when the sources of this wisdom were stopped up [or sealed] by the Philistines, who are symbolic of the evil in humans . . . the spiritual and mental powers were weakened. But when Abraham's son Isaac came, he followed the example of his father and taught the people of his generation to return (*la-shuv*) and dig into that Well (*be'er*) of Living Water [the Divine Source] through many marvelous acts and spiritual exercises. Hence, Scripture says, "And Isaac returned (*va-yashov*) and dug the wells (*be'erot*) of water."

Now all this came about through faith, which is the foundation of all; for a person must have complete faith that God fills the entire world and that there is nothing beside Him. And it is through this faith that a person yearns and desires to be attached to God. This [spiritual] state is also designated [by the term] *naḥal* [wadi or stream], whose consonants (*n'ḥ'l*) stand for *nafshenu ḥiktah l-Adonay* ["Our soul yearns for Y-H-W-H"; Psalm 33:20]. Through this figure of spiritual longing, attained through faith, one may be restored to their Divine Root, the Font of the Well of Living Water. Precisely this is what Scripture means when it states, "The servants of Isaac dug in the wadi," [alluding to] the *naḥal* of spiritual desire, as we have said.

In this selection, the preacher presents the spiritual life as rife with dangers and tasks—both the dangers of idolatry or false belief, and the recurrent task of individual (and even cosmic) repair. This theological issue is taken up in the preceding homily by means of the imagery of wells to illustrate, primarily, that God and His teachings are like a well of living water that nourishes all existence and the human being in particular. To disregard this reality is to depend on false truths, these being broken wells whose impure content derives from a cataclysmic event in primordial time when an initial emanation of Divine power had shattered their original containers and pooled within existence as negative forces that could still negatively influence humans—even after a more stable structure of world-being was created. These false wells are manifest in false beliefs or negative behaviors (symbolized by the Philistines). Thus, spiritually diligent persons will (like the patriarchs of old) dig down within themselves and purify their own inner well—a symbol of the character of their spiritual life and actions. To purify or properly dig one's well is to prepare oneself to be a container of the Divine source of life and be joined to its primal font. By contrast, to be a "Philistine"' is to be constrained by undeveloped instinct and will and fall under the influence of all that is separate from God—symbolized as the "Other Side" and its impure water.[29]

Another dimension of false religiosity is to think that all the phenomena of existence have a separate status and are sustained by independent life processes or influences. To have such an orientation is to be cut off from the Divine source of all (symbolized by the primal letter *aleph*). It is to live with a wholly natural view of things and their apparent multiplicity. This is the counterpoint, or the other side of true (monotheistic) belief, according to R. Menaḥem Naḥum. Digging one's inner well, however it was cognitively blocked, requires the belief that God alone exists and that there is nothing but God's life force that sustains all existence. This belief requires a wholehearted, repentant "return" to the well of God (symbolized here by Isaac and his action), and thus to right belief.

29. The figure of displaced waters is that of *mayyim mekhunasim* (or "stagnant" water, the opposite of "vital" waters. This theme is also taken up in *Sefer Me'or Einayim*, 1.28a.

This homily makes it abundantly clear that for the preacher and his devotees, Scripture is more than a record of historical events—in this case occurrences in the personal life of the patriarchs involving contentions over pasturage and cisterns. It is, rather, a fundamental teaching about the religious life of the formative spiritual masters of antiquity, who modeled reparative behavior in their own inner lives. In this regard, the biblical narrative is explicated via archetypes related to wells and water. The most primal Divine well is referred to as the *be'er* of sustaining life and is graphically marked by the letter *aleph* (/'/), whereas the shoddy wells of the "Other Side" are called *bo'rot*. Both formulations occur in the book of Jeremiah, and the preacher pays close attention to their spelling and pronunciation. Although each one is spelled *b-'-r* (*bet-aleph-resh*), the first is pronounced *be'er*, the second *bo'r(ot)*. For him, this difference is both rhetorically decisive and pedagogically significant for the spiritual concerns of this sermon. Namely, the homily turns on the fact that the consonant *aleph* (marked as /'/) is articulated (as a glottal stop) in the positive term *be'er* but is not articulated (though written) in its negative variant. The didactic implication drawn is that false belief disregards the Divine *aleph* (a hieroglyph of the Divine unity) and is also engaged in multiplicity—since the grapheme *bo'rot* not only ignores the letter *aleph* but is itself a plural noun.

Altogether, R. Menaḥem Naḥum teaches hermeneutically: he inculcates a spiritual lesson for the theological repair of his disciples' souls and, in the process, demonstrates how to read Scripture for its deeper, pedagogical instruction. This is no mean feat because despite the apparent superficiality of the Pentateuchal narrative, his homily is nothing less than an exegetical revelation that sacred Scripture contains teachings that bear on a person's spiritual life and a theology of radical monotheism. In disclosing these crucial religious instructions, the homilist integrates spiritual hints from the full range of the biblical canon—supplementing his major citation from the Prophets (Jer. 2:13) with others from the Writings (Prov. 16:28 and Psalm 33:27). In addressing his adepts with his pedagogical voice and Scripture with his exegetical eye, the master gives personal expression to the latent spiritual content of Scripture. Attentiveness to the potential directives concealed in assorted cues undoubtedly corresponds to the teacher's great longing for spiritual direction. From this inner desire, the sources of Scripture speak anew and address the devotee—a revelation from the eternal potential of God's word.

A Concluding Consideration

A final query imposes itself: Where do we stand in relation to the yearning for spiritual direction so evident in the Ḥasidic literature of a bygone era? Can its voice of instruction still resonate with our modern condition despite the chasm of epistemic differences that separate us from textual testimonies that are often fragmentary and opaque in nature? What might remain for moderns who seek to access the wisdom latent in these sources without compromising intellectual or psychological integrity? Is it possible to hold onto both (the teachings of these sources and our contemporary intellectual situation) and thereby foster new moments in the appropriation of this heritage? This is my hermeneutic hope and its challenges. It requires, I believe, cultivating a new disposition for spiritual study and a readiness to regard the difficulties of interpretation as a prompt for self-transformation. On this basis, the voices of the text will stimulate a personal response of thoughtful reflection in each reader seeking to recover spiritual meaning from the sources.

Two strategies take up the challenge of first receiving a text on its own terms and then appropriating it as a spiritual instruction (for the modern reader). Of special importance is the hermeneutical practice advocated by the philosopher Paul Ricoeur. It requires two distinct moves: first, an attentive philological engagement with the language of the text and its content so as to estimate its textual intent and intuit its apparent purport or goals, then an engagement with this textual content with a so-called second naivete (or innocence)[30]—a hermeneutical disposition that strives to cultivate a capacity to receive this

30. For the term and its hermeneutic character, see P. Ricoeur, *The Symbolism of Evil* (New York: Harper & Row, 1967), 351. This usage was preceded by Peter Wust, in *Naivität und Pietät* (Tübingen, 1925), now in *Gesammelte Schriften* (Münster: Regensberg, 1964), 2:25–352, who contended that a return to the primacy of piety

(older, different) text through its own (primary) gestalt. For Ricoeur the challenge is not to get "behind" the language of the text in order to retrieve some presumptive historical or social reality but to stand "before" its verbal presentations and be affected (without presupposition) by the thrust of its terminology and concerns. In this process, the engaged interpreter will try to reformulate what is "said" in contemporary terms, and thereby appropriate the material by comporting it with modern psychology and philosophy.

This hermeneutical procedure will be personally transformative, since the concerns of the text are now recast in terms that engage one's vital, existential being. The primacy of the received text and the primacy of one's interpreted response are thereby experienced in dynamic correlation. The textual content has a "say" (an inaugural provocation) with respect to how the reader reformulates its hermeneutic evocation, and if or when the "interpreted voice" of the text stimulates one's human core, it will express its spiritual truth through one's own "interpreting voice." Such is the hermeneutical circle that guides understanding. By becoming subject to the text, the reader's subjectivity is reciprocally evoked. The literary "source" and its "reader" will thereby testify to each other: the text inaugurates its vocal testimony (as a spiritual directive) through the integrity of its interpreters, and the latter respond in due measure. In this way, the received reality of the religious teaching becomes "objectively real" in the subjective soul of a reader even as the reader's contemporary condition provides the catalyst for each creative appropriation of the traditional content.

A second (related) strategy is to take the complex hermeneutic factuality of the source as the point of intellectual departure and allow that to condition the process of personal development that may coincide with the appropriation of its textual meaning. What is that factuality? In the present case it is the fact that each homily is composed of citations, allusions, and fragments from the cultural past that have been revised, condensed, or transformed from an original oral address into a literary instruction. Accordingly, the latter-day reader must discern the way that these enunciations, once addressed to a

---

(particularly the wonder of existence) must bypass stultifying doctrinal confessions and metaphysical attitudes.

circle of intimate disciples, have become transcribed segments for subsequent recipients. Thus, an initial attempt at hermeneutical recovery will involve a shift from the eye (that looks on the letters of a page) to the voice (that activates the verbal content). In addition to determining the given phrasing or terminology, interpretative competence will involve an appreciation of the topical resonance of the sources cited—their allusions and overtones. These are the verbal ciphers that must also be evaluated so that the voice of the master can again (in this written mode) guide a student's spiritual formation. The process of exegetical appropriation then becomes an integral part of personal transformation as one strives to integrate the cultural idiom into which the topics were rendered.

Taking the factuality of the literary content as the primary condition of hermeneutic possibilities means engaging the exegetical event as a "spiritual practice"[31]—a process that involves evaluating the epistemic constraints on "making sense" of a passage—and attending to the dialectics that link textual knowledge to spiritual development.[32] Integrity requires deliberate self-monitoring so that the language of the particular text is "read" (appropriated) in terms appropriate to itself and to one's modern situation. Patience and self-reflection are crucial. Exegetical engagement is thus multifaceted, and assessing "textual information" is directly related to the process of "self-formation." Guided by these considerations, hermeneutic practice can sponsor a contemplative mode of spiritual development, both singly and with a study partner. If the latter, the "hermeneutic between" (the reflective "give and take") becomes an occasion for the emergence of interpersonal meaning. This event may also be the setting for the incipience of a new spiritual community. This gives the hermeneutical process an added ethical valence.

31. With this notion I acknowledge the stimulus of P. Hadot, *Philosophy as a Way of Life*, trans. M. Chase (Oxford: Blackwell, 1995), esp. chaps. 3–4.

32. This is akin to what P. Rabbow, in *Seelenführung: Methodik der Exerziten in der Antike* (Munich: Rösel, 1954), 17, referred to as *Innerwendung* (inward orientation)

Conclusion

FORMS OF PRESENCE

Presence is primary in every respect. It is an omnipresent resonance pulsing in the depth of being, and it comes to receptive awareness in infinite ways and levels.

Naturally, what is "sensed" and "seen" is the particular presence at hand in its many kinds and forms. Presence is primordial for each species, each according to their nature—from the tropic "nurturance" of simple organic elements pervading existence, teeming in compounds or cellular singularities—to the rich environmental "saturation" of world-being, organically sensed or perceived by animals attentive to the vibrations of physical place and the smell of other creatures, or to the elemental "surround" that presents itself diurnally to human consciousness, experienced as so many different physical impingements or claims of attention. Each species is intransitive with respect to itself but simultaneously transitive in response to the pulsations of life to which they are bound and responsive. Duration and endurance exact daily tasks on each life-form and condition their inherent vitality in response to environmental factors and the drive for survival. There is a primary impulse that strives for successful adaptations and their inculcation (by imitation or instruction) across the generations. Presence is, therefore, repeatedly reconfigured into distinctive episodes that elicit primacies of attention emergent from the outer world in which each life-form is embedded. Hence, all presence is invariably copresence, the dynamic interdependence of one element with another. Aristotle was certainly correct when he said that *energeia* is primal. Hence, presence is actuality effectuated by the interactive dynamism of life-forms in their many local and translocal habitats.

The motility of organic life is one mode of its being—be it the need for food and light or dependence on water and warmth. As some primordial tropism, these forms bend toward what is needed and variously succeed or fail to endure. The motility of animals is similar and different: in response to the primacy of environmental presence these creatures display a primary sense of alertness, an attentive attunement to all the resonances perceived to bear on their survival. It is this quivering vitality of smell and sensation that elicits the drive for food or flight. Human beings are different and traverse an arc from animal needs, in both active and sublimated forms, to modes of reflective consciousness that can, in the best of circumstances, evaluate specific situations and engage in considered judgments or purpose. This means that sensed primacies do not elicit only neural reactions in humans but can cultivate habits of heart and mind—which involve patterns and determinants of value. Accordingly, presence may open up a space of attentive awareness wherein a variety of cultural values may transform or challenge instinct and habit. Given this singular quality of the human species, our *energeia* take the form of "work-in-action" bringing a species effecting potentiality into some new or renewed actuality. Aristotle perceived this dialectic as well.

In light of these considerations, we may offer concluding reflections on both the emotional and reflective primacies of the preceding chapters and consider their emergence and dynamics. The first of these is the most fundamental and refers to the initial presentiment of presence elicited by degrees of awareness. Beyond bland numbness or distraction, the multiple features of existence induce a felt presence: a kind of vibration of "the real without" (in the external world) and "the real within" (in one's mind or consciousness).

This simultaneity of awareness is crucial to our embodiment in the physical world—feeling external stimuli and processing them in mind and heart (from nameless aches to their verbal articulation). Accordingly, experience is not some dualistic split between a subject and an object but a unitive sensation that "feels-thinks" in integral, if alternating, bands of lived consciousness. I would characterize this personal resonance of a felt "other" and mental "inner" as "the lyre of Orpheus," since it conjoins registers of sound with inner significance both at the level of tonal shock or musical vibration and at the level of verbalized meaning—the ways tonalities reverberate and make sense as segments of (internal or social) communication. Like some lyric string, we vibrate between internal and external factors—feeling frightened or perplexed when the external impulse has no resonant internal coordinate, and feeling distraught or empty when inner thoughts and sensations seem without resonance in the public sphere. Thus, when Gaston Bachelard spoke of being aware of a "sudden salience," he puts us in mind of some natural event that "speaks to our soul," and thus, for him, this is the occasion when poetry is born through a conjunction of a worldly sound or shape and the language that reshapes consciousness. This is a heightened moment for singular individuals, but it is also within the ken of most persons who can reflect on their interactions with the world. Thus, presence is a multiform unity wherein particular episodes (primacies in their own right) come to some resonant and palpable awareness.

The second aspect of our relationship to the world is when something—an object or creature—stops us in our tracks and we feel addressed by its presence or summons. In this modality, exteriority has a certain inaugural primacy, and it makes a claim on consciousness. This sense of address, processed within memory and mind, is more than some "experiential event" that can be noted or transformed into an aesthetic response. It is rather "normative" in its import and conveys a moral ought that can have a social or natural valence. Struck by the moment, one is now bidden to act in a certain way toward some "other"—persons or nature. This being so, I would characterize this modality of experience as "the tablets of Moses." It involves some felt demand, which is dispositive with respect to what must be done or undertaken. Hence the event has some axiological significance whose life value must be translated into action. If it is the case that the integral dynamic (of "inner-outer") begins with some external experience, its normative claim stems from some spiritual interiority—wholly natural, if we think that values are an endowment of our creaturely nature or are alternatively social or religious, if we suppose (or believe) that values are inculcated by tradition or revelation. For a radical social ethics, the face or the presence of another person is the embodiment of a transcendent-natural event that imparts an imperative and stimulates action; for a religious ethics, the face or presence is an inviolable "image of God" that commands respect. From this perspective, a value-based interiority is primary, and it is the factor that responds to worldly events and influences decisions and actions. Other than ethics, such interior factors may include sorrow or memory, which perceive the external world through their own evocative lens. The endowed sensibility of an artist, or any other person, before a scene or object in the world seems to be conditioned from their soul-scape outward; hence internal factors share an integral primacy with external conditions.

The third modality of presence to be considered takes us to the mythic figure of "Hermes the messenger," the crosser of boundaries (as per a popular etymology of his name). Such activities make him an emblem for the ever-creative activity of hermeneutics, whereby one shuttles between external experience and its meaning, between life sensations and their vocal explication, or between events in the world and their comparative import. Readers of texts must carefully negotiate the lexical and contextual sense of linguistic elements, and similarly, speakers engaged in communication frequently request clarifications in order to determine what was said or intended. The process of interaction is especially to be noted in these cases. We are ever at a spiritual nexus between occurrence and meaning. Even when we are struck by some natural salience, we strive to integrate it into our mental matrix. Fortunately, we are not alone: many significant others offer models and guidance. Such powerful personalities constitute our primary community and its resources. It is from them that we learn and experience the relationship between texts and life—between forms of discourse and enunciation and their actual human embodiment.

A final thought about models: our teachers greatly influence our destiny. What we bear within, despite the inevitable revisions born of our nature and life conditions, is the inestimable memory of how these individuals engendered a path or vision—either by example or hint. The qualities of influence are not to be judged by attaining the same goal but rather by the gift of insight or the vision of a new horizon. What we retain (in both heart and mind) is the afterbirth of this formative generativity, one that resonates over a lifetime. These stimuli of word and gesture are the facts and presences that have shaped us and which we recall with gratitude. Our teachers are primacies of the human spirit evoking lived reflection on forms of discourse and their expression in the world. This is a sacred circle into which we are initiated. I acknowledge my dear teachers, sacred guides each and all, with greatest gratitude.

Acknowledgments

In the making of some books, this one in particular, inner silence and the rhythms of mood are necessary components; equally vital are the chosen words of a few. I have been blessed with a life companion, my dear wife, Mona, who has provided the space for my private world to sink its roots and has nurtured it again and again with loving comments and honest responses. For this gift of a lifetime, repeatedly renewed and varied, I am so profoundly grateful. As with all my work, this, too, dearest Mona, is yours in every sense, and it is dedicated to you in love, once again, for our shared lives together.

Among others whose words have been stimulating and graciously offered, I wish to thank my brother, Dr. Jon Fishbane; Dr. Chaim Kranzler; and Professors Eli Holzer and Omer Michaelis. Their thoughtful comments and evaluations of the human and theological concerns of this work, and particularly its phenomenological and psychological focus, are greatly appreciated.

I also wish to thank Kyle Wagner, my editor at the University of Chicago Press, both for his friendship and his gracious professional involvement at every stage in the emergence of this book.

Finally, I acknowledge the Academic Studies Press for permission to reuse chapter 4. The original publication was Michael Fishbane, "Monotheism and Idolatry: Theological Challenges and Considerations" in *Idolatry: A Contemporary Jewish Conversation*, edited by Alon Goshen-Gottstein. Academic Studies Press, 2023.

Michael Fishbane
July 2024

Index

Aaron, 95, 201–2n12
Abgrund, 181
Abraham, 28, 137, 140, 173, 237–38
Absolute Reality, 123
absolute transcendence, 90
"abyss," 6; as "no-thing," 175
Achilles, 140, 142
acquired learning, 129
Aeneas, 142
Aeneid (Virgil), 142–43
Aeschylus, 19
Agamben, Giorgio, 150n19
aḥor, 104
aḥor va-qedem, 103
Akiva, R., 55
aleph, 239–40
allegory, 66, 228, 230, 235n27, 236
All-in-All, 79, 115
aloneness, 195
'al pi peshuṭo, 214
ancestral wisdom, 57
aniconism, and radical transcendence, 94–95
anokhi, 99–100
Arendt, Hannah, 154–55
Aristotle, 67, 137, 196, 244–45
ascetism, and communal practice, 202
Athens (Greece), 137
attention, 37, 40–41, 52, 53, 99, 115, 142, 219; attentiveness, 5, 42, 44, 63, 118, 126, 240; attentive regard, 111, 114; to breath, 12; consciousness, 58; and eyes, 126; presentational force, 127; redirection of, 130; reflective regard, 128
Atum, 87
Auerbach, Erich, 137
Aurelius, Marcus, 4, 35, 41, 41–42n8, 43n14; appropriate action, 42; attentiveness, 44; consciousness, of radical transcendence, 44; cosmic perspective of, 44–45; as "indifferent to indifferent things," 42; interconnectedness of things, 42–43, 46; meditative practice of, 43; present, focus on, 42, 42n11; shared pathos, 43n16; and transcendent wisdom, 45; and transience of material things, 42–43
Auschwitz, 152; as unsayable, 150n19
Austin, J. L., 93
authenticity, 3–4, 157, 187
'avodah be-gashmiyyut, 121
awe, 3, 45, 99, 225
Axial Age, 36

Ba'al Shem Tov, 105, 192
Babylon, diviner's manual of, 61
Babylonian Talmud, 55
Bachelard, Gaston, 7, 16, 128; and sudden salience, 246
Baḥye ibn Paquda, Rabbeinu, 206

"Ba-ʿIr Ha-Hareigah" (In the City of Slaughter) (Bialik), 149
Baudelaire, Charles, 16
be'er la-ḥay ro'i, 122
being-in-the-world, 35
Berger, P., 218–19n2
Bergson, Henri, 112–13; attention to life, 130n48; flow of existence, 128; lived time, importance of, 110; lived vitality, notion of, 110; theory of creative evolution, 111
Dov Ber (Friedman), R., of Mezeritch, 192–93, 227–28, 233–35, 237; as Great Maggid, 50, 103–5
"Besorah" (Message) (Bialik), 168–69
between, 184–88, 190; between things, 2, 183; of interrelations, 191; one thing or another, 192; "thing and thing," 181
Bialik, Chaim Nachman, 1, 5–7, 135–36, 146–49, 157–58, 161–62, 165–69, 172n29, 175n32; abyss, profound sense of, 175; ancient language, reappropriation and transformation of, 172; ecstatic visions, memory of, 170–71, 176–77; *ke'ilu*, use of, 170n22; literary strata of, 172; *mah* (what?), query of, 174–75; personal and immediate experience, emphasis on, 171, 174–77; poetry, and language of unsayable, 174–75; sacrificial offerings, language of, 173; self-aware "I," 174; translucence as recurrent trope in, 160
Bildung, 221
Blumenberg, Hans, 162n9
Book of Zohar, 77, 97–98, 125, 126n41, 158, 204–5, 223, 231, 232n22
breath, 11–12, 18, 28–29, 31, 58
Buber, Martin, 97n23, 178, 181, 181n8, 182, 190n28, 192–93; "Absolute Thou," 183–84; between, notion of, 6, 179, 184–88, 190–91; consciousness, transformation of, 185; crisis of European spirit, 179–80; *Einschwingen ins Andere* (bold swinging), 189; elemental togetherness, 189; eternal Thou, as ever-present, 187; intentional movement, 188–90; interhuman realm, 188; I-Thou, 185; man and man, relation between, 186; mystery of presence, 183; Nietzsche, influence on, 180; ontology of the interpersonal, 190; partnership and existing whole, 188; personal making present, 188–89; presence, 187; *Seelungverfassungen*, 189; turning toward, 189
Bucke, Richard, 157
Buddha, Gautama, 36

Cairo (Egypt), 196
Chaim Volozhiner, R. (R. Chaim of Volozhin), 158–59
centering, 130–31
Cézanne, Paul, 47
cipher *k*, 105
coffin texts, 87–88
cognition, 105, 105n38, 106, 233–35; mortal, 101–2; as seen, 14; as sight, 14; spiritual, 53, 104; types of, 14; vocalic, 12
Cohen, Hermann, 96–97, 97n23
consciousness, 7, 16, 41, 43, 48, 58, 63, 78–81, 93–94, 102, 106, 114, 125, 127, 193; of approximation and similitude, 70; human, 123; illumination of, 160; lived time, 122; mystic, 49; ordinary, 122; of radical transcendence, 44; religious, 122–23; Sabbath, 123–24; significance of moments, 128; spiritual, 121; spiritual transformation of, 50; transcendental, 124; transformation of, 185; world building, 59–60
consolation, 13, 23, 30, 33, 39, 136; cognitive, 34; Divine, 21–22n14
cosmic transcendence, 45
creative energy, 130–31
Creative Evolution (Bergson), 112

creativity, 1, 7, 79, 111–12, 135, 158, 164, 170–71, 173, 177; cosmic, 237; Divine, 115, 117; hermeneutical, 6; literary, 63; primal force, 115; primal spark of, 148; "seeing as," 122n32; self-creativity, 181; Source of, 80; stimuli of 128; supernal, 53; transcendent, 105; verbal, 162, 167; world-forming process of, 110
cry of life, 11, 17, 30; lamentations, as source, 12; as primordial, 11; as scream, 4
cube, 48, 54

Daniel: Gespräche von der Verwirklichung (Buber), 179–82, 193
Dante, 30
Das Problem des Menschen (Was is der Mensch?) (Buber), 186
David, King, 13, 77, 80–81
David ben Meshullam, R., 24, 28
Dazwischen, 192–93
death, 42–43, 47n26, 110–11; as ultimate leveler, 38–39
Decalogue, 95, 99, 119, 122
depth, 48, 56; of being, 57; of God, 50; as reality of independent worth, 47; of Scripture, 49–50
Depth of All-in-All, 49–50
derashah, 222, 227–28; hermeneutic authority of, 229–30
"Der Heilige Weg" (The Holy Way) (Buber), 181–82, 185–86
Descartes, René, 47
despair, 12, 16, 20, 22–23, 29–31, 33–34, 37, 41, 43, 145–48, 160, 181; crisis of, 21; nihility of, 18
Deuteronomy, 33, 92n16, 197–98, 213
devequt, 202, 202–3n15
dialogue, 15, 137, 160, 176, 179, 186; authentic, 187–90; in Song of Songs, 68; as testament, 6
dibbur, 226–29, 232; Word of God, 50–51
difference, 67; cognitive states of, 125; between good and evil, 125, 125n39; likeness in, 81; between manifestation and *hyponoia* (deep sense), 79–80; monotheistic, 85–86, 101, 103; and otherness, 17; and pathos, 126; of persons, 185; relatedness, 178; between things, 15; and unity, 80
Dilthey, Wilhelm, 180, 220n4
"Dim'ah Ne'emanah" (Bialik), 147n17
"Din Ha-Shir" (The Judgment of Poetry) (Mirsky), 31–32
discourse, 17, 34, 233, 248; and enunciation, 247; inner, 42–43; homiletic, 6; theological, 72
Divine Absolute, 41
Divinity, 78–79, 83, 98, 195, 197, 206; Absolute Reality of, 48–49; creative energy of, 113; Divine actuality, 106–7; Divine agency, 92, 103; Divine *aleph*, 240; Divine beneficence, 19; Divine bliss, 209–10; Divine commandments, 89; Divine compassion, absence of, 28; Divine core, 118; Divine creation, 89; Divine creativity, 115, 117, 237; Divine depth, 53–56; Divine desire, and Ultimate Source of Unity, 115; Divine disclosure, 103; Divine emanation, 236; Divine energy, 205, 226; Divine gradations of primordial emanation, 231–32; Divine illumination, 117; Divine immanence, 54–56, 77, 166; Divine inherency, 88; Divine intentions, 62–63; Divine language, 50, 158–59, 176–77, 225, 233; Divine light, 115, 235–36; Divine model, 226; Divine mystery, 81; Divine ontology, 172; Divine personality, 62; Divine phenomena, 61; Divine plenitude, 85–86, 97, 99, 101; Divine power, 208, 239; Divine powers, 89, 91; Divine Presence, 54, 97, 103, 236; Divine providence, 37;

Divinity (*Continued*)
Divine Reality, 49, 51–52, 63, 96, 101–2, 106, 121–22, 124n35, 125, 236; Divine revelation, 172, 227; Divine reverence, 45; Divine seeing, 126; Divine self-expression, 226; Divine Silence, 24; Divine source, 239; Divine Speech, 49, 115; Divine totality, 57; Divine transcendence, 95, 97, 104–5; Divine truths, 235; Divine unity, 117, 125–26; Divine vitality, 113–15, 121, 123; Divine Voice, 177, 221, 223; Divine Will, 118, 123–24; Divine Whole, 51; Divine wisdom, 120, 143–44, 208–9, 211, 235; Divine Word, 173; Divinity of All, 49; human epistemology, 103; immanent within the creation, 115–16; mystical fullness of, 51; through Scripture, 50; shapes, as expression of, 86; world-being, 80
Dov Ber (Friedman), R. (the Great Maggid of Mezeritch), 102–5, 200, 207, 209–10, 225
du partzufin, 103
durée (duration), 111

earthly immanence, 45
Ecclesiastes (Qohelet), 4, 35, 41, 43–45, 234; living intentionally, 40
ego identity, 194
Egypt, 55–56, 60, 74, 86–88, 95, 138, 140
"Eḥad Eḥad uve-Ein Ro'eh" (One by One, and without Seeing) (Bialik), 160, 168
Ein Sof (Infinity beyond being), 25; *sefirot* (gradations), 226
"Elements of the Interhuman" (Buber), 187–88
Eliezer, R., 55
Elimelekh (Lippmann), R., of Lizhensk, 200, 206
Eliot, T. S., 158
Elohim (Divine Name), 99
Elohim al domi le-dami (God, do not be silent at my blood), 24–25
elohim ilmim (Divine muteness), 153
emotional intelligence, 129
empirical attentiveness, 62–63
empiricism, 61
energeia, 244–45
Enuma Anu Enlil, 61
Epictetus, 39, 42, 45n23
Euclid, 54
Europe, 180
exegesis, 114–15
experience: feels-thinks, of lived consciousness, 245; felt demand, 246; felt other and mental inner, 245–46; "tablets of Moses," 246
Exodus, 73, 75, 87n5, 88–89, 173, 211, 213, 228, 230, 232; molten calf, 97
exteriority, 246
Ezekiel, 225

felt demand, 246
Fez (Morocco), 196
flash worship, 89–90

Gadamer, H.-G., 219n3
Galicia, 200
gaze: contemplative, 110, 114; of eye, 109–10; frontal, 110; "suchness," 110; "thing" seen, 110
Gemeinschaft, 185–86
Genesis, 50–51, 172, 174; Divine speech, 115
Genette, Gerard, 138–39
genuvti yom, 172
Gerona, 198–99
Geschehen, 107
Gespräch (Dialogue), 190
Gesprochenheit, 191
Gestalten, 52–53
"Gillui ve-Khisui ba-Lashon" (Revealment and Concealment in Language) (Bialik), 174
God Alone, 207

Godhood: cognizance of, 102–3
God in all being, 117
God in all things, 115, 118
Goethe, Johann Wolfgang von, 44
Golden Age, 143
Golden Calf, 95
Golem, 94
Governance of the Solitary (ibn Bajja), 196
Great Chain of Divine Being, 50–51, 236
Greece, 60, 137
Greek age, 19
grief, 139, 145–46, 150, 174; collective, 30; sacred, 29
Guernica (Picasso), 29; as raw lamentation, 30
Guide of the Perplexed, The (Maimonides), 96, 196–97

"Ha-Bereikhah" (The Pool) (Bialik), 169–70
"Halefah 'Al Pana" (There Passed over Me) (Bialik), 176
Ha-Elohim ("the God"), 37–38
Halakhic practice, 121
Halevi, Judah, 198
Hanukkah, 75
Ḥasidic dynasty of Gur, 114
Ḥasidic hermeneutics, 236
Ḥasidic homilies, 5, 222–23, 225; exegetical revelation, 228; *mamaloshn* (mother tongue), 224
Ḥasidism, 6, 49, 105, 200, 225, 233
Hebrew Bible, 19
Hebrew Scripture: weeping, role of, 5
Heidegger, Martin, 190n28
hermeneutics, 220, 222, 247; attentive philosophical engagement, 241; engagement with textual content, 241–42; hermeneutical creativity, 6; hermeneutical hubris, 93, 96; hermeneutic humility, 108; hermeneutic theology, 104; human being as microcosm, and created universe as macrocosm, 236; lived hermeneutics, 7; meaning, flow of, 225; patience and self-reflection, as crucial, 243; as primary and formative, 219; religious, 221; as sacred act and process, 221; shift from eye to voice, 243; spiritual, 217; world-building consciousness of, 59–60
"Hermes the messenger," 247
"Hetzitz ve-Nifga" (He Gazed and Died) (Bialik), 175
hiketeia (supplication), 15
hishtadlut (striving), 120–21
hitkallelut, 124n35
ḥiyyut (life force), 113–14, 118, 120, 122–24, 126
ḥokhmah (wisdom), 38
Holocaust, 31, 150, 179
"Holy Jew," 99–100
Homer, 137; Homeric gaze, 63; Homeric poetry, 66; Homeric similes, 15, 63–64, 64n12, 65, 67, 69
Hosea, 91, 94n20
Husserl, Edmund, 104, 128n45; intention, 189

Ibn Bajja, 196
ibn Ezra, R. Abraham, 37n4
ibn Gabirol, Shlomoh, 143–46, 147n17, 153n23, 198–99; "if" clauses, role of, 151
Ich und Du (I and Thou) (Buber), 183, 187; authentic personhood, leitmotif of, 186; lived actuality, 182
identity, 62, 67, 83, 86, 137–39, 141, 145, 152–53; ego, 194; personal, 3–5, 68; personal lyrics, 143; reclaiming of, 142; and tears, 142–43
idolatry, 5, 84–86, 91, 94, 94n20, 97, 99, 101, 105, 239; cognitive, 96; collective, 95; demand against, 90; epistemological, 107–8; Golden Calf, worship of, 95; idol maker, 92–94; linguistic, 96

Iliad (Homer), 4, 15–16, 63, 66, 71, 138–39; mythopoetic summons, 64–65; poetry-induced participation, 64–65
imitatio dei, 204
immanence: Divine, 53–56, 56n37, 77, 102, 113, 166; earthly, 45, 226–27; godly, 49; human meaning and signification, 105; phenomenal, 106; realm of *Shechinah*, 50, 226–27; transcendence, distinction between, 48, 85–86; transcendent, 103
"'Im Petiḥat Ha-Ḥalon" (At the Opening of the Window) (Bialik), 162
"in between" zone: of mind and body, 149–50; mystery of, 178–79
Infinite Other, 80
insight, 191; centering point of, 131; epistemic, 46; gift of, 247; individual, 12; mystical, 45; revelatory, 229–30; and sight, 128, 162; spiritual, 51–52, 114
intention, 2, 14, 40, 65, 117–18, 127, 185; dialogical, 188; personal, 15; positivity of particular, 189–90; reflective, 129
interiority (*penimiyyut*), 121
Isaac, 122, 137, 237–38
Isaiah, 91, 93, 95–98, 100, 231
ish emunot, 121, 124
Israel, 28, 53, 66, 72–73, 86, 88, 137, 201, 209–10, 213; as God's holy seed, 26

Jacob, 140–41, 172, 215
James, William, 156–57
Jaspers, Karl, 36
Jeremiah, 91, 172n28, 173, 206, 240
Jerusalem (Israel), 137
Jewish mysticism, 48–49, 113, 235
Job, 18–19, 20, 172, 175n32; lamentation of, 21–23; "Why?" 30
Joseph, 140, 140n8, 141–42
Judaism, 84, 113, 159, 182, 195, 227n15, 233n25

kabbalah, 106n42; Kabbalistic hermeneutics, 170n23, 236
Kabbalists of Provence, 198–99
Kalonymous Kalman Epstein, R., of Krakow, 200, 202–11, 213–15, 217
Kandinsky, Wassily, 131
Kant, Immanuel, 59, 189
Kierkegaard, Soren, 137, 195
Kishinev pogrom, 148
Klee, Paul, 131
koaḥ ha-po'el (power of actualization), 115–16
"Kokhav Nidaḥ" (A Remote /Abandoned Star) (Bialik), 147, 167n18; as self-disclosure through tears, 148

lament, 22–23, 25, 26, 30, 32, 145, 149; as desperate acts of language, 27; as evocation of emptiness, 18; language of, 24; as primal shriek, 28
lamentation, 13, 21–24, 29, 33, 155; cry of life, 12; grammar of, 34; as imitation of death, 30; as language of silenced dead, 26; as primal expression, 18
Landauer, Gustav, 181, 185–86
language, 156–58; despair of pain, articulation of, 23; fear of failure, 13; incantational character of, 14; lament of, 16–17; personal identity, 5; representation of, 29; silent verge of, 177; simile structure of, 15
Lavelle, L., 47n26
Leidensgeschichte (history of sorrows) of Jewry, 148
Lévi-Bruhl, L., 60
Levi, Primo, 30–31, 153; "if," use of, 151–52
Levi Yitzḥak, R., of Berditchev, 231n20
Leviticus, 200–202, 204–5, 213, 215
likeness, 62, 66, 68; in difference, 81; as simile, 58, 69–70; as "thing itself," 5
linearity, 47

linguistic ontology, 157–58
L'intuition de l'instant (The Intuition of the Instant) (Bachelard), 128
literary phenomenology, 137
lived experience, 4, 16, 106–7
Logos, 12
Logos of Divinity, 13
Logos of things, 46
longing, 11–12, 15, 18, 21, 45, 68–71, 76, 139, 157, 160–61, 164, 168; for care and compassion, 136; and limit, 13, 17; for meaning and significance, 17; for *nostos* (return), 65; poetic, 148; silence, 167; spiritual, 171, 237; for spiritual healing, 147; to be heard, 33; unfathomable, 80; for wholly other, 80
"Lo Zakhiti Ha-Or Min Ha-Hefqer" (I Didn't Merit Light by Accident) (Bialik), 173
Luria, R. Isaac, 200, 223
Lurianic Kabbalah, 103, 162n10

magical thinking, 13–14
Mahler, Gustav, 131
Maimonides, 96, 195, 198, 200, 203, 204n17, 206, 206n21, 216; Code (*Mishneh Torah*), 197; as "Great Eagle," 196–97; *Guide of the Perplexed*, 96, 196–97; individual perfection, as elite few, 197; Law and Tradition, 197
Ma'or va-Shemesh (R. Kalonymos Kalman Epstein), 200
Marceau, Marcel, 29
materiality, 121
meaning, 4, 6, 13, 37–38, 60–62, 76, 80, 93, 108n49, 176, 178–79, 220, 222; creative correlation, 70–71; of dialogue, 186; esoteric, 212; failure of, 22; hermeneutical flow of, 225; interpersonal, 243; interpretative discernment, 219; occurrence, 247; personal, 63; search for, 34; significance, 17; signification of, 87, 105; spiritual, 241; textual, 17, 242; theological truth, 96; verbal, 14; verbalized, 245–46
Meditations (Aurelius), 41, 42n9, 43n14; shared pathos, 43n16
meditative reciprocity, 130
memory, 28, 137, 149, 152, 247; shared, 138; and tears, 141, 143, 153–54
Menaḥem Nahum, R., of Chernobyl, 237–40
menuḥah (rest), 125
Me'or Einayim (Menaḥem Naḥum of Chernobyl), 237
Merleau-Ponty, Maurice, 4, 47n26, 54, 56n38, 104–5n37; abyssal realm of being, 47; cube, use of, 48, 54; depth, 47, 56; "eye of God," 47–48, 56–57; perception, 46; phenomenology of, 51; phenomenology of perception, 129; spatial depth, 55
Mesopotamia, 60–61
Midrash, 222
Midrash Levicitus Rabba, 204, 214
Midrash Torat Kohanim, 201
mimesis, 70, 139, 141–43; literary, 137
mindfulness, 35, 53; transcendent, 40
Minkowski, Eugène, 110, 113; concrete experience, 111; lived synchronism, 111; lived synchrony, notion of, 114; lived time, 111
Mirsky, Aharon, 31–33, 153n24, 154; absence, evoking of, 153; identity, of death and loss, 153
Mishneh Torah, Sefer Ha-Mada' (Maimonides), 203
"Mi-Shomerim La-Boqer" (From Those Who Await the Dawn) (Bialik), 163
modernity, 84–85, 159, 176
monotheism, 85–86, 89, 97, 101, 103; God in all things, 119
monotheistic theology, 5
monotheistic universalism, 91–92
moral memory, 33
mortality, 11; death as ultimate leveler, 38

Mordechai Yosef Leiner, R., of Izhbitz, 100–101
Moses, 73–75, 89, 115, 198–99, 225, 231n20; *dibbur* (speech) and *qol* (voice), revealed at Mount Sinai, 228–32; as Divine spirit, 231; at Mount Sinai, 95, 226, 228–30, 232
Moshe Ḥayyim Ephraim, R., of Sudilkov, 105–6
mutuality, 6, 130, 179, 187, 189
mystery: and things, 99
mysticism, 55; *beli-mah*, 175, 175n32; Jewish, 48–49, 113; mystical experiences, 157; mystical hermeneutics, 97
mystic theology, 104
mythic plenum, 89–90, 101
mythopoeic thought, 60, 64–66

Nachmanides, 197; spiritual realm of "Thought," 198–99, 206
"Nadnedah" (The Seesaw) (Bialik), 176
naming, 12, 17, 52
Nefesh Ha-Ḥayyim (R. Chaim Volozhiner), 158
neo-platonism, 48, 115
Nicomachean Ethics (Aristotle), 196
Nietzsche, Friedrich, 180
normative inversion, 83
North Africa, 196
nostos (return to one's homeland), 15

Odyssey (Homer), 5, 65, 137–38, 141–42; "I am" speech, 139–40
Oneness of God, 119
ontological language, 176
ordinary time, 118
Or Ha-Me'ir (R. Ze'ev Wolf of Zhitomer), 50–51, 76, 76n17, 80, 228–29
otherness: of God, 90–91, 99

Palestine, 172
panentheism, 101, 113n9
panim, 104–5
Panofsky, E., 104–5n37
participation mystique, 60
perception, 5, 46, 54, 56, 80, 90–91, 129; through similes, 4
perspective, 47, 57; "view from above," 46, 52
phenomenology, 46, 51, 56, 112–14, 162; of depth, 54; of dialogical situation, 187–88; of literary formulations, 7; of perception, 129; of personhood, 109; of primary emotions, 8; of vision, 109–10
Phenomenology of Perception (Merleau-Ponty), 46–47n25
Philistines, 237–39
Picasso, Pablo, 29
piety, 18–19, 20, 26, 241–42n30; false, 28; filial, 211; public, 212; ritual, 22; spiritual, 199
Pirkei Avot (Ethics of the Fathers), 120
plagues, 86–87
Plato, 36, 66, 196–97
Poetics of Space, The (Bachelard), 128
poetry: as antidote to magic, 14; poetics of reverie, 16; poetic speech, 16; as unsayable, 174; verbal construction of meaning, 14
Poland, 200; Polish Jewry, 154
positionality, 4, 57, 109–10
posture, 45; bodily, 57; upright, 34, 109; of verticality, 41
presence, 2, 53, 185, 187; of another person, 246–47; as copresence, 244; degrees of awareness, 245; exteriority, inaugural primacy of, 246; felt presence, 245; Hermes the messenger, 247; modes of, 82; other, 246; as primordial, 244; and similes, 59; value-based interiority, 247
"Presence" (Buber), 183
presentational force, 127–28
present moment, 44n22; immediacy of, 41
primacies, 1–2, 217–18, 244–46, 248
primary experiences: analytic compo-

nent, 3; between things, 2; catalytic component, 3; dimensions of interiority, 3–4; poetic authenticity, 3–4
Proverbs, 214
psychopathology, 111
Pure Unity, 226

Qedoshim, 200, 210
Qohelet, 35, 36, 38, 45–46, 52; infinite Absolute and finite other, 41; intentionality, to live with, 40; living with anticipations, as sheer folly, 39; reaping the wind (*re'ut ruaḥ*), 39; time (*zeman*), 37, 39; world-weariness of, 37

radical monotheism, 240
radical transcendence, 85, 88–89; and aniconism, 94–95; Jewish philosophy, 96
Rashi, 77–78, 201–2
recitation, 17, 27, 139, 205, 225, 231; communal, 26
Renaissance, 47
rationality, 61–62, 66; instrumental, 97
rational thinking: as emergent phenomenon, 60–61
reflective intention: "the pause," 129
reflective regard, 128; as act of "seeing," 129
religious ethics, 246–47
religious hermeneutics, 221
reshut (liturgical request), 32n26
"Reshut Le-Qelalah" (An Invocation for Imprecation), 32–33
resignifications, 17
Rhetoric (Aristotle), 67
Ricoeur, Paul, 219n3, 241–42
Rilke, Rainer Maria, 107n44, 131, 176, 180
Rodin, Auguste, 47
Romanticism, 159–60
Rosenzweig, Franz, 107n45, 183

Saadia Gaon, R., 96
Sabbath, 116–17, 120–23, 125–26; transcendental consciousness as inner principle of, 124
Sachs, Nellie, 150
sacred and profane, 156, 173
Schlegel, Friedrich, 158
Scholem, Gershom, 94
scientism, 97
Scripture, 26, 36, 51, 71–77, 86, 105–7, 114–15, 122, 125, 138, 151–52, 155, 172–73, 201, 203–5, 214, 216–17, 219, 222, 235–36; allegorical meanings, 233; depth of, 49–50; Divine message of, 228; Divine word of creation, 226; as fundamental teaching of religious life, 240; Image of God, 237; *Remez*, 233; *Sod*, 233; spiritual direction, 240–41; as verbal codification of Divinity, 49
Scroll of Lamentations, 154
Scruten, R., 100n28
"seeing as," 14
"seen as," 62
Sefas Emes (R. Yehudah Aryeh Leib of Gur), 114–17, 119–20, 122, 126n41
self-expression, 17
selfhood, 139, 197
Seneca, 42
Shekhinah, 50, 53, 77, 183–84, 198, 224, 226–27
Shelley, Percy Bysshe, 157
"Shemà" (Levi): fold of impossibilities, 152; memorialization, demanding of, 152; as rewriting of Scripture, 151–52; silence in, 152–53
Shem Tov, 196
Shimon Lavi, R., 98n25
Shu, 87
Shuma alu, 61
sight, 114, 127–28, 162, 178, 185; as construct of sense, 14; unsayable experiences, 47
signification, 92–93; of meaning, 87; and signs, 95

silence, 6, 11–13, 18, 25–26, 28, 30–31, 33, 65, 124, 145–46, 168–69, 176–77, 184–85; of being, 29; of existence, 40; of longing, 167; mute, 152–53, 164; pious, 20; ritual expression, 23; silent indifference, 126; of sorrow, 21, 167; of the soul, 143; of splendor, 163
Simḥah Bunem (Bonhardt), R., of Przysycha, 99–100
similes, 1–3, 16, 26, 31–32, 64–66, 152, 170n22, 178; as antidote to verbal illusion, 14; "as if," 59; hermeneutical, 17, 59; Homeric, 15, 63, 64–65n12, 69; likeness of, 4–5, 58, 69–70; as metaphors, 14, 67; parables, 4; presence, 59; speaking in, 59; speech acts, 68
social ethics, 194, 246–47
sociality, 185
solecisms, 46
solitary self, 195
Solomon, King, 35–36, 71–73, 77, 80–81, 234–35
Song of Songs, 4, 15, 51, 53, 73, 76n17, 228; All-in-all, 79; allegorical tropes, 66, 75–76, 80–81; *derashah*, invoking of, 230; dialogue in, 68; erotic allusions, 71–72, 75; hermeneutical resonance of, 231–32; identity, 68; imagery of, 67–70; longing for interpersonal connection, 76; *mashal*, 72, 74–76; Midrash, 71; similes in, 66–70; spiritual teachings on, 76–80
"Song of Unity," 171, 171n25
sorrow, 1, 6, 12–13, 20, 23, 28, 136, 146–47, 154, 247; confession, 144; consciousness of, 21; cries of, 31, 174; of existence, 142; images of, 29, 175; longing to be heard, 33; in paintings, 29; silence of, 21, 167; tears of, 65, 139, 142–43, 149, 153
Spain, 143, 196, 198–99
spatial intersections, 55
speech, 3; and hearing, 6–7
speech acts, 13, 138
Sphere of Voice (Qol), 226
spiritual-religious awareness, 106
"standing in the world," 109
Steinbeck, A., 128n45
Steiner, George, 59n5
Stoics, 36–37, 39, 41, 46, 66
Straus, Erwin, 109–10; contemplative gaze, 114
sukkah: Divine immanence, symbol of, 56–57; as ritual place, 54–55
Sukkah: sugya of, 55
Sukkot, 54
Supernal Divinity, 236
Supernal Wisdom, 236
Symonds, John Addington, 157

Tales of Rabbi Nachman (Die Geschichten des Nachman), 191
Tales of the Hasidim, The, 191, 193
Talmud, 203, 223
tears, 144, 146, 148–49; and identity, 142–43; memory, 141, 143, 153–54; mysteries of absence, mourning of, 136; as primordial, 136; as silent cyphers, 135; and testimony, 141; and tragedy, 5
temporality, 112–13, 115
Tennyson, Alfred Lord, 157
theomacy: Divine battles of plagues, 86–87; second commandment, 86
"There Is No One to Recite the *Kaddish*" (Arendt), 154–55
thingness, 99
This Is a Man (Levi), 151
thoughtful discrimination, 129
Thus Spoke Zarathustra (Nietzsche), 180
time, 23, 37, 49–50, 89, 97, 117–18, 127–28, 145, 149, 160–61, 217; beyond, 125–26; flow of existence, 111; historical and eschatological, 56; human time, as vale of sorrow, 136; "if" statements, 151; infinite,

44–45; lived time, 110–11, 114, 122; mindful of, 40; night sky, 146–47; ordinary, 129; oriented to, 110–11; present, 42; profane, 129; segmented, 114; space-time, 56–57; spiritual adept, 112–13; "time for all things" under heaven, 39; vitality of, as near-mystical omnipresence, 112
Torah, 72–74, 77, 119–20, 198, 200–201, 204–5, 214, 231–33; allegorical figures, 235; concealment of Divine reality, 236; *dibbur* (speech), 228; Divine Will, 124; fundamental laws of, 210; God's esoteric truths, 235; of Heaven, 158; mysteries of, 78; parabolic character of, 234–35; as primordial, 159, 226; *qol* (voice), 228–29; renewed in each generation, 229–30; scholars, 215–16; speaking Torah, 223, 226; as supernal, 236; supernal revelation, 228; teaching Torah, 223; Torah of Moses, 115–16, 158, 226, 229, 236–37; and Tradition, 117–18
Torat Kohanim, 202
transcendence, 93; cognitive, 97; immanence, 48–49, 85–86; letter *k*, 100–101; mystery of, as Divine plenitude, 97; transcendent bond, 100n28; transcendent creativity, 105; transcendent immanence, 103; transcendent mystery, 100–101, 106; transcendent otherness, 103, 105n38
Troyes (France), 27n19
Two Sources of Religion and Morality, The (Bergson), 112
tzaddik, 224, 230–33, 236; as charismatic agent, 227; primary task of, 235; source of teachings, 225; "speaks Torah," 226
tzimtzum, 102–3

"Ulay Dema'ot" (If Tears) (Ibn Gabirol), 143–45; doubt and despair, working through of, 146

Vaihinger, Hans, 59
Varieties of Religious Experience (James), 156
"Ve-Im-Yish'al Ha-Mal'akh" (And Should the Angel Ask) (Bialik), 160, 162
verticality, 41
Virgil, 142–43
yitron da'at (benefit of mental awareness), 38
Vivante, P., 64n12

Waste Land, The (Eliot), 158
Weber, Max, 97, 107–8n46; demystification of the world, 159; *Entzauberung*, notion of, 107n44
Weitzman Institute, 94
Whitehead, Alfred, 95, 108n48
"Winter Songs" (Bialik), 171
Wittgenstein, Ludwig, 59
Wolfson, E., 170n23
"Word That Is Spoken, The" (Buber), 190
Word of Thought, 226
world-being, 58, 80, 105, 236, 244
World of Speech, 226
World War I, 180
World War II, 29
Wust, Peter, 241–42n30

"Yam Ha-Demamah Poleṭ Sodot" (The Sea of Silence That Emits Secrets) (Bialik), 167
Yeats, William Butler, 159
Yehudah Aryeh Leib Alter, R., of Ger, 113, 116, 121, 125–26, 126n41; lived time, 122
Yehudah bar Ilai, R., 73–75

Zaehner, R. C., 156
Ze'ev Wolf, R., of Zhitomer, 50, 76, 76n17, 80, 228–31, 231n20, 232; *dimyon*, 77–79; *dugma*, 77–78
Zeitlin, Hillel, 170n22

zikr (remembering God at all times), 198–99
Zohar (Splendor) (Bialik), 164–67, 169, 170n22, 234
Zoroaster, 36
Zusammenhang des Seelenlebens (interconnection of spiritual life), 180, 182–83
"Zweisprache" (Dialogue) (Buber), 185–86